Working Harder Isn't Working

Working Harder Isn't Working

How we can save
the environment, the economy,
and our sanity by working less
and enjoying life more

Bruce O'Hara

New Star Books
Vancouver
1993

Editor: Audrey McClellan
Cover design: Kris Klaasen / Working Design
Cover illustrations: Barbara Klunder
Diagrams: Stuart Morris

Printed and bound in Canada by Best Gagné Book Manufacturers
  2 3 4 5   97 96 95 94

Publication of this book is made possible by grants from the Canada Council, the Department of Communications Book Publishing Industry Development Program, and the Cultural Services Branch, Province of British Columbia.

New Star Books Ltd.
2504 York Avenue
Vancouver, B.C.
V6K 1E3

Canadian Cataloguing in Publication Data
O'Hara, Bruce, 1952 -
   Working harder isn't working!

   Includes bibliographical references and index.
   ISBN 0-921586-33-7

1. Four-day week — Canada. 2. Hours of labor — Canada.
3. Work sharing — Canada. 4. Canada — Economic conditions — 1991-
* I. Title.
HD5110.2.C2043 1993   331.25'72   C93-091900-9

Acknowledgments

As this book came into being it grew harder and harder to refer to the author as "I." Increasingly, I wanted to speak for the author as "we," not from any royal pretensions, but simply in recognition of the extent to which this book had become a collective effort.

It was my partner, Lynne Primrose, who came up with the title on the cover, and the last quote on the final page — which is fitting, given that her influence and support show on every page in between.

Though I am not kind in my assessment of most economists, I wish to thank for their invaluable advice three economists who do the profession proud: David Weston, Johan Schuyff, and Michael Mascall.

I thank my friends, and the volunteers of the **Work Well Network**, for their support, ideas, and patience through the long process of birthing this book, particularly Martin Gavin, Catherine Shapcott, Catherine Cardinal, Robert Thompson, Nancy Greene, David Stott, Kathie Gibson, Tim Roberts, Marie Fortier and Stephen Purcell.

I am grateful for the support of Audrey, Rolf and Karen at New Star Books: when a publishing team shows such passion and commitment it's hard not to think of it as "our" book.

Finally, I must acknowledge the writers and thinkers whose ideas I have borrowed so liberally: Wendell Berry, John Cobb, Herman Daly, Erich Fromm, Hazel Henderson, Mel Hurtig, John Maynard Keynes, Michael Lerner, William McGaughey, John Ward Pearson, Neil Postman, David Riesman, Anne Wilson Schaef, Juliet Schor, Lester Thurow, and Paul Wachtel. If this were an academic treatise, most every paragraph would require at least one citation.

I hope we have created a book you will enjoy.

Table of Contents

Working Harder Isn't Working

1

The Dream That Disappeared

The future isn't what it used to be.
ARTHUR C. CLARKE

Do you remember that rosy vision of the future we had in the 1950s? Computers and automation were going to create abundant wealth. Technology would free us from the drudgery of work.

Most predictions then were that a three-day workweek would be the norm by the 1990s. (The norm for Dad, that is; the idea that Mom would need to work for pay wasn't even considered!)

The 1960s cartoon series *The Jetsons* was a tongue-in-cheek time capsule of our fantasies of future life. George Jetson ostensibly had a job, but it was more an occasional, somewhat nostalgic hobby than a serious responsibility. Jane Jetson spent much of her time getting made up in outlandish hairdos, or ordering about the household machinery. For the Jetsons, life was one big vacation.

That was our idea of the future: an age of leisure and material abundance. There would be more time for family life, for contemplation, and for worship. We'd be able to relax and play. Articles of the day predicted that the biggest problem we would have in the 1990s would be figuring out what to do with all our free time.

That future is now. Instead of one breadwinner working 24 hours per week, most families now have *two* breadwinners *each* working 40 hours per week. Despite extra work hours, real family income has been falling for more than a decade. Stress management, not leisure counselling, is our major collective preoccupation. The economic elite upbraids us that in days ahead we must work longer and harder still — for less money — if we are to remain competitive in the "new global economy."

What happened to that wonderful future we were promised? Why do we have the age of stress instead of the age of leisure? How could the futurists have been so wrong?

In predicting an age of leisure, futurists made two assumptions. The first assumption was that technological progress would generate an increasing ability to create more wealth with less effort. This has happened: the average Canadian worker today produces twice as much per hour as his/her 1950s counterpart. The futurists' technical predictions were accurate: our productivity increases have been such that, by now, we could have had both a three-day workweek and a healthy increase in our standard of living. With two breadwinners per family, a two-day workweek could generate a higher standard of living than we had in 1970.

This brings us to the futurists' second assumption, which was that government would manage the economy sensibly and rationally, intervening as necessary to maintain a healthy economic balance.

If you'd asked 1960s futurists how they knew that people would work less in the future — and not more — they would have had a clear answer: "It would be stupid not to work less. If we don't work less, modern technology will start to produce too much — more than can be sold. Unemployment will grow by leaps and bounds. Rising unemployment will increase the expenses of government at the same time it reduces the number of taxpayers, causing taxes to soar. The economy will become less and less efficient, and more prone to recession and depression. The country will use up its natural resources far too quickly. Working *more* would push us into even worse problems — and faster." Our friendly futurists may well then have dismissed further discussion by saying: "The government couldn't possibly be that stupid!"

The ills of our modern economy are just what any futurist would have forewarned: TOO MUCH. We have more planes, buses, and trains than we have passengers to fill them; more banks, stores, and gas stations than customers to patronize them. Hundreds of factories, mines, and mills shut down every year, temporarily or permanently, because we produce so much more than can be sold. Our warehouses are bursting with surpluses of grain, cheese, and agricultural produce. Millions of our people are out of work.

For years, we have been told that if we just work harder and more productively, the economy will get better. Canadians have done so, and the results of this strategy are clear. Working harder has made the surplus of labour much larger, adding hundreds of thousands of people to the unemployment rolls.

Working more productively has created huge production surpluses throughout the Canadian economy, and pushed thousands of businesses to the edge of bankruptcy — or beyond.

It takes a perverse kind of genius to turn an increasing ability to generate wealth into a declining standard of living — but we have done so. We have created a monstrous paradox, where the more efficient technology becomes, the more inefficient the economy gets; a crazed treadmill where the harder we work, the poorer we become.

Using the "Work harder" prescription of the economic elite, we have dug the Canadian economy into a deep hole of overproduction and unemployment. What prescription do they offer us now? "Dig deeper."

In this book, I will explain how and why our current policies have failed. I will show clearly that working harder is the problem, not the solution. Finally, I will offer a step-by-step plan to save our sanity, the economy, and the environment — by working less and enjoying life more.

■ MY INTEREST IN EMPLOYMENT ISSUES

I first became interested in the issue of work hours in the early 1980s. As a professional counsellor I was struck by how many of my clients (and friends) represented one of two extremes. Some had no work; unemployment slowly but steadily ate away at their sense of self-worth. The rest were at the opposite extreme; work consumed so much time and energy that it ground them down and burned them out — particularly those people in families with young children where both spouses worked full time. This constant juxtaposition of unemployed and overworked clients made it clear to me that we had to find healthier ways to distribute the available work.

Initially, I imagined starting an organization to lobby for a reduction in the standard workweek. As I read more about employment issues, I discovered *work options*. Job sharing, phased retirement, banked overtime, and sabbaticals eased work stresses at the same time they reduced unemployment. Work options offered the possibility of incremental change that felt more manageable than the all-or-nothing hurdle of changing the standard workweek.

About this time, the Canadian Mental Health Association produced two reports: *Work and Well-Being*, and *Unemployment: Its Impact on Body and Soul*. These documents presented a larger picture matching my own experience. Canada was turning into a nation of the unemployed and the overworked, and both groups were suffering.

I approached the Victoria branch of the CMHA with a proposal for an agency to promote work options. They liked the idea and, with funding from Canada Employment and Immigration, Work Well was born. Work Well's mandate was to promote flexible work schedules through public education, the creation of resource materials, and case study research. We also assisted individual clients to make work option proposals to their employers and provided employers and unions with consulting advice. I wrote *Put Work In Its Place* as a self-help guide. As a way of practicing what we preached, all the Work Well staff worked flexible hours; I worked a three-day week.

During that time there were gratifying changes. The majority of our clients were happier and healthier as a result of cutting back their work hours — as was I. Several hundred other people benefitted from new jobs.

Organizations which had stubbornly resisted the earliest of our clients' efforts to gain approval for job sharing now offered it routinely. Public and corporate awareness of work options had risen considerably.

Although work options were helpful at an individual level, it became obvious that we could not nickel-and-dime our way to the promised land. The economy was getting sicker faster than the spread of work options could move us towards wellness. Prolonged high levels of unemployment had so damaged the economy that few people could afford to work less.

■ A NIGHTMARE VISION: THE FUTURE-BY-DEFAULT

During the years I was at Work Well, I talked to thousands of people about work issues. Between Work Well workshop participants and individual clients, I heard about the hopes, wishes and struggles of a wide spectrum of Canadian workers. At conferences and work-shops on the future of work, I explored employment issues with economists, government bureaucrats, human resource managers, social planners, corporate executives, and union leaders. I engaged in dialogue with the public in radio talk-show promotions of *Put Work In Its Place*. I devoured any written materials I could find.

It was then that the nightmare vision began to emerge. Originally, I thought our failure to embrace the leisure vision was a missed opportunity. It soon became clear to me that the unwillingness to let our lives get easier has made them *actively harsher*.

I came to see that many of the apparently separate evils of our age — degradation of the environment, escalating debt, persistent militarism, a declining standard of living, burgeoning social unrest, and rising taxes — are all tied to our failure to work less.

■ THE SMOKE SCREEN OF 'ECONOMIC POLICY'

It also became apparent that the reason that employment issues have not been properly addressed in the public forum is that work has been framed as an economic policy issue—almost a technical or engineering question — rather than a quality of life or social justice issue.

With a few notable exceptions, most books on economics are written in dry, academic style, filled with obscure jargon, reams of confusing statistics, copious references, and footnotes that run off on multiple tangents. Reading the stuff qualifies as an act of masochism. Most people decide to leave such matters to the experts.

Perhaps the tunnel-vision that afflicts most modern economists is a function of rampant specialization. To say that most of today's economists can't see the forest for the trees is to be too kind by half; most of them can only barely make out the trees for the branches. Even those few economists able to write with wit and flair seem to lose their cutting edge as they become well known.

I am not a professional economist. I came to economics through the back door of my concern for mental health issues. I have none of the experts' credentials. I am able to talk about economic issues in plain and simple language. I have the outsider's ability to see the big picture — and I can talk about what it means to your life.

We have given too much power to the experts. It is time we took our power back. The term "economics" in the original Greek translated to "of the home" — and referred to the subject of family finances. At the level of family finances, we all have a fair understanding of economics. At the big picture level that this book addresses, the trends are clear enough that fancy mathematics are not required. As Bob Dylan said: "You don't need a weatherman to know which way the wind blows."

The Path To A Better Future

In this book I will take the reader through the five steps I see as essential if we are to understand what's wrong with the Canadian economy and how to fix it:

❶ Tell the truth about how bad it is.

❷ Clearly define exactly what's wrong.

❸ Evaluate possible solutions.

❹ Examine the blocks to implementing solutions.

❺ Develop a clear and concrete vision for the future.

Step One may make you depressed — or angry. Step Two can feel a little bit like a textbook, but it provides the "aha" of understanding. Step Three will appeal to engineers and fix-it types. Step Four is a pleasure for anyone who is fascinated by human nature. Step Five feels good for everybody. Each step is different; each is necessary.

■ STEP ONE: TELL THE TRUTH ABOUT WHERE WE ARE

Our response to Canada's economic problems has been hampered by deep official denial of the scope and severity of our economic difficulties. Part I of this book confronts that denial by telling the truth about the extent of Canada's economic plight:

- 🌢 A look at the stress triangle: stress for the overworked, stress for the unemployed, and stress on the environment;

- 🌢 An itemized accounting of the price that working people pay to live in a high-unemployment economy;

- 🌢 An accurate assessment of the levels of unemployment and economic insecurity in Canada.

■ STEP TWO: DEFINE WHAT'S WRONG

Part II examines the fundamental bind which is inexorably destroying the North American economy. Our technological, work-obsessed society requires constantly expanding production, while a fragile and stressed environment demands that we consume far less — and we cannot do both. This underlying conflict creates a series of self-aggravating problems:

- 🌢 The paradox of efficiency: the more efficient technology becomes, the less efficient the economy is;

- 🌢 The vicious circle of unemployment, where high unemployment creates more unemployment;

- 🌢 The dark shadow of persistent inflation and its underlying cause: real estate speculation;

- 🌢 The unravelling of the global economic order: not "competition," but chaos;

■ STEP THREE: EVALUATE POSSIBLE SOLUTIONS

The problem of overproduction is not a new one for market economies: environmental limits have simply sharpened a long-standing
struggle. In Part III, I will examine a range of interventions which
have been used over the past 200 years as instruments to help maintain a dynamic balance between production and consumption. In
addition to showing where and how these various strategies have
been used, I will rate them according to their effectiveness, examine
their side effects (both beneficial and harmful), and assess their
potential for restoring the Canadian economy to health. Such interventions include:

- Limits on who can work, and limits on the hours of work;

- Ways to foster consumption: advertising, disposables,
  militarism, government spending, and debt;

- Interest rate policies, and controls on production;

- Mechanisms which protect certain groups from a declining
  economy;

- Non-solutions: Canada's economic policies.

■ STEP FOUR: WHAT'S IN THE WAY?

Part IV will attempt to answer that nagging question which has probably already surfaced for many readers: why are we doing this to
ourselves? I had initially assumed the problem of more sensible
work scheduling was technical; mechanisms were needed for getting
shorter schedules into place, and for making them effective. I have
since come to see that there are deep-seated reasons, both personal
and political, why we have turned our backs on the leisure vision.
Although some of the process has involved powerful interest
groups, the condition in which we find ourselves is not simply a case
of the rich and powerful pushing their interests at the expense of
working people. At least in part, we must echo the immortal words

of the comic-strip character Pogo: "We have met the enemy, and they is us."

In this section I will examine how the past and the present have conspired to defeat the future:

- 🌢 How our history has made us suckers for work;

- 🌢 The dynamics of work addiction, and addictive organizations;

- 🌢 Faulty values around work and self-worth;

- 🌢 The politics of scarcity — how we sold out the future;

- 🌢 The dead-stick future: where inertia will take us if we continue on our present course.

■ STEP FIVE: RECLAIMING THE FUTURE

The biggest flaw in our 1950s picture of the future was the naive assumption that the age of leisure would somehow just happen. Change, even when positive, is scary. Canadian politicians have ducked the challenge of the future and become apologists for the status quo. We have drifted into our current malaise largely because we have lacked a positive, concrete vision for the future.

While it is obvious to virtually everyone that working harder isn't working, the alternative, working less, has not received serious consideration. Ironically, our failure to work less has created an economy so dysfunctional it now appears we can't afford a shorter work-week. It's an illogical truism of our times that a more efficient and productive technology requires us to work harder and faster.

The practical step-by-step plan I present in Part V will change that, open a strong public debate, and create a new vision of the possible. I present my vision not as an end product, but as a starting point. What shorter working hours offer us is a chance to begin talking about the future again, not with resignation, but with excitement.

Readers tell me that Part V is far and away the most exciting and inspiring section of the book — and yet those same readers also say that it is the understanding gained in Parts I to IV that gives it its power. If you're one of those people who eats the icing first and the cake later — by all means read Part V first and come back to the rest.

In the concluding section of the book you will find:

✔ A detailed proposal for implementing the four-day workweek — and further reductions beyond;

✔ Proposals for reclaiming our national sovereignty;

✔ A plan for undoing the damage caused by our current craziness;

✔ Proposals to further strengthen the environmental friendliness of shorter working hours;

✔ A new worth ethic: values and practices to reclaim community, pleasure, and play;

✔ The politics of abundance: how to create a coalition for change;

✔ What to do until the revolution comes.

An extensive "Notes and Sources" section at the end of the book gives additional detail for each chapter section of the book, including more complete statistical information, reference sources, and suggested readings.

AN EMANCIPATION PROCLAMATION

Only a few years before slavery was abolished in the United States, it was considered an essential part of the economy. How did an economic institution as basic as slavery go from normal to unacceptable within a few short years? Part of the change came from courageous individuals, who were willing, as the Quakers say, "to speak truth to power." Part of it was collective readiness: the end of slavery was an idea whose time had come.

For three years, I resisted writing the book you now hold. What finally prodded me to action were the changes I noticed in the people around me. In great numbers, they are rethinking the role of work in their lives, becoming convinced that we must change how we live.

I trust my home community of the Comox Valley is not an isolated enclave of enlightenment. A consensus for change is forming, so deep and powerful that it will sweep aside our somnambulant leaders — or drag them along into a new vision of Canada.

It is not too late to reclaim the future we once imagined. The age of leisure was not a pipe-dream, but simply the road not taken.

If we are to create a future of leisure and abundance, we must begin moving in that direction. Shorter working hours will end another form of slavery. We must build the necessary political will to enact a shorter workweek.

Lives rich in spirit and love, full of pleasure and play, are our birthright. It is time to claim what is ours.

Prosperity/leisure is not an either/or choice; in the 1990s we must create the means to have them both — or we will wind up with neither.

PART I

WHERE DOES IT HURT?

For the past 40 years we have turned our backs on the vision of a future of abundant leisure, attempting instead to expand consumption *ad infinitum*. Insofar as this expansion of materialism has been insufficient to keep the workforce employed 40 hours per week, we have endured high levels of unemployment and a lacklustre economy.

The ethic that "we just have to work a little harder and everything will turn out okay" dies hard in a work-addicted society. The one problem which more work *cannot* solve is a surplus of labour. Until we understand the extent to which we have been harmed by a labour-surplus economy, change is unlikely.

The personal costs of living in a sick economy have grown up slowly and discretely, in a multitude of nibbling burdens, large and small. We've been paying these costs so long, it's easy to forget they do not exist in a healthy society. Only by making a cumulative tally can we begin to appreciate the magnitude of the price we pay.

The first step towards reclaiming the future of our dreams is to recognize our self-inflicted wounds.

2

The Stress and Pain Triangle

The nineties will be a decade in a hurry; a nanosecond culture. There'll only be two kinds of managers: the quick and the dead.

DAVID VICE

An economy with high unemployment creates hurt all round: stress and struggle for those who are working; pain and deprivation for the unemployed; damage and degradation for the environment.

Stressful Work

When unemployment is high, those who are employed are squeezed. High unemployment pushes their wages down. At the same time, high unemployment raises the costs of UIC, welfare, education, health care, and policing — which drives taxes way up. The average worker has to run faster and faster — simply to keep from falling further behind.

■ FAMILY BUSYNESS

Most married women in the 1960s and 1970s entered the workforce by choice, drawn by wishes for self-fulfillment, independence and a higher standard of living.

A side effect of falling wages is that in recent years many households have *needed* a second income to cover basic expenses. Families which try to make ends meet on one income first see their ability to save disappear. Later they need to cut out luxuries, and finally to forego what they had previously considered necessities.

When the family budget won't stretch any further, married women have had few options for interesting and remunerative part-time work. Given our one-size-fits-all attitude to work scheduling, most women have been obliged to return to full-time work. Men have also had few options to reduce their employment load to accommodate domestic and parenting tasks.

The result is that the total workload of the typical Canadian adult (i.e., job plus housework) has risen by more than 40% in the past 40 years. Particularly for single parents, and families with young children, the 1990s is the era of exhaustion.

The classic symbol of family life in the 1990s is the refrigerator chart, where the logistics of the dual-earner home are laid out in terse code. Who will take Nathan to the daycare and who will pick him up? Which babysitter will come in after school? Who will drive Jennifer to her baseball game? Who will do the grocery shopping? Who will pick up dinner at the deli on the way home? Smart couples will schedule in time alone together. When both partners work full time, if it isn't written down, it probably won't happen.

High stress is the immediate impact of this lifestyle: personal stress, stress in relationships with our partners, and stress in relationships with our children. Our lives are so overcrowded that the agitation of rush-rush seldom leaves. Many Canadians have had marriages go down the drain and been too busy to notice. They come home from work one day and find the furniture gone and a note from their now ex-partner: "Have a nice life — I couldn't stand it any more."

Parents don't have enough time to be parents. They try to make it up to their children with horse-riding lessons, Nintendo games, designer clothes, and "quality time." The result of this neglect is children who know more about keeping busy than about intimacy.

Teenagers in particular often feel they have no place, and no chance to do anything productive in our economy. Vandalism and self-destructive acts become the outlets for their anger and despair.

Parenting becomes a recurring financial burden, as young adults who had moved out are often forced by joblessness to return home. The resulting juxtaposition of over-stressed parents and their under-stimulated offspring is often an unhappy one.

■ DETERIORATING WORKING CONDITIONS

When unemployment is high, employers are in a stronger position to "put the screws" to workers. Many of us are required to do more work in less time. Employers are less accommodating about allowing special working arrangements. "Voluntary" overtime becomes less voluntary. Salaried workers (particularly middle managers) get pressured into working evenings and weekends. Sometimes the threat is explicit: "If you're not willing to toe the line, I am sure there are hundreds of people out there who would love to have your job."

Ironically in these times of high unemployment, most North Americans are working longer hours — often for less money. In the past generation the average workweek for full-time workers in North America has increased by about three hours. (This is in sharp contrast to Europe: in France and Germany, a full-time worker works an average of six hours per week less than we do.)

When unemployment is high, job mobility is restricted. In his book *Working*, Studs Terkel interviewed hundreds of workers from a broad variety of occupations. A striking number of those people were bored with their jobs but felt they had no other choices. How many people do you know who are stuck in jobs they hate? Are you one of those people yourself?

A healthy economy includes a healthy level of job mobility. When people get tired of a job, they can change careers to find work that is new and challenging. When so many people are out of work, it's hard to switch to a new career because most openings are filled by people who already have experience in that field. Rising educational requirements mean that changing careers may involve the time and expense of several extra years of schooling.

■ THE BURNOUT BLUES

The biggest health costs many of us pay are not our Medicare premiums. Insomnia, eczema, digestive upsets, asthma, traffic accidents, back pain, and heart troubles are often the physical symptoms of over-stressed lives. The health crises of those dear to us — be they alcoholism, suicide, ulcers, or a nervous breakdown — may also have their roots in stress and overwork.

High unemployment creates a culture of scarcity. One in six Canadians now lives in poverty. It's hard to feel good about what my job gives me when I know so many other people are deprived. It's hard to feel safe in a country where so many people are desperate.

■ THE LOST GENERATION

Much has been made of the aimlessness of the generation which follows the baby boomers, sometimes called "Generation X" or the "Lost Generation." Rather than blaming the young, we should take a hard look at the world we are leaving our children.

If young people are to have any hope of decent jobs, they must spend long years at school. Many of us over 40 were "grandfathered" into professions that now have inflated educational requirements. The young must spend extra years in school and assume crushing student loans to pay the *de facto* entrance fees to their chosen careers. Sometimes even after all that schooling, there are no jobs. Those who do manage to snag a plum job often fall victim to layoffs: the last hired are the first fired.

Most of those who can't (or won't) spend forever in school end up in "McJobs": low wage, part-time, and casual jobs in the service sector. Short-term employment as waiters, cleaners, and sales clerks is interspersed with periodic unemployment.

Buying a home has also become a luxury beyond the reach of many of our young people. Speculation in the housing market may have given baby boomers a retirement nest-egg, but it has made home ownership a debt trap for the young.

It is our children who will pay for our environmental negligence. I think the young have every right to be angry. We have eaten the apple — and left them the core.

Painful Unemployment

Unemployment is the mirror image of overwork. Where most employed Canadians have too much structure in their lives and too little time, the jobless have too much time and too little structure.

Over the years, my work as a counsellor and employment counsellor brought me into contact with people who have suffered deeply from unemployment: people who had lost their homes; men and women whose marriages hadn't been strong enough to survive such stress; parents who couldn't afford Christmas presents for their children, and who had to send them to school in old clothes.

I saw individuals who were upset with themselves for venting anger and frustration on their children or their spouses, but who did not know what to do with those feelings. I saw men and women who had lost confidence in themselves, who knew they were sabotaging themselves in their job searches, but felt helpless to do otherwise.

Some people developed rashes and stomach troubles. Others developed insomnia — or found themselves sleeping all the time. Some people who had never had a problem with alcohol, could not stay away from the bottle.

For young people, who had not developed a solid sense of self as good workers, self-doubt often went deep. Lacking purpose, young people often over-generalized: "I have no use or value as a human being."

Older workers battled a different demon. Their fear was that they would never work again. Being out of work made them feel useless, discarded, and old.

Some themes kept recurring. The sense of being stuck was one. Unemployment was a limbo land where a person's time was his own but not his own.

Most people experienced a slow but relentless pressure on their confidence and sense of worth. Many described unemployment as a hole that dug itself deeper over time. The longer a person was in that hole, the fewer resources she had for climbing out.

Isolation was another common theme. People missed workplace

contacts, yet would cut themselves off from friends and family members because they felt unworthy.

Shame was another almost universal response. People told themselves, "If I'm unemployed it must be my fault; there must be something wrong with me. It must be a punishment for not working hard enough, for trying to change careers, for not getting enough schooling."

The need to matter, to make a difference, to create, and to give are all profound human needs. Some of the deepest pain I've heard from unemployed clients related to feeling unproductive and unable to contribute.

Some individuals coped well with unemployment. They kept contact with friends, engaged in volunteer work, relaxed, taught themselves new skills, and found creative ways to enjoy themselves without spending money. They plugged away steadily at the job of finding a job and held tenaciously to the memory of being a competent worker. Even those people found that it hurt to be unemployed. They said that the longer they were out of work, the harder it was to feel good about themselves and not to slide into despair and self-sabotage.

Unemployment can have a profound impact on mental health. Epidemiologist Harvey Brenner has gathered statistical data which indicates that current levels of joblessness are creating an extra 20,000 admissions to Canadian psychiatric wards every year.

■ MY PERSONAL EXPERIENCE OF LONG-TERM UNEMPLOYMENT

My own experience with extended unemployment was gentle in many ways, in that I didn't have a mortgage or children to support. Nonetheless, the process and the feelings I went through are typical.

I moved to Victoria at the height of the 1981 recession, at a time when the economy was actively contracting. I found it scary to apply for a job and be told that hundreds of people had applied for the same position.

As I ran through the weeks of my UIC claim, I felt a mounting sense of anxiety. My partner at the time was also new to Victoria and having difficulty finding work. Even after we put ourselves on a strict budget, our expenses exceeded our income. Soon there was an outstanding balance on my credit card, and each month it crept upwards, usually on unplanned expenses.

My car disappeared early in the process. Insurance would cost money I didn't have, and selling it brought a small infusion of cash.

Unemployment was ambiguous "free time." Most leisure activities required at least some money. When friends asked us out to lunch, we might go, but only to have a cup of tea, claiming we had eaten at home. The beautiful countryside of Victoria surrounded us but, with no car and no money, it felt a long way away.

It was hard to make solid plans, because a job interview or temporary work could disrupt any arrangements. We couldn't afford to take courses. We each found value in volunteer work but felt limited to roles where we could easily be replaced.

The lack of income expressed itself in other ways. We each found a certain amount of part-time and temporary work, but the money from that work was not "ours" the way it had been when we had regular jobs. It first had to pay down the credit card bills. Any extra income was "rainy day money." Furniture and clothing were luxuries that would have to wait. Gifts of cash from relatives back east usually went for groceries.

The longer I was out of work, the harder it was to give a good job interview. It was painful to hear myself, sounding unsure, an edge of pleading in my voice. Sometimes, I tried to *act* confident. I can only presume my act was unconvincing — I didn't get the jobs.

Eventually UIC ran out and my charge card hit its limit. We both found casual work, but it was sporadic and didn't cover our bills. Reluctantly, we applied for welfare.

Welfare had lots of shame attached to it. My naive prejudice was that only lazy, scummy people lived on welfare. Now *I* was on welfare. It became even harder to feel confident or worthwhile selling myself to an employer. I felt like I was sinking into a trap, scared I would be permanently caught in this marginal world.

It was hard to be social when I felt useless and unproductive, and I withdrew somewhat from friends. My partner and I began arguing. I found myself giving up my place in line in banks and grocery stores — other people's time was more valuable than mine.

I used to take the bus out to a ritzy section of town and go around door to door, asking if people needed a handy man. I got little bits of work that way. (One doctor's place was so big there were always new weeds to pull!) The pay was low and UIC or welfare deducted much of what I earned. Even so, it felt better to *earn* my money.

We were on welfare only a few months when each of us landed more substantial jobs. (My job was temporary, but gave me that foot-in-the-door I needed.)

I felt the effects of unemployment for more than a year after I was back at work. It took 18 months to pay off my credit card, buy new clothes, pay for an overdue trip to the dentist, and save for a used car.

It took a similar period of time to recover emotionally. At first I felt like an impostor being back at work—that I must somehow have fooled my new boss into giving me the job. I slowly shed the habit of being anxious about money. There was a gradual process of reclaiming my own time, planning for activities and vacations. I could buy furniture; I could build a future.

Joblessness had not been without its compensations. I had an abundance of time with my partner. I enjoyed and learned from my volunteer work. Overall, though, the experience was painful. Unemployment cast a long shadow over that period of my life.

Millions of Canadians live under such a shadow. Few families have escaped completely unscathed; the threat of it hangs over all of us. As an employment counsellor, I found it was the people who felt most secure in their jobs who crashed the hardest when the unthinkable happened. None of us is really safe.

Environmental Degradation

As the economy worsens, it makes more demands on the environment. As more families send a second spouse into the workforce, there are more commuters on the road, more fast-food meals and litter. For every toddler who toilet-trains in disposable diapers, 1.5 tons of non-biodegradable waste is added to landfills.

Rather than allowing the unemployed to lighten the burden of the overworked, we have clung doggedly to the 40-hour workweek, seeing growth as the only way to create jobs for the jobless.

The myth of the permanently expanding economy demands continually expanding consumption, as though the environment had no limits. In the process, we have depleted and poisoned the earth. The unthinking worship of economic growth has created several environmental crises:

- ✺ Uncontrolled use and release of CFCs into the atmosphere threatens the ozone layer;

- ✺ Increasing use of fossil fuels has created a greenhouse effect which threatens to flood coastal areas of Canada and fry the rest of the country;

- ✺ Excessive consumption of fossil fuels is poisoning our lakes and forests with acid rain;

- ✺ Current farming and forestry practices wash away topsoil and decrease soil fertility;

- ✺ Rapid consumption is depleting natural resources such as fish stocks and forests;

- ✺ The World Health Organization estimates that nine-tenths of all cancers are triggered by pollution.

What is perhaps most scary about these environmental crises is that by the time their full impact is clear, it will be too late: the damage will be irreversible. Our relationship with the environment reminds me of the story of the fellow who jumped off the top of a 32-storey building. As he zoomed past the 16th floor, he was asked how he felt, to which he replied, "I feel just fine — so far!"

Ecologists are very clear: if we want our planet to be habitable in 40 years time, we must make major changes in how we live, *immediately*.

Unfortunately, our current economic configuration makes jobs and the environment an either/or choice. Environmental concerns get brushed aside when a new factory promises to bring jobs to an economically depressed community. We hesitate to save the old-growth forests as parks because jobs would be lost. The jobs of east coast fishermen are more important than conserving the

northern cod — at least until there are no more cod. We are caught
in a bind: if we use less, waste less, and recycle more, people will lose
their jobs.

It is essential that everyone who cares about the Earth understands
this: unless we take jobs and the environment off their collision
course, environmental changes will be too little, and too late. There
is only one way that we can simultaneously have more jobs *and* put
less stress on the environment: shorter working hours.

THE TRIPLE IMPERATIVE

The employed are stressed out.
The unemployed are in pain.
The Earth is dying.

A shorter workweek can save them all.

3

The Financial Costs
We All Pay

*What we are getting in our lives is less for more. The
process of earning and spending more and more dollars
to achieve increasingly less meaningful results is a
disheartening one for those who have been brought up
expecting to attain the reverse.*

JOHN WARD PEARSON

Those of us who are employed would like to believe we haven't paid
a price to live in an economy where unemployment is high. Our
governments have been only too happy to support us in that belief.
Nothing could be further from the truth.

What follows is a laundry list of the financial costs we've all paid
to have less leisure. It may seem, as you read through this chapter,
that I have made some bold and unwarranted assertions about the
personal costs of living in a labour-surplus economy. However, the
larger picture I draw in Parts 2 and 3 will clearly tie the personal costs
outlined here to our collective unwillingness to work less.

■ DECLINING HOURLY WAGES

The most striking cost we've paid is that wages are pushed down
when unemployment is high. For the past 15 years, wages have been
falling behind the rate of inflation.

Our reactions to money are emotional rather than rational. If I get a 6% pay increase, my natural reaction is to feel good about my raise, and to think I am better off. If, however, the inflation rate is 7%, I have actually suffered a 1% drop in real income.

An income drop of 1% or less per year may seem minor, but when income slips consistently it becomes substantial. Over the past 15 years, average real wages in Canada have dropped by 10%. (The reader is reminded that "Notes and Sources" to support these figures are at the back of the book.)

North American workers have greatly improved their productivity in recent years. If average wages reflected this increase in production, real hourly wages should have risen 20% over the past 15 years. In a healthy economy, this would have happened.

When unemployment is high, however, the benefits of increased productivity are not passed on to workers; their reward has been to see their hourly wages go down instead.

If wages had reflected productivity increases over the past 15 years, full-time workers would have to work about 25% less to earn their current weekly wages. Put another way, the most direct impact of high unemployment on our lives is that each full-time worker now works 10 hours every week for free.

Canadians have done what they could to maintain their standard of living. Statistics Canada reports that real, average, after-tax family income fell by only 4% between 1980 and 1991. However, considering that we have an older and more skilled workforce, that we are working longer hours, and that we have more workers in each family, this decline in income is scary. The average family is running as fast as it can — and still losing ground.

■ RISING UIC AND WELFARE COSTS

High unemployment has another direct impact on workers' take-home pay. For most workers, seven cents out of every wage dollar goes to pay UIC contributions, if we include contributions employers make on employees' behalf. This figure somewhat overstates the cost to the average Canadian family — given that not everyone has to pay UIC. The average Canadian household's share of the cost is about $2100, or about 4% of family income.

Ten percent of British Columbia's population is now on welfare, even though B.C. is considered to be a wealthy province. Other provinces carry a similar and rising welfare burden. Welfare costs are paid for through a variety of federal, provincial, and municipal taxes. The cost of all these taxes can be estimated at about $1600 per year per Canadian household. For an average Canadian, this translates into roughly 3% of annual income. Combining welfare and UIC, a typical full-time worker works almost three hours each week to pay people who aren't working!

Some people may respond by blaming the "lazy bums" on welfare, discounting that most of Canada's unemployed would jump at the chance to work those hours themselves.

■ HIGHER FAMILY EXPENSES

Falling standards of living have forced many Canadian families to add a second breadwinner. Unfortunately, two full-time workers in a family with young children often proves to be an inefficient solution.

When the stay-at-home spouse returns to a job, the initial breadwinner loses that person as a tax deduction. In financial terms, this means that the entire second income is taxable; somewhere between one quarter and one third disappears in taxes.

Daycare and after school baby-sitting costs must be subtracted from the second income. If the second job requires a second car, this also increases family expenses. If a family does more eating at restaurants, buys prepared foods, replaces rather than mends clothes, and buys house-cleaning and car-maintenance services, expenses will rise in pursuit of income.

Canadian data suggests that these items add at least $14,000 in new expenses to the family budget. In other words, when the second spouse goes back to work full time, only that part of their annual income in excess of $14,000 represents an increase in disposable income. The first $14,000 of the second income goes towards paying the added expenses resulting from the second job.

It would be unfair to count the increased tax load of dual-earner homes in a cumulative list because this would, in effect, double-count all of the other costs that result in higher taxes. As well, if we want to consider what the average family would pay, we must allow for the fact that some families have only one breadwinner, and many do not have young children. Taking these factors into account we might estimate that the average Canadian family spends about 5% of its income on the costs associated with having a second breadwinner.

■ EDUCATIONAL INFLATION

When unemployment is high, occupations which are easy to enter are flooded with workers, driving down wages in those occupations. Professional associations respond by erecting barriers of educational qualification around their particular occupations.

Even when professional associations do not demand more schooling, high unemployment creates a demand for extra schooling. A master's degree is not strictly required for many positions in the social services, but applicants with an MA jump the queue when a job opening appears. How many of today's university and college students are really after extra skills and how many just need a very expensive piece of paper?

Only a small proportion of the cost of our universities and colleges is covered through tuition. One reason education has been eating up more of our tax monies is that we must pay for higher educational requirements that are designed to keep people out of particular occupations. It costs taxpayers more than $20,000 in public funds for every young person who must spend two more years in school to jump through the MA or PhD hoop.

About 2% of your gross income goes into paying for excess education. That's another three-quarters of an hour you work for nothing every week, as a consequence of high unemployment.

■ HIGH HEALTH-CARE COSTS

Harvey Brenner is a Harvard University epidemiologist — a researcher who studies the patterns behind the occurrence of disease. In studying hospital records, Brenner found that rates of admission mirrored changes in unemployment levels. Brenner also found that increasing levels of overwork measurably increased hospital admissions.

In Canada, we have managed to have the worst of both worlds — an economy in which most of the population is either unemployed or overworked. Brenner's evidence suggests that about 20% of all admissions to Canadian hospitals can be attributed to unemployment. Brenner wasn't able to quantify precisely the effects of overwork, but estimated that they were comparable to those for unemployment. A conservative estimate would be that 30% of current health care costs can be attributed to either unemployment or overwork — about $1800 annually for each Canadian household. This extra tax burden could be avoided if we led more balanced lives.

In personal terms, you work about 1.5 hours every week to pay for the illnesses wrought by unemployment and overwork.

■ RISING CRIME

Harvey Brenner also found a correlation between high unemployment and high crime rates. Brenner's figures suggest that 40% of all crime in Canada, and more than half of all murders, have their roots in high unemployment.

The only country in the world with a larger proportion of its population in jail than Canada is the United States. Statistics Canada reports that policing and prisons cost more than $7 billion in Canada last year. It costs taxpayers $40,000 a year for each inmate. If we assume that the private costs of crime — property losses, insurance premiums, and private security measures — are at least as much as the public costs, then the cost of crime generated by unemployment last year was $570 for each Canadian household. Another half hour of your workweek gone.

■ COLLECTIVE INSECURITY

Politically, we have an unparalleled opportunity to turn swords into ploughshares. With the collapse of the Soviet Union, we have the chance to stop the insanity of the arms race. The *$1 trillion* that the world has been spending annually on the military could be turned to peaceful and constructive purposes. Some of the 11 cents of each federal tax dollar that funds the military could go to more useful purposes — like staying in your own pocket!

Sadly, military spending is like a drug for our sick economy. We know that horrific weaponry puts us all in danger, yet without the "fix" of military spending, North America would have even higher unemployment. Another half hour of your workweek gone!

■ HIGH PRICES

As we will see in Chapter 6, high prices are a side effect of an unhealthy economy. Most businesses are operating at far less than capacity, which decreases their efficiency and adds 5% to the cost of most consumer goods and services. A conservative estimate is that 2% of the average family's income disappears in this way. Another 45 minutes of your workweek pays for the high prices engendered by a sick economy.

■ INFLATED HOUSING COSTS

In Chapter 8, rapid inflation of real estate prices is shown to be an indirect result of high unemployment.

Those of us who own homes revel in rising house prices because they increase the value of our assets. It feels great to think that a home bought for $50,000 is now worth $150,000. But are you really better off? You're still living in the same home. If you sell, any new home you buy is going to cost you more to buy. If you die, your children's inheritance is still the same home as before, or its equivalent. (Economists use the apt term "the money illusion" to describe this mirage of wealth which inflation creates.)

Buying your own home protects you from the most immediate damage caused by inflating real estate prices. It doesn't increase your in-pocket wealth. Only people who own multiple homes make bankable money in real estate.

The long-term effect of inflating real estate prices has been to increase the portion of the workforce's income that goes to housing. The effect is felt most keenly by young couples buying their first house, but anyone who trades up to a larger home will also feel the pinch.

■ HIGH ADVERTISING AND PACKAGING COSTS

Saturation advertising and excessive packaging are not necessary in a healthy economy. In a crowded marketplace, however, it takes more advertising to get the customer's attention. These costs must be reclaimed in the price of the advertised products. Large and flashy packaging gets the consumer's attention; it also ends up in landfills. Advertising costs in Canada amount to about $860 per family per year.

It's easy to see how our children are manipulated into buying toys, clothes, and breakfast cereals that are a waste of money. It's harder to admit we are manipulated in exactly the same way — to buy toys which are far more expensive.

At issue is not the number of gadgets we may *choose* to buy, but the degree to which we are *conned* into buying, in an economy so unhealthy that producers must resort to such manipulation in order to survive.

■ RAPID INFLATION AND HIGH INTEREST CHARGES

We will see in Chapter 8 that rapid inflation is another indirect consequence of our failure to work less. Inflation shrinks the value of savings. Inflation erodes the buying power of everyone who lives on a pension or fixed income. Inflation leaves most of us struggling to catch up, as prices go up faster than wages.

In a sick economy, high interest rates are required to keep inflation under control. When interest rates were sky-high, the economic penalty they exacted was painfully obvious. If you had a $50,000 mortgage and interest rates averaged 14% instead of a more reasonable 8%, during the life of a 20-year mortgage you paid an additional $48,000 in interest charges. High interest rates cost you almost as much as the principle!

In recent years interest rates have come down so much that it's easy to forget that they are still very high. If we correct for inflation, Canadian interest rates give a 6% rate of return — double what banks have historically considered fair.

The average Canadian household owes $43,000 in mortgages and consumer loans. High interest rates cost an average family an extra

$1300 per year. High interest charges on the public debt also cost Canadians dearly — by a conservative estimate an additional $1900 per family, per year. As an average Canadian, you work another 2.5 hours each week to pay the added costs brought about by high interest rates.

■ DEBT CHARGES

As we will see in Chapter 9, high unemployment has so damaged our wage structure that the government had to borrow large sums of money to keep the economy afloat. Now we're stuck with the bill.

Annual interest charges on Canada's public debt amount to $6500 per household. We've already said that at least $1900 of that is really due to high interest rates, which leaves each household with $4600 in debt charges.

If each of us paid about 40% more in income taxes, our governments would be breaking even — i.e., keeping up with the interest charges on past debt. Given that such a tax increase would be political suicide, governments have been running up the tab instead — which, of course, means that both debt and interest charges continue to grow.

The combined indebtedness of the federal and provincial governments is increasing by more than $4600 per household, per year — more than 8% of the average family's income! Eventually that debt must be paid off — if not by you, then by your children.

IN SUM: THIS HURTS!

The total cost figures which follow are for the average Canadian family. If you are older, a unionized worker, with no (or grown) children, and own your own home outright, the total costs you must pay may well be one-third lower than that shown. At the other extreme, if you are young, have children in daycare, and are a first-time home-buyer, your total costs may well be one-third higher. If you are a typical Canadian, your wages since 1977 have fallen 25% behind your productivity. In addition, a sick economy then exacts more costs (shown in the table on the next page) from what's left:

Type of cost	% of income
UIC contributions	4%
Taxes for welfare costs	3%
Added education costs	2%
Added health costs	3%
Added crime costs	1%
Taxes for unnecessary defence costs	1%
Second breadwinner costs (minus taxes)	5%
Excess advertising/needless purchases	3%
Inflated housing costs	3%
High consumer prices	2%
High interest charges	6%
Interest on the public debt (deferred)	8%
Total	41%

Even if we exclude the deferred interest charges on the public debt, one third of your income disappears in costs associated with a labour-surplus economy.

If we take the combined effect of lower wages and higher expenses, Canadians' net incomes are about half of what they would be in a healthy economy.

THE FULL COST TO YOUR WAGE DOLLAR		
25¢ goes to lost earning power	25¢ (one-third of what's left) goes to extra expenses	50¢ is all that's left

If you are a typical Canadian, half of your workweek is spent paying the cost of living in a labour-surplus economy. Having a job does not protect you from the economic effects of high unemployment!

4

The True Scope of Unemployment

There are three kinds of lies: lies, damned lies, and statistics.

BENJAMIN DISRAELI

The official rate of unemployment in Canada hovers around 11% of the workforce. This translates to more than 1.6 million people — the entire working age population of all four maritime provinces.

Frightening though the official jobless figures are, they severely understate the true level of unemployment in Canada. Successive federal governments have tried to manage the unemployment problem with public relations and information management, rather than economic reform. Unwillingness to admit the true extent of unemployment has undergirded our failure to realistically address our economic problems.

The Real Rate Of Joblessness In Canada

The world of employment statistics is strange and confusing. Some statistics are based on the population as a whole. Others are based on the working age population. Some are based on the "labour force" (defined as the total employed plus those who would like to work) or on the actual working population (which may or may not include part-time workers). Some of what would be most pertinent to know has been measured only indirectly.

All of this makes the task of disputing Canada's official jobless figures somewhat difficult and complex. I have tried to keep numbers simple in the main text. If you want more detail or mathematical rigour, please refer to the "Notes and Sources."

How does Canada Employment arrive at Canada's official unemployment rate? One week out of every month, Statistics Canada surveys 62,000 Canadian households which have been carefully selected to form a representative sample of the Canadian population, and extrapolates from this sample to arrive at the official rate.

StatsCan's *Labour Force Survey* asks every person over the age of 15 in each sample household a series of questions. If respondents indicate they had a job during any part of the survey week (including self-employment), they are considered to be employed. Respondents who report that they did not have a job and actively sought employment during the survey week, are considered unemployed. The employed and the unemployed together make up the labour force. Anyone who falls outside these two categories Statistics Canada classifies as "not in the labour force."

Does this method make an accurate tally of all the unemployed in Canada? No, it's not even close. Let's look in detail at some of the people it leaves out.

■ DISPIRITED WORKERS

The government only counts as unemployed those people who are actively seeking employment. They leave out the people who want to work but who have been out of work so long that they have given up looking. StatsCan reluctantly admits that such workers do exist, and have even given them a rather apt title: "discouraged workers." They then do their best to minimize the numbers of discouraged workers by defining the term narrowly, counting only people who have given up looking for work in the past six months. By this definition, discouraged workers increase the "adjusted" unemployment rate by about one percentage point, from 11% to 12%.

We need a broader category, which I shall call "dispirited

workers." A dispirited worker is anyone who would look for work (and would work) if she believed that work were available.

Who are the dispirited workers? There are several main groups:

●* Older workers who "retire" early on inadequate pensions after being laid off or fired;

●* Single mothers who get trapped on welfare;

●* Teenagers and young adults who can't find employment and who either are on welfare or continue to live at home, supported by their parents;

●* Homemakers who would prefer to be working but who have found it impossible to get back into paid jobs;

●* Elderly widows with incomes below the poverty line.

How many Canadians are dispirited workers? There has been no direct tally of these groups, so an estimate must be based on indirect information. An Organization for Economic Cooperation and Development (OECD) study of western industrialized democracies found a strikingly consistent pattern: every time 10,000 people are added to the official unemployment rolls, 10 to 15,000 people mysteriously drop out of the labour force. The converse is also true: when the number of unemployed goes down, thousands of people "not in the labour force" coincidentally decide that they now want to work.

Does this apply to Canada? Since the recession hit in 1990, about 500,000 people have been added to the unemployment rolls. Sure enough, in a sharp break with the previous trend, the "not in the labour force" category has also grown by 750,000. Are you willing to believe it was a coincidence that three-quarters of a million people just happened to decide to take a break from working at the same time the economy slumped? Of course not.

Some of those people who left the workforce have gone back to school at least semi-voluntarily, and some have accepted early retirement offers — but it appears likely that most just decided there weren't jobs out there, so why look?

While the OECD study gives us strong evidence that high unemployment causes a lot of people to become dispirited workers, it doesn't tell us how many. Fortunately, the U.S. Bureau of Labor Statistics did a follow-up survey of people categorized as "not in the labour force" in that country. They found that within a year, about 20% had either worked or sought work. Researchers studying the data estimated that at any given time, about 13% of the people listed as "not in the labour force" want to work, and will work if given an opportunity.

If we take 13% of the 7 million Canadians "not in the labour force," it works out to over 900,000 people who should be listed as "unemployed" instead. This bumps up the true unemployment rate by six percentage points!

■ INVOLUNTARY STUDENTS

A second group not included among the unemployed are involuntary students. Education is such a lofty ideal in Canada that we have difficulty seeing it as other than a useful activity. However, in talking with students of various ages, my best guess is that one fifth of Canada's student population is in school under duress. These students are not in school for training or increased job prospects it might bring but because it's easier on one's pride to be doing *something*. Student loans need to be repaid some day but they're less demeaning than welfare. The current recession has intensified the trend. Says Doug Higgins, who follows education trends for Statistics Canada, "There's no jobs out there, so they think, 'Well I may as well pick up some education'."

Young people are also savvy enough to know that it is less damaging to their future employability to be "unemployed" studying anthropology or English than to be jobless for a comparable period. Being a few years older and having displayed the initiative to get a degree improves their chances in a tight job market. Our colleges and universities are functioning as expensive parking lots for bodies for which we have no place in the labour market.

About 5% of the working age population is in college or university. Twenty percent of that group translates to an additional 1% of the workforce which is unemployed in everything but name.

■ MARGINAL EMPLOYMENT

A third uncounted group is the scarcely employed — more than 6% of Canada's workforce works 14 hours per week or less. We don't know how many of that specific group are involuntarily under-employed. Surveys do show that about one third of all Canadian part-time workers would prefer to be working full time.

If we take one third of the 6% of the workforce that is barely employed, we could estimate that an additional 2% of the workforce is seriously underemployed.

■ COUNTING THE UNCOUNTED

What happens when we take the total of these various groups?

Unemployed group	% of workforce
Officially unemployed	11%
Dispirited workers	6%
Involuntary students	1%
Involuntary marginal part-time	2%
Total	20%

The harsh reality is that one in every five Canadian workers lacks substantive employment — more than 3 million people. If you find yourself among the unemployed, the underemployed or the misemployed, you don't need to feel quite so alone. You have plenty of company. Canada's unemployed represent the entire working age populace of six provinces: all of Newfoundland, P.E.I., Nova Scotia, New Brunswick, Manitoba, and Saskatchewan.

Of necessity, estimates are built into the figures I have given. Unemployment may be as high as 25% or as low as 17%. In either case, the real level of Canadian unemployment is much higher than the official rate.

To place these numbers in a historical perspective, we must consider that Statistics Canada estimates Canadian unemployment during the last depression peaked at 19% in 1933, and averaged about 11% in the period from 1936 to 1940.

The True Scope Of Employment Insecurity

What happens if we extend our tally to include all those who have insecure or unsatisfactory employment?

The Washington-based Economic Policy Institute has done an American tally of all those who are unemployed, underemployed, working below their skill level, those who are earning poverty-level wages, and those in temporary or insecure employment. They estimate that such "distressed workers" amount to 40% of the U.S. labour force. Two in every five American workers are in trouble.

Accurately estimating the number of Canadian workers employed below their skill level is difficult. However, if we leave out that one group, we can create a comparable tally for distressed workers in Canada.

The first group we can consider is workers with only seasonal or cyclical work — in fishing, forestry, construction, and the hospitality industry. There are almost 3 million temporary layoffs annually in Canada, so we must assume the number of Canadians with seasonal or intermittent unemployment is large — perhaps 6% of the workforce.

There is also a group of workers at the bottom end of the service sector. For years, inflation has risen faster than the minimum wage in most Canadian provinces. When unemployment is high, desperate people are willing to work for less than a living wage. This means businesses can operate which would not be viable if fair wages were paid. If low-end fast-food restaurants and the like paid decent wages, their prices would have to be higher. Fewer people would use those services and fewer such businesses would exist. The low end of the service sector is unemployment in disguise.

The low end of the job market is sizeable. Information from the Canada Council on Social Development suggests that any wage less than $7 per hour is below the average poverty line. At least 8% of the full-time workforce has hourly wages of $7 or less.

There is a further group of underemployed people we must add to our tally. Approximately 10% of the workforce works part time between 14 and 29 hours per week. Given survey information that almost one-third of part-time workers would like to be working full time, this suggests that another 3% of the workforce is under-employed.

One third of Canada's self-employed have incomes below the poverty line: a further 5% of the workforce to add to the total.

Unfortunately, though I was able to adjust some of the calculations to eliminate double-counting, there are some serious overlaps between the groups listed, particularly between underwaged work-ers and those with intermittent employment. One approximate way to correct for double-counting is to remove underwaged workers from the total.

What is the total of all these groups?

DISTRESSED GROUP	% OF WORKFORCE
Unemployed or marginally employed (previous table)	20%
Seasonal or cyclical work	6%
Underwaged	8%
Underemployed	3%
Non-viably self-employed	5%
Aggregate total	42%
Less estimated overlap	8%
Net total	34%

One-third of Canada's workforce has an insecure and problematic relationship with employment. If you have felt irrationally anxious about losing your job, you can go easier on yourself. Nervousness is understandable when we realize that one out of every three workers is in trouble.

ECONOMICS IS TOO IMPORTANT TO LEAVE TO THE EXPERTS

The next time the "spin doctors" in Ottawa try to claim an unemployment rate of 10%, you can translate that statistic into plain English: one out of every three Canadian workers is in trouble.

Economic policy is not some distant thunder in Ottawa. It affects our financial well-being, the struggles of our daily lives, and our security.

> Economic policy is too important to be shrouded in jargon or left to the experts. It is important that all of us, as citizens and voters, understand how we arrived at our current unhappy state.

It is to that task that we now turn.

PART II

WHAT IS THE PROBLEM HERE?

For many years, successive governments have glossed over the problems of the Canadian economy. The politicians say that nothing is really wrong with the economy — it just needs "a little fine-tuning."

Governments have responded to our economic problems in the same way they dealt with problems in the east coast fishery for northern cod. For years they denied any problem with the cod fishery. Then they downplayed the problem. Then they studied the problem. During all those years they were doing almost nothing to *solve* the problem. Government's efforts were focused on public relations and politics. "How can we make it *look* like everything is okay, or that the problem is under control?"

By the time the federal government finally admitted something was wrong, the problem had grown so bad the government had no option but to shut down the entire fishery. With no guarantee that fish stocks will ever recover, a way of life may have disappeared forever.

Following the same pattern, this government could take the Canadian economy down the drain. When it finally admits something is wrong, it will be too late. "Last one to leave, turn out the lights."

In the next five chapters we will explore fundamental problems within the Canadian economy. That's the first step to ensure that our government doesn't take our economy the way of the northern cod.

5

TOO MUCH:
The Problem of
Overproduction

Our basic economic dilemma has three elements:

❶ **A market economy gets sick whenever we produce more than we can consume.**

❷ **Our technological, work-obsessed society is constantly expanding its ability to produce.**

❸ **There are limits to our ability to consume.**

The Limitations of a Market Economy

For many years, anyone who talked about the limitations of the free market system risked being branded a communist. I'm still not sure I can discuss the limitations of a free market economy without being accused of wanting to trash it. So let me briefly digress with a metaphor.

A backyard vegetable garden can be an effective food production system — within certain limits. One of the most obvious limits is that a garden will only grow properly if it gets the right amount of watering.

The amount of watering doesn't have to be exact; a garden which is a little bit dry or a little too moist will still grow lots of food. So long as there is an approximate balance between how much water we add, and how much water the garden uses, everything is fine. That being said, a vegetable garden clearly does have an *effective operating range*: too little water, and plants wilt and wither; too much water, and rot, mould and mildew set in.

When I say that vegetable gardens grow well only when they get the right amount of water, I am not saying that vegetable gardens don't work; only that they need to be managed properly in order to produce a bumper crop.

In similar fashion, when I say that a market economy has an effective operating range, I am not saying that market economies don't work; only that they too need to be kept in balance to work properly.

■ A HEALTHY ECONOMIC BALANCE

The effective range for a market economy is when the total amount that can be produced is roughly in balance with what can be consumed. When an economy's overall capacity to produce and consume goods is in balance, the free market shows great flexibility in correcting specific surpluses and shortages.

The incentive structure in a free market system makes it responsive to changing needs and tastes. If too few vacuum cleaners are being produced, the price goes up. More companies will be motivated to make vacuum cleaners, and fewer consumers will be willing to buy them. On the other hand, if too many toasters are produced, the price is driven down. If the price of toasters is low, some toaster manufacturers will re-tool to produce something that commands a higher price: vacuum cleaners, perhaps.

A market economy's ability to balance relative needs and put energy where it is most required has made it the economic system of choice for most of the world's nations.

However, the incentives in a market system only work when there are both surpluses and shortages in the economy—a situation which happens whenever total production is roughly in balance with total consumption. When this is so, energy flows quickly from areas of surplus to areas of scarcity. Both surpluses and shortages are corrected quickly, which means prices remain fairly stable.

What happens if we venture outside the effective operating range of a market economy?

■ THE EMPTY SHELVES ECONOMY

The empty shelves economy is like a vegetable garden where the soil is parched and dry. When everything is in short supply, the self-correcting nature of the market breaks down. Producers of the least needed items have little incentive for switching to another commodity, because they can still sell all they make. Because of this, items in shortest supply will remain unavailable until prices for those items rise phenomenally. What results is a situation in which the market is ineffective at priorizing, and prices fluctuate wildly.

During World War II there were shortages of almost everything, which resulted in unstable prices. There was inflation, hoarding, and persistent shortages in critical areas. When there was a scarcity of everything, the market mechanism became erratic and ineffective in priorizing production and consumption.

Being at war gave government the clout to take drastic action quickly. Wage and price controls, rationing, and production quotas suspended free market operation until production rose to approximately meet demand. (We may have been "defending freedom" but we had the good sense to know when the authoritarian approach of a managed economy was required!)

Only on rare occasions has the North American economy suffered from underproduction. Overproduction, on the other hand, has been a chronic problem.

■ THE CROWDED MARKETPLACE: OVERPRODUCTION

The crowded marketplace is like a garden that is very, very soggy. When there's too much of everything being produced, there is little incentive for businesses to switch commodities — everything is hard to sell. Once again, the market system becomes ineffective at priorizing where the economy puts its energies, with the result that prices again become unstable.

When there's too much of everything, a market economy slides into a tailspin. The economy grows inefficient, unemployment rises, inflation erupts. In the worst cases, a depression ensues.

It's not a complicated process—we can see it at a local level. When there are four gas stations on a corner that can only support two, all four stations will fare badly.

When the economy has only specific surpluses, this kind of situation usually corrects itself quickly. If there are too many gas stations, one or more of the shop owners will get tired of working long hours for little return, and will close their business down. They'll convert the premises into an auto body shop, or tear them down and put up a video store. Or they'll move to another town where there's a shortage of gas bars. The remaining businesses can then operate more efficiently, at or near full capacity.

When there's too much of everything being produced, there's nowhere to hide. You can't go anywhere else because every market niche is overcrowded. All the owners can do is hunker down and hold tight. They'll do what they can to garner a larger piece of a too-small pie, cut their expenses as much as they can — and hope the other guy goes broke first.

The problem in an overcrowded marketplace is not with the level of wealth available, or the capacity to produce wealth. North America had more capacity to produce goods and services in 1930, during the Great Depression, than in 1928. It's just a design limitation of a market allocation system that the economy does badly whenever more is produced than can be sold.

All these negative effects happen only when production outstrips the ability to consume. If production and consumption are kept in rough balance, a market economy is as happy and bright as a well-tended garden.

Increasing Productivity

Technology and social changes have been steadily increasing our ability to produce.

Improvements in productivity have been most striking in the industrial and manufacturing sectors. Faster machinery, automated equipment, new materials, improved processes, and robotics have all dramatically increased the amount each worker can produce per hour. Output per hour for industrial workers in North America has been doubling every 21 years.

The B.C. forest industry is a good example. Logging produces half the number of jobs per volume of timber cut as it did 30 years ago. Newer pulp mills can produce more paper than the old ones with half the workforce. In newer sawmills, each log is automatically measured and cut to produce the most value for the least waste, so today's sawmill can get more lumber out of each log, in less time.

Substantial increases in productivity have also been seen in the white collar sector. White collar jobs have been revolutionized by computers and office machines. It is not uncommon among small businesses to find a secretary, switchboard operator, and book-keeper replaced by one person who does all three jobs.

Computerized drafting programs can produce building plans in a fraction of the time it would take an architect to draw them by hand. A good desktop publisher can produce in a couple of hours as much as a manual typesetter did in a full day. Banking machines increase not only the number of clients each bank employee can serve, but also the times at which the service is available.

Changes in technique have been almost as important as changes in hardware. Just-in-time delivery programs have reduced inventory costs in many industries. Management-by-objective techniques mean that fewer supervisory staff are required.

Even in the service industry, improvements in technique have increased workers' ability to produce. Restaurants have developed streamlined meal preparation procedures which enable staff to produce more food in less time. Hair-cutting franchises rely on new barbering procedures which enable staff to produce attractive haircuts in less time. Self-serve arrangements in the retail sector increase the number of customers each worker can serve. The average hourly output for all Canadian workers has doubled since 1950.

■ AN EXPANDING LABOUR FORCE

Changes in the size of the workforce have also increased our productive capacity.

In the past 40 years, married women have re-entered the labour force *en masse*. A norm of one breadwinner in a family of two adults and three or more children has been replaced by two breadwinners in a family of two adults and one or two children. Since 1969, the average full-time workweek has increased by more than three hours.

It doesn't take a math genius to realize that the total output of our economy will rise inexorably if:

❶ **Workers work more productively every year;**

❷ **We have more workers every year;**

❸ **Those workers work the same or more hours.**

In ideal models of the free market system, growth continues *ad infinitum*. The more workers produce, the more they consume, in a never-ending expansion of the economy. In real life, there are limits to our ability to consume.

The Limits of Our Ability to Consume

It's easy to increase indefinitely the amount we produce. However, our needs are not so flexible. In my imagination my needs may seem infinite, but in fact I have limited time, energy, and desires. Anything I buy requires time and energy to purchase, use, and maintain, and this constrains my willingness to consume. Beyond a certain point, possessions become a drain on my life rather than a benefit.

If I worked as a framer in construction, and switched from using a hammer to a nail gun, I might double the speed at which I could frame houses, but it's likely I'd still only want one house for myself. I might desire a condo in Maui, but the expense and hassle of caring for a second home would not be worth it.

If I worked in a factory that made hiking boots, the introduction of computer-controlled cutting equipment might well triple the rate at which I could cut the leather pieces that are assembled into boots. I wouldn't buy a new set of boots myself though, until the old ones wore out.

If I worked as a quality control inspector in a factory that made chocolate chip cookies, the introduction of automated sensing equipment might increase fivefold the number of cookies I could inspect. I'd like to eat five times as many chocolate-chip cookies, but my waistline would demand I should eat fewer, rather than more, cookies.

Productivity expands more readily than consumption. This is the wall against which the modern economy breaks, time and time again.

Frederik Pohl has written a delightful science fiction story entitled *Midas World*. The premise of the novel is that machines have been invented which produce unlimited consumer goods, without the requirement of human labour. To head off economic catastrophe, this mythical society has made consumption a legal and moral duty. Rather than working, the denizens of Midas World are kept busy from dawn to dusk, using and wearing out as many consumer goods as possible. (Rich people are allowed to live in smaller houses, eat less, and wear less ostentatious clothes.)

Midas World describes, in a whimsical way, the fantasy land of economists: a society where consumption expands as readily as production.

■ ENVIRONMENTAL LIMITS

Beyond our finite needs as individuals, we face another, more profound, obstacle to non-stop growth: the limits of the planet's resources.

The current structure of our economy requires that we must continually produce more, use more, waste more, just to keep unemployment from rising further. Meanwhile, the environment is demanding that we consume and waste much less, or the planet will soon be uninhabitable.

Some pro-growth economists have tried to argue that growth and a sustainable relationship with the environment are not mutually exclusive. Four of the most common positions are outlined below — along with their fatal flaws.

❶ **The workforce is shifting from manufacturing to service and information jobs, which do not necessarily require raw**

material use, so job growth may not require increases in raw material usage. This argument has a certain whistling-in-the-dark element to it. It asks us to forget that most services indirectly use large amounts of both energy and resources, and that most of those "clean" service workplaces have dumpsters full of garbage out back. This argument also overlooks the fact that technology is now eliminating service jobs as fast as they can be created. (Look at the layoffs of the 1990s: airline personnel, bank tellers, architects, managers, sales clerks — all services!)

❷ **Technology is making products smaller, lighter, and more energy efficient, which means growth can occur without using more natural resources.** Unfortunately, we are decreasing the person-hours of time needed to make modern appliances even faster. Newer automobiles weigh about 20% less, as the techno-optimists so gleefully report, but they can be made in one-third less time, so the tonnage of raw materials needed to keep an auto worker employed is still rising.

❸ **Environmentally sound practices such as recycling, reforestation, and organic farming are labour intensive, and will create job growth while taking better care of the environment.** The statement is true, but the effect is inadequate to the task. Sound environmental practices could create hundreds of thousands of jobs over the next decade. During the same period, technological advances are expected to eliminate millions of jobs.

❹ **Technology will find new sources of energy and raw materials as old supplies run out.** (This argument has great appeal for technophiles.) Unfortunately, it falls short on two grounds. As an example, let's look at oil. Advances in technology mean that we continue to find new oil reserves. Unfortunately, as we exhaust easily available supplies it takes more and more energy to find new supplies of oil, and more energy to extract and refine them. In *Beyond Oil*, John Gever estimates that by the year 2005 these difficulties will have reached the point where it will take one barrel's worth of oil energy to find and extract each barrel of new oil — at which point, if not before, technology will no longer be able to replace oil energy supplies which are used up. Furthermore, even if we could find more oil, we must greatly reduce the burning of all fossil fuels if we are to prevent an environmental nightmare via the greenhouse effect.

Each of these pro-growth arguments contains a grain of truth. However, their cumulative effect covers only a fraction of the gap between our current high resource usage and the much lower usage inherent in a sustainable relationship with the environment.

All four of the main trends outlined by the techno-optimists were as true in 1980 as they are now. Since 1980 growth rates have been very low, and unemployment levels have risen sharply, yet the use of energy and resources has continued to rise. Imagine how rapidly resource use would have increased if the economy had grown large enough to put all the unemployed back to work!

If we look at global trends, the picture is even clearer. As the developing world tries to catch up with a high-consumption North American lifestyle, increases in consumption here will be multiplied across the globe. Only by establishing a low-consumption lifestyle here can we hope to persuade the rest of the world not to climb aboard the Suicide Express. Technology does not provide an escape from the limits to growth. Only by consuming far less can we hope to avoid environmental catastrophe.

In years past, it was merely difficult to continuously expand consumption; now it is essential to our survival that we find ways to balance production and consumption without growth. Or, better still, to find ways to sharply reduce both production and consumption.

THE BIG SQUEEZE

We are caught in an impossible set of demands:

❶ **If we are to have a healthy economy, we need to consume as much as we produce.**

❷ **If we are to employ an expanding workforce, working longer and more efficiently, we must produce more goods and services every year.**

❸ **The protection of the environment demands that we reduce consumption drastically — and quickly.**

This basic contradiction has been squeezing us harder and harder. We have curtailed production as far as we can — and thrown 20% of the workforce out of work. We have expanded consumption as far as we dare — so much so that the planet may not be habitable for our children's children. Yet the economy is still drowning in over-production, only a short step away from collapse.

> If the Canadian economy were a garden, it would be drowning under six inches of water. The roots are rotting; the leaves mildewed; the fruits and flowers black with mould. Prospects for the harvest are dismal.

Clearly, we need to cut back on watering and perhaps install a drainage system. How do we restore balance? In Part III we will explore options on how to do that. First, though, we need to take a closer look at those economic equivalents of rot, mould, and mildew: inefficiency, unemployment, and inflation.

Then, a quick look at the global economy to see how the neighbours' gardens affect our own.

6

Efficient Inefficiency

Only on a very short-term basis will a market economy produce more than can be sold. Factories very quickly cut back on production and lay off staff once unsold inventory starts to overflow storage facilities. Overproduction soon changes to surplus capacity and surplus labour: under-utilized factories, farms, and shops, and under-employed or unemployed workers.

Unused production capacity and unemployment are two sides of the same coin. Both are forms of waste: a waste of expensive equipment and facilities, and a waste of human energies and talents. In this chapter we will examine both forms of surplus and the degree to which they create an inefficient economy.

The Extent of Surplus Capacity

For the past decade, even in good years our economy has operated well below capacity. In 1988, the best year in the past decade, Statistics Canada reported that Canadian industrial output briefly reached 87% of capacity. Even at the peak of the economic cycle, one eighth of Canada's industrial capacity was wasted.

This figure still manages to understate the true extent of wasted capacity. Retail stores, banks, service and commercial enterprises, and small businesses are not included in the above statistic. All indications are that each of these sectors operates much further below capacity.

Unemployment represents a further waste of resources. Even in the good year of 1988, the official unemployment rate hovered around 8%, which we know from Chapter 4 translates as a true unemployment rate of about 15%.

If we consider the combined effect of unemployment and overcapacity, we would have to estimate that the Canadian economy is operating at 80% capacity or less — at its best. Even in good years, the Canadian economy produces 20% less than it could have if it had operated at full efficiency.

In recent years, the level of waste has been higher still. In 1992, StatsCan reported that the industrial sector operated at about 78% of capacity. The service sector operated at even lower efficiency — as evidenced by a multitude of half-empty stores and restaurants. Real levels of unemployment hovered around 20% of the workforce. Overall, we may estimate that the Canadian economy produced only about two thirds of its full output capacity. If the Canadian economy had operated at top efficiency in 1992, it would have produced 50% more than it did.

The Mechanics of Inefficiency

To understand the mechanics of inefficiency, we need to look more closely at the example mentioned in the previous chapter: four gas stations at an intersection which will properly support two.

Let's imagine that all four gas bars offer top-notch service. At full capacity, each can serve 200 customers a day. Each business has an overhead of $400 per day in fixed or irreducible expenses — rent, utilities, telephone, and the wages of a minimum staff complement. At full capacity, each customer's "share" of this overhead works out as $400 ÷ 200, or $2.00 each.

Let's suppose there are only 400 customers a day needing gas. That's enough to keep two stations operating at capacity. Unfortunately, there are four shops splitting the market, each of which gets roughly 100 customers a day.

The same $400 overhead must be covered by fewer customers. Now the average customer's share of the overhead is $400 ÷ 100, or $4. To cover costs, an owner would have to charge $2 more for each tankful of gas.

The owners may raise prices, but with all four stations hungry for business it's unlikely they'll be able to raise prices by the full $2 per tankful. Instead, they'll take less profit out of their businesses, work longer hours, and cut back the work hours of their employees. They'll pressure staff to work faster for less money.

It's possible to make a ballpark estimate of the costs of current levels of overcapacity. If fixed overheads make up 20% of a manufacturer's costs for a certain product when that business is operating at capacity, overheads will rise to 25% of the manufacturer's costs if the business is operating at 80% capacity. That extra 5% in costs can be made up in only two ways: higher prices for the consumer, or lower profits for the manufacturer.

The effect on business profits is much larger than might immediately be apparent. A small business owner may only make a 5% profit margin on sales. If her firm's cost per item rises by 5%, and a hungry marketplace restricts increases in the sales price to 3%, it slashes the owner's income by 40%.

Often the only way an individual company can regain its profitability is to reduce its costs by installing labour-saving equipment. What then? The company can produce as much output as before but with fewer staff. Perhaps it will lay off some of its employees — increasing the surplus of labour. Perhaps it will raise production levels enough to keep all of its employees working, and lower prices enough to steal away most of its competitor's customers. Its competitors then are less efficient, less profitable, and have more surplus capacity. Some of them may even go broke — converting overcapacity to unemployment.

Here we have a paradox: whenever a company takes steps to improve its efficiency, it creates changes which either increase market overcapacity — making other companies less efficient — or increase unemployment — making the entire economy less efficient.

Whenever surplus capacity increases, businesses are caught in a squeeze. Even when they raise prices and push their employees harder, profits are likely to shrink. Surplus capacity makes for bitter lose-lose battles, as organizations struggle to apportion the costs of inefficiency between customers, employees, and shareholders.

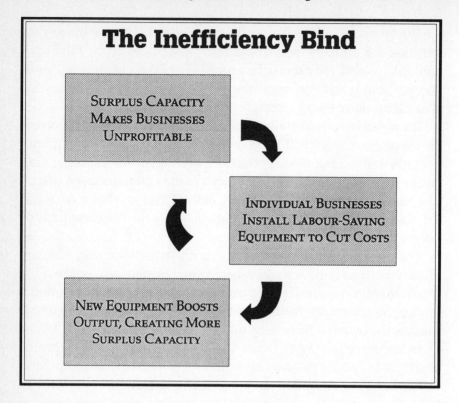

The Inefficiency Bind

SURPLUS CAPACITY
MAKES BUSINESSES
UNPROFITABLE

INDIVIDUAL BUSINESSES
INSTALL LABOUR-SAVING
EQUIPMENT TO CUT COSTS

NEW EQUIPMENT BOOSTS
OUTPUT, CREATING MORE
SURPLUS CAPACITY

National Inefficiency

Chronic overcapacity means few job opportunities are available when workers are laid off. Many cease to be taxpayers, becoming instead a drain on the public purse, first on unemployment insurance rolls and later as welfare recipients.

Rising unemployment increases the overhead costs of running the country: there are fewer people able to support the government through taxes, and increasing numbers who must depend financially on government support. Should workers, taxpayers, or the jobless bear the brunt of the cost of the inefficient use of our human resources? Much blame and name-calling results as we struggle to apportion burgeoning social expenditures.

Confidence Lost

At best, overcapacity makes a market economy inefficient. At worst, it creates the economic equivalent of cardiac arrest.

Confidence is the lubricant which keeps a market economy in motion. Only insofar as I have confidence that I will have an adequate income next month will I spend most or all of this month's paycheque.

Surplus capacity undermines confidence. When business profits are falling and unemployment is rising, cautious individuals and businesses cut back on their discretionary spending to create a savings buffer in case next month's income is smaller — or non-existent.

If enough people reduce their spending, a vicious circle develops. Consumers spend less because they fear an economic downturn. Reduced spending causes the economy to contract, making consumers

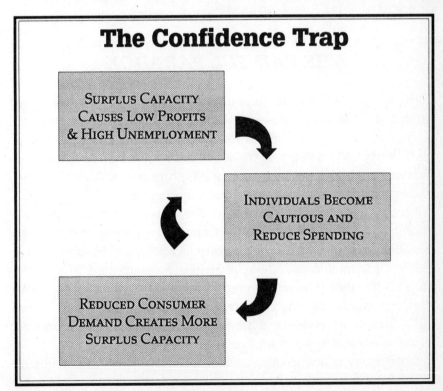

The Confidence Trap

SURPLUS CAPACITY
CAUSES LOW PROFITS
& HIGH UNEMPLOYMENT

INDIVIDUALS BECOME
CAUTIOUS AND
REDUCE SPENDING

REDUCED CONSUMER
DEMAND CREATES MORE
SURPLUS CAPACITY

more fearful. They spend even less, beginning another round of contraction. If the cycle continues long enough, the economy can spiral down into a recession. If confidence erodes to the point of panic, a depression ensues.

It is important to remember that North America had more capacity to generate wealth in 1931, in the midst of the Great Depression, than it did in the 1920s boom years. The production facilities, human talents, and natural resources of wealthy nations were all still there. The missing element was confidence, the "animal spirits" that keep an economy in motion. Once the circle of confidence is broken, it's hard to get an economy moving again.

Just as overcapacity and unemployment erode consumer confidence, so does lack of confidence reduce consumer spending and aggravate overcapacity. Eroded consumer confidence has now so paralysed commercial exchange in Canada that one out of every six Canadians lives in poverty — even though we clearly have the necessary labour, resources, and expertise to generate a high standard of living for all our people.

THE PAINFUL PARADOX

Inefficiency is everywhere. If you go into a shop and there are more sales clerks than customers — that's inefficiency. When you stop for a bit of lunch at noon and the restaurant is nearly empty — that's inefficiency. When you are stressed to the verge of a heart attack by overwork, while your grown son or daughter is pushed to the edge of despair by unemployment — that's inefficiency.

Because we fail to understand the nature of our economic dilemma, we have configured the Canadian economy in the worst possible fashion, so that it turns every technological blessing into a curse. Unworkable economic strategies have created a horrible paradox: the more efficient our technology becomes, the more inefficiency it injects into the economy as a whole. Each time I, as an individual, work longer and harder, it makes the national economy less efficient and less productive.

Inefficiency is not an intrinsic feature of the market mechanism. When kept in its proper operating range, a market economy is very efficient. Inefficiency builds up whenever the economy is designed in such a way that production chronically outstrips consumption. We can state this limitation on a market economy's operating range in the form of a design constraint:

> **To function efficiently, a market economy must be structured so that an approximate balance between production and consumption is always maintained.**

7

The Unemployment Blues

*The trouble with being unemployed is that
you never get a day off.*

P. CORRIGAL

Unemployment is the long-term result when the ability to produce outstrips the ability to consume. The growth of surplus capacity is restrained because it makes businesses unprofitable. Companies close money-losing factories; some businesses go broke. Beyond a certain point, excess capacity will convert to unemployment until the balance between production and consumption is restored.

We have now reached the point where the only way we can keep the employed working 40 hours per week, and limit production to what can be sold, is to have permanently high unemployment.

Persistently high unemployment is not just a human tragedy. It is also a disaster for the economy, especially for the interests of working people. High unemployment sets in motion cycles which have two profound effects:

❶ Declining wages for the working population;

❷ Built-in overcapacity.

The Incredible Shrinking Paycheque

Labour is a market commodity like any other, and when there's a continuing surplus of labour, the value of labour declines relative to other commodities. If there are lots of hungry, out-of-work people on the job market, employers can find good staff even at bargain-basement wages. People may be so desperate for work that they are willing to be strikebreakers, which puts unions under pressure to make wage concessions.

Inflation often makes this process invisible. Workers may get a raise in pay each year and still be worse off because the cost of everything they buy is going up faster than their wages.

The way in which wage changes are measured has also obscured the magnitude of average wage losses. Statistics on changes in hourly wages in Canada are generally determined by tallying the wage settlement contracts negotiated by large Canadian unions. When measured this way, wages in Canada have almost kept pace with inflation. If you're a unionized logger or pipefitter, your real earnings are about the same as they were a decade ago.

Unfortunately, millions of Canadians have been shifted out of high-wage jobs. Over the past 15 years, Canada has seen four major job shifts: from large businesses to small ones, from industrial jobs to the service sector, from full time to part time, and from waged employment to self-employment. In each case, the new jobs involve lower average hourly earnings.

It's hard to determine exactly how far the average Canadian hourly wage has fallen over the past 10 years, but based on both Canadian and American evidence, a figure of 10% could be considered conservative.

■ THE VICIOUS CIRCLE OF UNEMPLOYMENT

When prices go down, it causes the supply of most market commodities to shrink and thus brings supply and demand back into balance. If house prices go down, for instance, many would-be vendors will keep their homes off the market. This equalizes the number of buyers and sellers and stabilizes prices.

Unfortunately, when wages drop, the demand for employment doesn't shrink. When wages drop, the supply of labour increases as individuals work longer hours in an attempt to maintain their standard of living. The classic example is the former housewife who says, "I had to go back to work — we couldn't make ends meet on one paycheque any more." In the past 15 years we've seen the labour force growing faster than the population, as declining wages push more families to add a second breadwinner.

While most commodity surpluses are self-correcting, a surplus of labour is self-aggravating. High unemployment leads to lower wages. Lower wages mean that workers work longer hours, and more people are forced to enter the labour force. Since the number of jobs available hasn't changed, both trends result in more unemployment — setting the stage for even lower wages.

Here we have another paradox. If I work more hours, I expect to

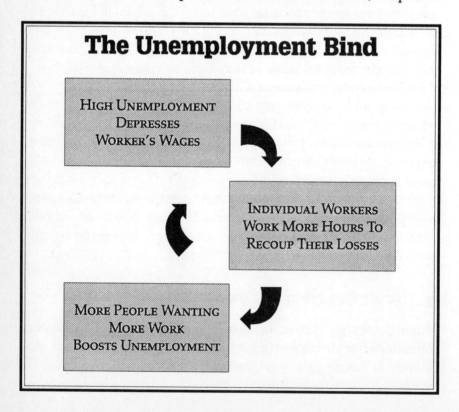

The Unemployment Bind

HIGH UNEMPLOYMENT DEPRESSES WORKER'S WAGES

INDIVIDUAL WORKERS WORK MORE HOURS TO RECOUP THEIR LOSSES

MORE PEOPLE WANTING MORE WORK BOOSTS UNEMPLOYMENT

be better off financially. However, when everyone works more hours, the value of my labour goes down. This is the treadmill on which we find ourselves — working more, and earning less.

The Imbalance Between Wages and Prices

A market economy is in balance when people's incomes enable them to buy an amount of goods and services roughly equivalent to what they produce.

When unemployment is at reasonably low levels, wages rise with productivity. Employers must pass on most of the extra income that results from increased productivity, or their employees will leave and work for someone who is willing to reward workers according to their ability to produce. When workers' purchasing power rises in step with productivity, everything that is produced can also be sold. The increase in what workers produce is matched by an increase in what they can afford to buy.

When high unemployment persists, wages do not reflect gains in productivity. They tend to decline in real dollars, even when productivity is rising — as has happened in the past several years.

■ THE WORKER AS CONSUMER

When productivity rises at the same time wages are falling, the economy is headed for trouble.

I remember hearing of a conversation between Henry Ford II and the head of the United Auto Workers' Union, the gist of which went something like this:

Henry was gloating to the union leader, "These new robots work 24 hours a day, 7 days a week. They don't get sick. They don't take holidays. They don't take coffee breaks, lunch breaks, or smoke breaks. They don't go on vacation. They don't go on strike. They're perfect."

The UAW leader looked at him and said, "Henry there's one other thing those robots don't do."

"What's that?" asked Henry.

"They don't buy cars," replied the UAW leader.

Contrary to what might be assumed, rich people make lousy consumers. If $10 million is spread among the 1000 employees of a factory, those workers will buy hundreds of cars, homes, televisions, tools, groceries, and haircuts. The money will generate new business for thousands of factories, restaurants, farms, and insurance agents, circulating throughout the economy.

If the same $10 million is given to the rich factory owner, what will be purchased? Perhaps an extra BMW, a luxury condo somewhere warm, the services of a scullery maid—and a great deal of real estate and investments. The rich person will purchase only a small number of goods and services. While he might keep one investment banker employed, the rich person will not make purchases that keep the economy moving.

Working people form the backbone of consumer spending. When their wages are so low that they can't afford to buy all they produce, the "recycling" of the economy is interrupted. The economy starts producing more than can be sold. (The effect is further magnified when a significant portion of the workforce is unemployed, or living on subsistence wages.)

When unemployment is high, wages are pushed down. The owners of corporations have lower expenses, and can make high profits. Wealth moves away from the working classes and accumulates with the rich. The recirculation of wealth is interrupted.

This whole problem is not new. During the early part of the nineteenth century, the introduction of the factory model increased productivity greatly, creating high unemployment, which, in turn, pushed wages down. The new technology provided an increased potential to create wealth, but economic growth was lacklustre until activities within the labour movement reduced the over-supply of labour, causing wages to rise. Once workers could buy all they were making, healthy economic growth was possible.

A similar situation occurred in the Depression of the 1930s. During the Depression, productivity increased faster than workers' wages. Workers produced more goods than they could afford to buy. Production outstripped the purchasing power of the workforce even when millions of people's basic needs were unmet.

The economy was stuck in a bind. As long as unemployment was high, wages stayed low. So long as wages were low, the economy's

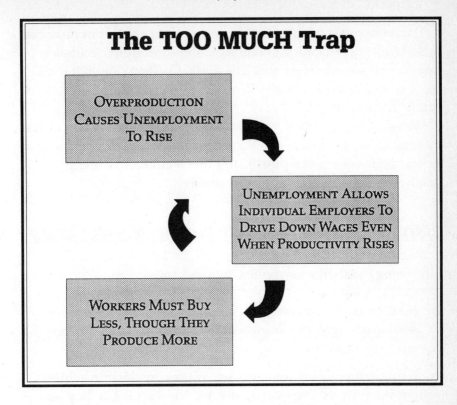

The TOO MUCH Trap

OVERPRODUCTION CAUSES UNEMPLOYMENT TO RISE

UNEMPLOYMENT ALLOWS INDIVIDUAL EMPLOYERS TO DRIVE DOWN WAGES EVEN WHEN PRODUCTIVITY RISES

WORKERS MUST BUY LESS, THOUGH THEY PRODUCE MORE

ability to produce outstripped the purchasing power of the population, resulting in a sick and stagnant economy. It took World War II to end the cycle. Once much of the population was off at war and there was a booming demand for war materials, wages rose to match workers' productivity. Only then was that essential balance restored between what could be produced and what could be sold.

An economy in which wages do not reflect productivity has a built-in flaw: It can never be healthy.

■ THE OBESE ECONOMY

The science of economics was developed within the context of the expanding empires of Europe, in an age of mechanistic thinking. The accumulation of capital was seen as the purpose of all economic activity. Our ways of thinking about the economy haven't changed much since, despite what we now know about ecology and systems theory.

The economy is not a collection of unrelated events but rather an ecology of interrelated activities. It is the constant recirculation of money that generates growth. The market system does not require the accumulation of capital — it works as well as it does in spite of capital accumulation.

Wealth is to the economy as stored fat is to the human body: a little bit squirrelled away here and there provides resilience and a source of energy for the future, but if too much collects in one place, it distorts the organism and impairs vitality.

THE UNEMPLOYMENT DOUBLE-WHAMMY

Reviewing briefly the key points in this chapter:

❶ In a market economy, high unemployment results in declining wages. Declining wages, in turn, cause unemployment to rise further.

❷ If high unemployment causes wages to decline while productivity is increasing, the workforce cannot buy as much as it produces, and the economy stagnates.

The problems described in this chapter do not occur when unemployment is kept low. They should not be seen as necessary evils of a free market economy, but rather as an operating constraint. It is a design limitation of a market economy that it works badly when high unemployment is allowed to persist.

> **To remain healthy, a market economy requires that unemployment be kept low.**

8

The Inflation Balloon

*In the dicta of Adam Smith, the individual search for
profits would always promote the nation's economic
growth. But in practice a problem developed. Too often,
Adam Smith's "invisible hand" became the hand of the
pickpocket. Free unfettered markets had a habit of
discovering very profitable but nonproductive activities.*

LESTER THUROW

The traditional explanation for inflation is that when an economy is
growing too fast, shortages of a wide variety of goods result in widespread price increases. These price increases then work their way
through the entire economy in a domino effect.

This theory has fallen out of favour in recent years. Throughout
much of the 1970s, the economy experienced "stagflation" — high
inflation in a stagnant, sluggish economy. It was hard to blame inflation on rapid growth when the economy was shrinking.

Newer theories on inflation focus on two elements: an inflationary
psychology, and a trigger or engine that starts and drives the spiral.

The inflationary spiral is a classic feedback loop. Once inflation
starts, it quickly begins to feed on itself, with higher prices leading
to higher wages and vice versa. A "psychology of inflation" develops, with all players in the economy regularly raising the price of
goods, services, or labour, based on the assumption that the cost of
everything else will rise.

Economists believe that an inflationary spiral also requires some
out-of-the-ordinary increase in prices, both to get the cycle started

and then to keep it going. Huge increases in the price of oil were seen as the engine behind the high inflation of the early 1970s.

Traditionally, wage increases in excess of gains in productivity have been seen as the trigger for inflation, but since wages have fallen behind the rate of inflation for many years, this explanation is increasingly suspect.

Is there another engine for inflation that would make more sense? Raw material and food prices have trailed the rate of inflation, so they don't seem like good candidates. Oil prices have also fallen behind inflation in recent years. In only one segment of the economy have price increases consistently exceeded inflation: land and housing prices.

Increases in real estate prices quickly reverberate through the economy. When it costs more to buy a home, it drives up what the home-buyer demands in wages or small business income. When the cost of property for factories and malls goes up, so do the prices that must be charged for the products they make and sell.

The speculative growth of real estate prices has been the real engine for inflation.

What's happened to cause real estate prices to rise so precipitously? The inflation of real estate prices, and the more general inflation that results from it, are a function of an undue accumulation of capital.

Investment Within a Healthy Economy

Limited amounts of great wealth accumulate in a healthy economy. When unemployment is low, workers bid up wages until most investors make only modest profits. In a healthy economy, there are enough opportunities for lucrative investment in new factories and businesses to absorb most of the limited investment wealth available.

In a healthy economy, the wealthy *do* invest some of their money in real estate and existing stocks, but mostly as a safe place to park their wealth rather than as a means of generating income.

In a healthy economy, the primary determinant for house and stock prices is what economists call *use value*. The value of a particular stock is decided primarily by the dividends it pays. The purchase value of a rental property is determined primarily by the rental income it generates. The price difference between a large lot and a small one is decided primarily on the basis of concrete differences: the level of privacy, amount of garden, and so on. In other words, the price of stocks and real estate is determined primarily by their usefulness relative to other commodities.

Canada has no shortage of land or building materials. There should be no reason for across-the-board inflation in real estate prices, if the economy were sound. There would be fluctuations in the value of real estate as particular neighbourhoods are perceived to be more, or less, desirable. Individual properties would appreciate if they had been spruced up, and depreciate if they had been allowed to run down. Overall though, the price of real estate would remain stable, reflecting the stability inherent in prices that are based on use value.

Unfortunately, we do not live in a healthy economy.

Investment Within an Unhealthy Economy

When unemployment is high, wages become depressed. The result is that owners of factories and corporations have lower expenses, and can make higher profits. Since the rich have limited abilities to consume, most of this extra wealth must go into investments. When this growing pool of wealth goes into the traditional avenues for investment — building new stores and factories — production quickly outstrips consumption. The stagnation of the crowded marketplace appears.

As will be illustrated in Chapter 14, corporate concentration enables large companies to generate high profits from existing production facilities even in a crowded marketplace. However, there are few opportunities for lucrative investment in new or expanded production facilities. The economy is in trouble precisely because there's already too much being produced.

A bad combination ensues: a growing pool of investment capital, yet few opportunities for investment in new facilities. Where does this wealth go? In an unhealthy economy, excess investment capital goes into stock and real estate speculation.

When the wealthy begin to invest unusually large amounts of capital in real estate and existing stocks, the laws of supply and demand cause prices for those commodities to rise. The expectation that prices will continue to rise then draws more investment capital into real estate. A speculative boom develops, with prices being driven progressively upwards by the hope or expectation that they will be even higher in the future.

The primary determinant of stock and real estate prices in such a circumstance is no longer their use value, but their *speculative exchange value*. A surplus of investment capital is thus the fuel for rapid inflation in the price of real estate and stocks.

■ SPECULATION DOESN'T MAKE MONEY — IT *TAKES* MONEY

Rising stock and real estate prices appear to be marvellous money machines that generate great profits out of nowhere. In truth, insofar as rising prices are the result of speculation, no new wealth has been created. The on-paper profits that come to real estate speculators always involve a loss for someone else.

Commodity speculation of any kind functions exactly like an old-fashioned chain letter.

In a typical chain letter, the recipient is requested to send $1 to the top name on an enclosed list of five names. The recipient is then to stroke the top name off the list, add her own name to the bottom, and mail off the letter to 20 friends or relatives. If the chain survives to the point where your name reaches the top of the list, thousands of people will get letters and each will send you a dollar.

On the surface it looks like a great money machine: invest one dollar and get back thousands! In fact, no new wealth is generated. For every dollar that someone on the front of the chain gains, someone at the end of the chain must lose a dollar.

All speculation works in precisely the same way. It doesn't create new wealth. It merely transfers wealth from those at the end of the chain to those earlier in the chain.

We like to think of money as the reward for the creation of wealth. When money motivates people to either create or share wealth, it serves a socially useful purpose. If investment money is used, for instance, to open a new factory that makes bicycles, the profits from that factory may be seen as a reward or commission for creating the new, concrete wealth of thousands of bicycles. Similarly, the wages of the workers at that factory can be seen as their reward for assembling the bicycles.

If a person builds an addition to his home and subsequently sells that home for a higher price, that profit can be seen as a reward for creating the concrete wealth of a larger house. If, instead, that person rents out the addition, the rental income is a reward for sharing the living space.

Speculation, on the other hand, does not create any new, concrete wealth. The gains from speculation exist only on paper. The only thing that speculation can be rightly said to reward is the good luck or the good judgment of finding one more person in the speculative chain from whom wealth can be taken.

We have developed a certain grudging respect for the wheeler-dealers who make their wealth speculating in stocks and real estate. We need to be clearer that speculation serves no socially useful purpose. Speculators do not create wealth; they merely feed on it.

Speculation is a form of gambling; it has the same something-for-nothing appeal as lotteries. Perhaps the reason we have not been clearer on the moral bankruptcy of speculation is that many of us secretly hope that we too can climb aboard the gravy train of speculative wealth.

I may see that my house has increased in value, and think that I am thousands of dollars richer. However, I still live in the same house, and there is no more money in my pocket than there was before. The speculative growth of housing prices has not significantly benefitted individual home owners, only professional speculators.

The Speculative Cycle and Inflation

There is an additional reason we should neither respect nor value speculation. Speculation is the source of the inflation which dogged our economy for so many years.

The buying frenzy of a speculative boom can temporarily jack up the price of real estate far beyond its use value. Wealthy speculators

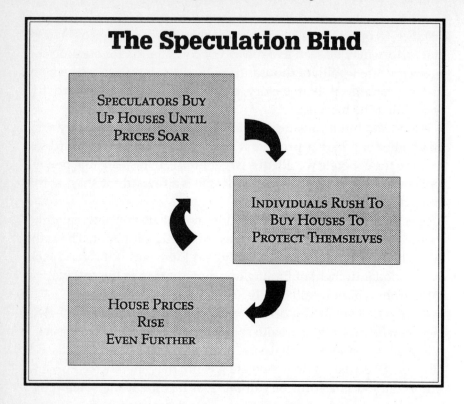

The Speculation Bind

SPECULATORS BUY
UP HOUSES UNTIL
PRICES SOAR

INDIVIDUALS RUSH TO
BUY HOUSES TO
PROTECT THEMSELVES

HOUSE PRICES
RISE
EVEN FURTHER

can buy up a large number of properties and carry them at a short-term loss. The shortage of real estate properties that results causes prices to rise. Once a speculative boom develops, prospective home-owners will often be stampeded into buying homes that are more expensive than what they are worth in use value. They will buy based on the fear that if they don't buy immediately, prices will rise so high they won't be able to afford a home at all.

Speculative growth in the stock market functions similarly. Throughout the early 1980s, the over-supply of capital created a speculative run-up of stock prices.

It would be bad enough if the inflation of stock and real estate prices were a one-time event. Unfortunately, higher real estate prices push up the cost of everything else — setting the stage for more real estate speculation.

Real estate prices can run only so far ahead of the price of everything else before people stop buying property. However, higher prices for real estate push up the costs of everything else in a general inflation of prices. Once inflation has raised the price of everything else, the price of real estate is no longer disproportionately high. Speculation in real estate can begin all over, setting the stage for the next round of inflation. Real estate prices and inflation ratchet each other upwards, like an inchworm working its way up a tree trunk.

Governments have tried, with limited success, to control this vicious circle using the blunt instrument of high interest rates. Because high interest rates make it harder to afford a mortgage on a house purchase, they take a lot of steam out of real estate speculation. This slows increases in the price of real estate, putting a damper on the main source of inflation.

Unfortunately, high interest rates themselves increase the cost of housing for anyone who renews a mortgage. High interest rates contribute to inflation almost as much as they curb it, so interest rates must rise painfully high before they impact on inflation.

In 1992 we saw a clear demonstration of the role of real estate

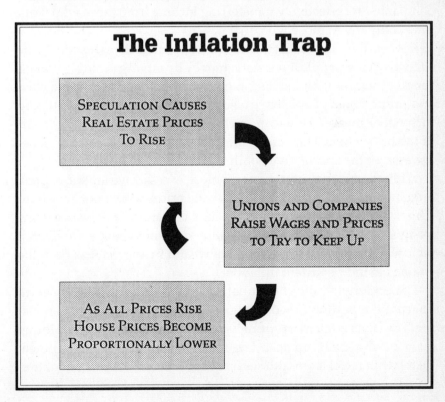

The Inflation Trap

SPECULATION CAUSES REAL ESTATE PRICES TO RISE

UNIONS AND COMPANIES RAISE WAGES AND PRICES TO TRY TO KEEP UP

AS ALL PRICES RISE HOUSE PRICES BECOME PROPORTIONALLY LOWER

prices on inflation. Across most of North America, the real estate bubble of the late 1980s burst, resulting in stagnant or falling real estate prices. As interest rates fell, so did the cost of home owners' mortgages, which further curbed increases in the cost of housing. Once rising real estate prices were no longer driving inflation — bingo — low rates of inflation.

Some people claim that rapid increases in stock and real estate prices are evidence of a buoyant economy; in fact, they reflect an unbalanced economy.

■ PROPERTY PICKS THE POCKET OF LABOUR

When stock and real estate price increases exceed the rate of inflation, they direct more of an economy's wealth to those who own stocks or property. Higher real estate prices mean that a larger share of a worker's income goes to rent and mortgage payments. When stock dividends run ahead of inflation while wages fall behind inflation, companies are effectively transferring income from those who work for a company to those who own it.

It is true that it's not just the rich who speculate in real estate. Quite a few working people have made money by buying multiple homes, renting them out, and selling them when prices rise. Middle-class and professional people have also made small fortunes speculating in the stock market. However, such people make up only a small part of the big picture. They are neither the source, nor the prime beneficiaries, of the speculative boom in stocks and real estate.

Without the fuel of a huge pool of excess investment capital, ongoing inflation in stock and real estate prices would not have happened. The fact that some middle-class investors have been carried along in the slipstream of the wealthy does not change the overall picture. The undue accumulation of wealth by the rich has been the engine behind persistent inflation.

The underlying effect of inflating real estate prices has been to increase the portion of working people's income that goes to housing. The effect is felt most strongly by first-time home-buyers. Homeowners who trade up to a larger home will also feel the pinch. Renters often feel it too, although a surplus of rental accommodation may limit the ability of new landlords to pass on increases in real estate prices.

The long-term effect of the inflation in real estate is to transfer wealth from workers to property owners.

■ WHEN THE BALLOON POPS . . .

Uncontrolled speculation in real estate makes a market economy unstable. Boom-and-bust cycles happen because there are limits to how far speculation can jack up housing prices. When real estate costs push ahead of inflation, more and more of the workforce's income is directed to paying for housing. As prices rise, first-time home-buyers are increasingly stretched — often beyond the bounds of prudent borrowing. As housing costs consume more and more of the family budget, less income is available for other purchases. Consumer spending is choked off; the economy stalls. Many of the people who lose their jobs are young home-owners already at their credit limits. They are forced to sell, the market is glutted, and prices tumble.

Looking at the historical record, speculation in real estate creates two separate cycles of economic instability. There is a short cycle every 10 to 15 years, where housing prices climb until they choke off consumer spending. Prices then drop sharply (though not as far as the total climb) and the economy slips into a recession.

Those who were left holding the bag in the real estate slump of 1981 know very clearly that someone always pays for the gains of the speculator.

There is also evidence of a long economic cycle, every 50 to 60 years. As housing prices climb over the decades, the economy builds up increasing levels of debt, both public and private. Eventually, the inexorable logic of compound interest causes debt to spiral out of control. A full-blown depression ensues; real estate prices collapse. By the end of the depression, bankruptcies have liquidated most debts — and the economy is ready to start a new cycle. It is not yet clear whether the real estate slump of 1991 marked the end of another short cycle, or the beginning of the end of a long cycle.

Recessions and depressions — and the pain that those economic contractions create — are a long-term consequence of uncontrolled real estate speculation.

SPECULATION AND INFLATION: GAMBLING WITH THE FUTURE

What have we discovered in this chapter?

❶ If wages decline while productivity is increasing, excessive amounts of investment capital accumulate, which then cause a speculative run-up of stock and real estate prices. Higher prices, in turn, fuel inflation throughout the economy.

❷ When stock and real estate prices run ahead of inflation, the wealth of the economy shifts from labour to property, aggravating the problem of overcapacity caused by falling wages, and eventually leading to economic collapse.

A healthy economy requires the prevention of undue accumulations of wealth.

9

The Unravelling of the Global Economy

*I sympathize, therefore, with those who would minimize,
rather than with those who would maximize, economic
entanglement between nations. Ideas, knowledge, art,
hospitality, travel — these are the things which should
of their nature be international. But let goods be
homespun whenever it is reasonably and conveniently
possible; and, above all, let finance be primarily national.*

JOHN MAYNARD KEYNES

In recent years, Canada's political leaders have maintained that increased exports are the way to solve the twin dilemmas of overcapacity and unemployment. The strategy of promoting exports has caused Canada to lower tariff barriers, linking us increasingly to a global economy.

Unfortunately, global trade has all the problems of the North American economy. As well, the world economy faces the problem of Third World debt. Finally, as an *open system*, the global economy is spiralling out of control.

Too Much All Over

All over the world there are more people working, and working more productively. This is particularly true in the newly indus-

79

trialized countries, where state-of-the-art factories leapfrog nations from labour-intensive craft shops to high-tech productivity superior to that of North America. The result has been an across-the-board surplus of goods and services in the world economy.

It is extremely tempting for countries to "dump" their surpluses overseas at less than the cost of production. While the dumping of agricultural products has received the greatest attention, most Canadian commodity markets suffer foreign dumping from time to time.

Dumping has had a destabilizing effect on many of our industries. Rather than seeing it as the problem, dumping should be seen as a symptom of overcapacity. It is the problem of TOO MUCH on a global scale.

Worldwide Unemployment

A second problem faced by the world economy is that overcapacity has created global unemployment which, in turn, has depressed wages worldwide. In most of the developing world, the labour movement is weak or non-existent; unemployment in the 25 to 50% range has driven wages way down.

This means that Third World countries can produce far more goods and services than their consumers can purchase. Their economies could not function without a high-wage export market.

Cheap labour in the Third World, meanwhile, exerts a downward pressure on wages in Canada.

Worldwide Currency Instability

Depressed wages have meant huge profits for the rich in the Third World, and resulted in inflation rates of more than 100% annually in many countries. (Only part of this hyper-inflation is fuelled by undue accumulations of wealth. Third World governments, even more so than our own, have a habit of printing money whenever they run short — a sure-fire recipe for inflation!)

Hyper-inflation in much of the world has destabilized world

currency markets, transforming them into arenas for speculation. The *Globe & Mail* reports: "Currency traders who specialize in little more than speculation buy and sell about $26 billion worth of money a day — enough to handle a month's worth of imports and exports. As traders buy and sell, the dollar rises and falls."

As currency traders take runs at one currency after another, exchange values fluctuate wildly. A Canadian exporter or importer may see his/her profit double — or disappear — in the time it takes goods to get from one country to another. The more unstable global currencies become, the harder it is for any Canadian business to plan for the future with any degree of confidence.

Third World Debt

All through the 1970s and early 1980s, Third World governments borrowed hundreds of billions of dollars from North American banks. The banks assumed that such governments couldn't go broke, so they kept loaning Third World countries more money each year. Some of the money went into establishing an industrial base. Much of it was wasted on impractical or poorly designed projects. A whole lot of the money went into the Swiss bank accounts of government officials and their friends.

Much of the Third World is now deeply in debt. To meet the interest payments on their huge debts, many developing nations have had to gear their entire economies towards earning foreign exchange, through unprecedented levels of raw material exports.

This hunger for foreign exchange has created low prices and instability in raw material markets. Wood, metals, agricultural products, and oil have all been subject to volatile markets.

Western governments, including Canada's, find themselves in a bind. It is our banks which loaned all those billions to the Third World. If Third World countries default on their loans, many of our banks will find themselves awash in red ink. We would like to protect raw material producers from low commodity prices, but putting up tariff walls would mean Third World countries couldn't earn the interest payments that keep our banks out of trouble.

Much of the Third World is having trouble keeping up with the interest payments on its debts. The loan principal is not being paid off. At some point the people of the Third World may become fed up with growing cotton for export instead of food for domestic consumption. At some point the Third World may decide it has more to gain by walking away from its debts.

If there is a bright spot in this whole messy situation, it is that, for several years now, Western banks have been writing off their Third World loans. The banks would still bleed if the Third World defaulted on its loans, but most would probably survive.

Even where the consequences of Third World debt are sweet, the aftertaste is bitter. North American consumers have enjoyed bargain prices on a whole range of agricultural goods, manufactured goods, and foreign-made crafts. Unfortunately, these same low prices have driven thousands of Canadian firms into bankruptcy, with the loss of hundreds of thousands of jobs.

As worrying as Third World debt is, it is not the worst problem of the global economy. The scariest aspect of the global economy is that no-one is at the wheel.

A Ship Without a Captain

When nations were divided from one another by high tariff barriers, they functioned as relatively closed and autonomous systems. The lower tariffs associated with the General Agreement on Tariffs and Trade (GATT) mean that boundaries between nations have become more porous. The world functions more like a single economy. Canada has allowed itself increasingly to be drawn into the open system of world trade.

Unfortunately, in the absence of effective world government, the global economy lacks overall organization. No one body has the power to set rules or to decide economic policies for the whole system.

The United Nations has shown little ability to address collective economic issues — differences in members' political philosophies mean it can't even agree on what's wrong, let alone act. The World Bank has some limited ability to bully the world's poorer nations.

However, it too has proven unable to confront collective economic problems. The world economy is a ship with no-one at the helm.

■ THE PLACE OF RULES IN A FREE MARKET SYSTEM

Why is the need to set rules and policies important? We receive a lot of right-wing propaganda to the effect that a free market works best when unfettered by rules. Rules have been portrayed as impediments to a fully competitive market.

To speak against this position, let us imagine a very competitive football game — one without rules.

At the opening kick-off, the Roughriders' quarterback is momentarily stunned when an opposing tackle hits him in the chest with a carefully thrown rock. He still has the presence of mind to jab a bony finger in the eye of the first Argonaut attacker, blinding him. He looses a short pass before being clotheslined by the next attacking linebacker.

On the next play, a Roughrider ruse involving a second football fails. The ball carrier is kicked in the crotch, and the Argonauts recover ... but I think you get the picture.

Rules are how we cooperate in a market economy. As with football, rules are designed to make competition safe, fair, and mutually beneficial. Rules set community standards that all players in the economy must observe. Rules are as essential to the proper functioning of a market economy as they are to a sporting game of football.

Businesses which observe workplace safety standards, install pollution controls, and pay employees a living wage have higher expenses than those which would shirk such responsibilities. Rules insure that responsible businesses are not at a competitive disadvantage.

Within a closed economic system, all players play by the same rules. A nation with tariff barriers protecting it from unfair imports can insure that all businesses adhere to community standards of health and safety rules, environmental protection, and worker rights.

Businesses within a closed economic system can still compete hard. They can compete to be the most efficient, to have the best products, to have the lowest prices, and to give the best service. They can't compete by skimping on safety measures or pollution controls, murdering union leaders, or paying their employees 60 cents an hour.

Trade barriers are essential when our trading partners lack safety, environmental, and employment standards. Trade barriers are also important insofar as we lack the ability to establish collective economic policies with our trading partners.

■ THE IMPORTANCE OF COHERENT ECONOMIC POLICIES

As Guy Dauncey has observed: "Globally, the financial crises which threaten us with crash and collapse express the vacuum of leadership at the global economic level."

There are no existing mechanisms for taking collective action to solve global overcapacity and unemployment. At the same time, in an open system, restoring an individual nation's economy to health is like bailing out a holed boat. Forces outside that nation's boundaries nullify and overwhelm positive changes made to the economy.

If we can skip back to our vegetable garden analogy for a minute, it may make the picture clearer. If my garden is waterlogged, I can fix the problem by watering it less, or by putting in drainage tiles. However, if both my neighbours' yards are flooded, my actions will only do a little bit of good; water draining in from either side will keep my yard soggy. In such conditions, if I can't get my neighbours to change, I'll need to build a small dike around the perimeter of my yard before I do anything else. Tariffs are the economic equivalent of a dike, and act in the same way to restore a nation's autonomy.

Many economists view the protectionism of the 1930s as a mistake. By aggravating the general collapse in confidence, protectionism did initially make the Great Depression worse. However, in the absence of any international ability to take collective action, it was the only way that nations were able to recover the control they needed to take corrective action. Without firm tariff boundaries, nations which corrected their over-production problems found their economies destabilized by trade with nations which had not done so.

Heavy protectionism can be expected again as the world economy continues to deteriorate. Nations which are heavily wired into world

trade will suffer more than those which have continued to do most
of their trading internally.

■ TRANSNATIONAL HARDBALL

The players who most benefit from the lack of community standards
and collective policies inherent in an open system are transnational
corporations.

The largest of the world's corporations have stock ownership
spread throughout stock exchanges on three continents. Such companies owe allegiance to no people, place, or flag; their only motive
is profit.

Transnationals have played hardball in the global economy,
taking their business wherever wages and taxes are lowest, and
safety and environmental rules the weakest. "Competitive poverty"
has resulted, with nations vying against each other, lowering wage,
safety and environmental standards to attract transnationals.

The only thing that has protected Canada from more transnational
blackmail is that countries which best fit the cheap and sleazy prescription are often unstable. It's bad for company profits if rebel
forces burn down factories, or nationalize them. Canada is secure
enough that it remains attractive to some transnationals despite its
higher, more expensive standards.

■ TRADING BLOCS AS OPEN OR CLOSED SYSTEMS

Canada has some legitimate reasons for wanting to be part of a larger
economic unit. Our country's population is small enough that the
domestic market for specialty goods is too small to generate economies of scale. We also have more of some raw materials than we
could ever sell domestically. Would membership in a trading bloc
give us larger markets and still allow the healthy autonomy of a
closed system?

There is no reason why a closed economic system must be limited
to a single country. What is essential is that all businesses within the
economic system be bound by the same standards, and that there be
some mechanism for setting economic policies for the entire bloc.

The European Economic Community (EEC) is an example of a trading bloc which has the means to manage its collective house. An international parliament in Brussels has the power to legislate hours of work, minimum pay scales, floor prices on agricultural goods, etc. Within its borders, the EEC has the necessary tools to control total production, set base prices on raw materials, and enforce uniform environmental standards.

Membership in the EEC would be advantageous for Canada, offering us both the benefits of a larger market and the integrity of a closed system. However, the trading bloc to which we do belong, the Canada-U.S. Free Trade Zone, should not be seen as similar to the EEC.

There is no North American parliament to make collective decisions or set collective policies. Furthermore, without safety, environmental, and employment standards that apply to all of North America, Canada is at a competitive disadvantage within free trade. Some U.S. states have abysmally low health, safety, and employment standards. Canada has the fool's choice of either standing by while Canadian firms lose out to unfair competition, or lowering our standards to match those of South Carolina.

In a similar way, if Canada taxes corporations enough to prevent undue accumulations of wealth, companies will simply move to Texas. If we control work hours to limit production, and the U.S. does not, their overcapacity will drive us into recession too. The proposed North American Free Trade Zone would throw us into direct competition with even lower Mexican standards.

Problems with both free trade deals will be explored further in Chapter 15.

Future Scenarios

Have you ever wondered why there are so many wars of separation these days? A deteriorating global economy generates political instability because most people lack a sense of the Big Global Picture. What they see is that they are working harder and earning less. In such a situation, it is easy to assume that if I have less, someone else must have more — and that they took it from me. It's an easy jump from there to thinking that my clan, ethnic group, or region would be better off on its own. Canada is not immune to such jealousies. Unless we insulate ourselves from a deteriorating global economy and fix the underlying imbalance in our economy, there is a good chance that Québec (or Western) separatism will tear Canada apart.

Where does the global economy go from here? In *Head to Head*, Lester Thurow documents the extent to which the world has already begun to split into separate trading blocs. Thurow suggests there is a high risk that worldwide protectionism will create a global economic collapse. My only disagreement is that a careful examination of the evidence would put the shoe on the other foot: global economic collapse is creating worldwide protectionism.

Thurow's only hopeful scenario for the future is that a united Europe will emerge as a powerful trading bloc of 850 million people. The European parliament would set collective rules and policies which would bring production and consumption within Europe back into balance. As the world's single largest market, Europe would then have the clout to set the rules for world trade. Europe would only trade with other nations if they instituted rules and policies similar to those of Europe. The European Parliament would, in effect, become the manager the world economy so desperately needs.

Thurow's vision offers hope, but is deeply disturbing for Canadians. Traditionally, Canada's rules and economic policies have been a hybrid, midway between the American and European economic models. Under free trade, we have been painfully restructuring our rules and policies to become more like Americans and less like Europeans. If Thurow is right, in 10 years we'll have to turn around and painfully undo those changes so that we can be allowed access to a new, European-style global trade network.

GLOBAL TRADE: NOT A SOLUTION, BUT A PROBLEM

Where does all this leave us? To summarize:

- ☛ Overproduction threatens to drive the global economy into a full-scale depression;

- ☛ Prolonged high unemployment has depressed wages worldwide, resulting in a world economy with a built-in tendency to produce more than it can sell;

- ☛ Hyper-inflation in much of the Third World exerts a destabilizing influence on world currency prices;

- ☛ Interest charges push Third World nations to export more and more, glutting world commodity markets and aggravating problems of overproduction;

- ☛ The problems in the world economy will not go away without collective intervention, and existing means to do so are woefully inadequate.

We are misled when Canada's political and business elite refers to international trade as "increasingly competitive." Global trade is falling apart, out of control, and headed for complete collapse. Only strong trade boundaries can limit the damage that a collapsing global economy will otherwise inflict upon us.

Only when we *limit* foreign trade, do we have the national autonomy we need to restore a healthy balance between production and consumption in Canada.

PART III

ELEGANT AND INELEGANT SOLUTIONS

Two statements summarize what's been said so far:

❶ Productivity grows inexorably in a technological society, while the growth of consumption is constrained by human and environmental limits.

❷ To perform effectively, a market economy must be structured so that production is roughly equal to consumption, and unemployment is kept low.

The conditions of the first statement clearly work against the demands of the second. Over the past two centuries, many strategies have been developed to deal with this dilemma. These strategies fall into three groups: measures which reduce the supply of labour; measures which increase consumption; measures which decrease production.

Over the next five chapters we will examine and rate several strategies of each type. Rating is important because some solutions clearly work better than others. *Elegant solutions* solve the problem in a direct way, with positive side effects. *Inelegant solutions* deal with our dilemma in a roundabout way, with negative side effects. *Stopgap solutions* are temporary fixes that cover up symptoms while allowing the problem to grow.

The *non-solutions* of the Canadian government are examined separately in Chapters 15 and 16.

10

Limits on Who Works

No Irish Need Apply.
ANONYMOUS BIGOT

Historically, one of the prime means of restricting the number of people who worked, thereby restricting production, has been to limit access to the workforce.

Major Exclusions From the Workforce

In the early 1800s the whole family worked. Children from the age of six, married women, and seniors were all part of the workforce.

We often see the introduction of child labour laws in the past century as being for the welfare of the child. In fact, much of the movement against child labour was driven by the need to reduce the supply of labour. The gradual abolition of child labour effectively reduced the size of the workforce by a third.

Throughout the latter part of the nineteenth century, and again after World War II, we saw a similar process with regard to married women. The rationale for married women leaving the workforce centred on the idea that women could make better mothers and homemakers if they weren't employed. Originally, it was only in rich families that women could afford to be without paid employment. As worker incomes rose, the trend spread down through class levels to a large majority of Canadian families. Eventually, a working wife was seen as a sign of the husband's financial inadequacy. Legal, practiical, and prejudicial measures strengthened the trend by marginalizing the married and single women remaining in the workforce.

The exclusion of married women was not complete; even in the 1950s, 25% of married women had paying jobs. Nonetheless, excluding most married women shrank the size of the labour force by about one-third.

There was some degree of public consciousness that the exclusion of married women from the workforce played an important role in reducing unemployment. After the end of World War II, for example, it was considered a patriotic duty for married women to leave non-traditional jobs to make way for returning servicemen. The trend towards single breadwinner families offset increases in productivity and kept the economy in a healthy balance.

Seniors were excluded from the workforce in a similar fashion. The public rationale was that retirement and its accompanying pension were rewards to an employee for long service. Pensions were also seen as health safeguards for seniors. What started as a benefit within a few collective agreements eventually became a national norm. The Canada Pension Plan and Old Age Security were instruments designed, in theory, to insure that every worker had an adequate income by age 65.

There was some public recognition that retirement was a way of opening up new job vacancies, particularly managerial positions. Within this context, many corporations established mandatory retirement rules.

Initially, mandatory retirement created only a minor reduction in the size of the workforce. With rising life expectancies and an aging workforce, its importance has grown rapidly. For many companies, early retirement has become the tool of choice for reducing workforce size. Looking at society as a whole, the institution of retirement has significantly reduced the size of the workforce — and will have an even greater effect in years ahead as the workforce ages.

Excluding certain groups from the workforce has been an extremely potent tool in curtailing our productive capacity. What were its side effects? There have been some salutary ones; children and retirees have been given time and energy for play, creativity, and leisure. When children had a stay-at-home parent available, they received more active and attentive parenting.

Economic Effects of Workforce Exclusions

The enforced exclusion of various groups from the job market has also had profoundly negative side effects. Women, children, and the old are all disproportionately represented among the poor in Canada.

In theory, women and children were supposed to be supported by husbands. The family was supposed to be an economic unit where resources were shared. In those few cases where a husband died or abandoned the family, our social safety net was supposed to take over.

In practice, male breadwinners are often miserly in the amounts they dole out to wives and children. The rate of family breakdown has skyrocketed. Estimates are that soon 20% of families will be headed by single moms. The safety net of welfare falls below the poverty line.

In theory, older workers were all supposed to have adequate pensions by age 65, with a social safety net protecting those few who did not. In practice, many Canadians do not, and will not, have adequate pensions when they retire.

Most pension plans have what is called a "vesting period" of five to ten years. If an employee changes jobs during that period, that employee loses pension rights. The way many plans are designed, even employees who leave a plan after 20 years of contributions may end up with a disproportionately small pension.

A second drawback with the exclusionist approach is that it invites abuse of excluded groups. This abuse takes place both through economic coercion and through negative stereotyping. Excluded groups find their status and influence reduced. Patronizing and dismissive attitudes are disguised as benevolent caretaking.

■ STEREOTYPING AND DISCRIMINATION OF EXCLUDED GROUPS

Women's wages in Canada are only two-thirds of their male counterparts'. Women are under-represented in managerial roles. Limited access to high-profile, high-status careers has undercut women's ability to enter political life. With only token representation in government and management, women have had little power to change conditions which discriminate against them.

The stereotyping of women as flighty, overly emotional, and preoccupied with trivia has been used by men to rationalize continued discrimination against women in the workforce. Gender humour isn't funny when its purpose is to "keep women in their place."

Seniors have suffered similar discrimination. Annual service increments mean that senior workers have the highest wages in many organizations. Many corporations use forced and early retirement as deliberate strategies to get rid of their highest-paid workers. The "voluntary" nature of early retirement is often suspect; many employees have turned down an early retirement offer of a reduced pension, only to be laid off shortly thereafter with no pension at all.

The exclusion of seniors from the workforce encourages ageist prejudices. The stereotype of doddering oldsters, indecisive, unable to take care of themselves, has been used to force seniors from their homes. Seniors are patronized with half-price movie tickets, but their serious concerns are dismissed.

John Holt argues persuasively in *Escape from Childhood* that children also suffer serious discrimination as a result of their exclusion from the workforce.

We pretend that we protect children from having to work. Yet as adults, we know there are all sorts of benefits attached to working. Working provides opportunities to learn and socialize, make income, and feel worthwhile. As adults without jobs we often find it hard to build a sense of ourselves as competent, worthwhile beings. The same is true for many children. The destructive behaviour of many teens may be a cry of pain: it hurts to feel useless. Conversely, some of the most solid and secure adults I know are people who had the opportunity as children to work at a family business or farm.

Child labour has an ugly image. Nonetheless, I am sure there are thousands of Canadian boys and girls who would much prefer child labour to child poverty.

We pretend that children and young adults are too irresponsible to work. Yet I have seen 10-year-olds on farms and in mom-and-pop stores who handled their duties more competently and conscientiously than most adults. The "irresponsibility" of children is a self-fulfilling prophecy. In *Centuries of Childhood*, historian Philippe Aries provides clear evidence that childhood as we now know it is a modern invention. In other places and times, children have proven to be competent and responsible workers.

This is not to suggest that all children would be better off if we plugged them into full-time jobs. It *is* saying that many of our children and young adults would be better served if offered a mix of work, play, and schooling.

Stereotyping children as cute and irresponsible enables the adult community to run roughshod over the legitimate rights of young human beings. Childhood is the training ground for all later forms of disempowerment.

The Unbalanced Society

Controlling the size of the workforce by excluding certain groups creates imbalances in the lives of both excluded and included groups. It was this pattern which first led me into the promotion of flexible work schedules.

Consider the division of labour that is rapidly becoming the norm in our society. Young people are being kept out of the workforce until their mid-20s by the use of inflated educational standards. Older workers past age 55 are being forced into "early retirement" in ever greater numbers.

As a result, the entire employment burden of our society falls on the age cohort from 25 to 55. This is the same age group that is also responsible for the raising of children and, increasingly, for the care of elderly parents. The "sandwich generation" is burning out under this triple burden. Meanwhile, the young and the old are suffering from *not* having jobs. Our current economic configuration is exactly opposite to how an economy friendly to the interests of families would be structured.

■ US-OR-THEM THINKING

Perhaps the strongest drawback to excluding specific demographic groups as a way to control productivity is that it invites an us-or-them mentality. When hard times hit, dominant power groups go looking for a scapegoat.

The extreme form of the approach is prejudice against identifiable minorities: blacks, Jews, the handicapped, homosexuals, natives, and immigrants. With this mindset, the only way I can have enough is if someone else doesn't get any.

ABANDONMENT OF THE EXCLUSIONIST STRATEGY

As a nation, we are increasingly aware that the exclusionist approach to controlling workforce size is unjust, and results in an unfair distribution of wealth and power. Charter of Rights challenges to sexism, mandatory retirement, and ageism are not just a function of that legislation, but of new attitudes towards minority rights.

When women, seniors, and teenagers are allowed to be full participants in the labour force, it will be more likely they will receive economic justice. It will be more possible to build a society where political power and influence are shared.

It is right and proper that we work towards the re-entry of excluded groups with all possible speed. What must be recognized, however, is that this re-entry cannot take place in isolation.

Children, seniors and married women were excluded from the workforce to reduce the supply of labour. It has been a disaster for Canada's economy to begin reversing those exclusions without a corresponding reduction in the workweek.

11

Sharing the Work

*So long as there is one who seeks work and cannot find it,
the hours of work are too long.*
SAMUEL GOMPERS

We humans have limited needs. The most direct and elegant way to restrict total production to stay within those needs is to restrict the aggregate hours that the workforce works. Reduced work hours, employee time-off benefits, impediments to overtime, and flexible work schedules have all been used to curtail the supply of labour.

Reductions in the Length of the Workweek

In days gone by, there was a much stronger awareness that a surplus of labour hurts not just the unemployed, but all working people. The quote at the chapter head is from Samuel Gompers, one of the founders of the North American labour movement, and typifies past attitudes of organized labour.

Through the period from 1860 to 1950, the workweek was gradually reduced from about 80 hours per week down to the 40 hours we think of as standard. Reductions were first negotiated in labour contracts and later given legal backing through employment standards legislation.

The standard workday was cut back in increments from 12 to 10 and finally to 8 hours. The standard workweek was cut back from 7 days to 6.5, to 6, to 5.5, and then finally to the current 5-day week.

In 1933, organized labour succeeded in getting the U.S. Senate to pass a bill which would have implemented a 30-hour workweek. Fierce opposition from the business community eventually caused President Roosevelt to scuttle the bill. This defeat marked the end of shorter working hours as a central economic strategy and laid the foundation for the consuming madness of recent decades.

■ SIDE EFFECTS OF A SHORTER WORKWEEK

Reducing the length of the standard workweek has been the simplest, most elegant solution to problems of overcapacity. Not only does a shorter workweek restore economic balance in times of surplus, but it is also a benefit to the workforce in and of itself. Extra time for family life and leisure is a boon for working people.

In the past, a shorter workweek has sometimes been accompanied by a reduction in take-home pay. This can be seen as a negative side effect, though the income loss was usually far less than the corresponding reduction in hours. However, the consistent effect of shorter work hours has been that the economy grows healthier; wages rise, and workers' income soon exceeds former levels. The usual alternative has been the slow erosion of wages characteristic of our own labour-surplus economy.

The argument could be made that a reduction in the standard workweek restricts a person's freedom to work long hours. However, we must consider the alternative to a shorter workweek, which is a large over-supply of labour. High unemployment and low wages are typical of a labour-surplus economy. In such an economy, people who can't find jobs don't feel very free. Neither do the people who are forced to work longer hours as their wages drop. The loss of freedom inherent in a mandated workweek reduction is usually smaller than the loss of freedom associated with living in a sick economy.

A shorter workweek, if clumsily implemented, can sometimes result in less efficient use of plant and equipment. When the shift was made from a six- to a five-day workweek in the late 1940s, some factories were closed an extra day a week, which left expensive plant and equipment idle. On the other hand, many firms shifted to rotating shifts to cover seven-day-a-week operation; these organizations actually made fuller use of facilities. A carefully thought-out reduction in the standard workweek can actually improve efficiency — a positive side effect, rather than a negative one.

Time-off Options

Work hours have been cut back over the past century by an expansion of paid time-off. These benefits can include statutory holidays, vacations, lunch and coffee breaks, sick leave, sabbaticals, paid educational leave, and maternity/paternity leaves. Cumulatively, these benefits reduce annual work hours by a considerable degree:

BENEFIT	AVERAGE REDUCTION IN WORK HOURS
Vacations	5%
Statutory holidays	4%
Lunches	5%
Coffee breaks	5%
Sick leave	4%
Maternity leave	1%
Sabbaticals	1%
Total	25%

Paid time-off benefits shrink the effective size of the workforce by about one-quarter. The spread of time-off benefits has had an important effect on controlling overcapacity.

Paid time-off began as perks negotiated in specific collective agreements. Once a time-off benefit became widespread in the labour market, federal and provincial employment standards were used to set minimum standards. (For example, two weeks of paid vacation per year is the statutory minimum in Canada.)

Time-off options have shown limited effectiveness in spreading employment because of how we have structured overtime in North America. (This problem is discussed further in the next section.)

Time-off benefits have obvious salutary side effects for the working population. Many of us live for holidays and vacations. Unfortunately, from the employer's point of view, time-off benefits can create scheduling nightmares. Most time-off comes in little chunks here and there, and arranging staff coverage for holidays, vacations, lunch breaks, and sick time has given grey hairs to more than one supervisor.

A second negative side effect is that statutory time-off often results in inefficient use of space and equipment. Extra statutory holidays, for instance, would help curtail total production, but for many businesses they would mean more time that plant and equipment were left idle.

The least disruptive form of time-off benefit is an increase in vacation time. Because vacation time comes in large chunks, it is less disruptive than longer lunch breaks or more statutory holidays. Other nations have used longer vacations to restrict the supply of labour. In France, the legal minimum is six weeks of paid vacation annually. Almost nowhere in Europe do employees get less than four weeks of vacation per year. Canada's statutory minimum of two weeks' vacation is miserly by comparison.

Europe also makes greater use of paid educational leave. Sometimes such leave is paid for through a national training fund; at other times it has been legislated as a required employee benefit. Educational leave has the obvious attraction that it increasing the skills of the workforce at the same time it reduces the surplus of labour.

Increasing the minimum annual vacation in Canada to five weeks would reduce average annual work hours by about 4%, which would significantly cut unemployment. Alternatively, requiring all employers to provide 10 days of paid educational leave per year would make a similar reduction in unemployment.

Impediments to Overtime

Overtime premiums, as originally envisioned, were designed to actively discourage employers from working their staff overtime. Impediments to overtime were designed to protect the health and family lives of workers, but also to insure that employment was shared around. The growth of fringe benefits has indirectly undercut the effectiveness of current impediments to overtime.

Over the years, the cost of benefits has grown. In most workplaces, it now makes up one third of labour costs. Most benefit costs do not grow when overtime is worked. Whether an employee works 40 hours per week or 60, the employer pays the same for medical and dental plans, statutory holidays, vacation, and sick leave.

It costs employers only marginally more to pay existing staff over-time rates than it does to hire permanent relief staff with their atten-dant benefit packages. Using existing staff means that an employer does not pay severance if extra work hours — and relief staff — are cut in order to scale back production. As a result, many workplaces cover most of their time-off benefits through overtime.

In workplaces where it is routine for employees to work eight to ten hours of overtime every week, the employment-spreading benefits of paid time-off have effectively been wiped out. The employees of such firms get attached to the luxuries that overtime work enables them to buy. To protect this extra income, unions will often fight against management proposals for paid relief staff.

As they are now structured, rather than being an impediment to longer hours, overtime premiums actively encourage the use of over-time to cover holiday, vacation absences, and illness. Increasing use of overtime means a *de facto* increase in the workweek for many workers. Such increases aggravate our economic dilemma.

Changes to how overtime is structured could make current or future time-off benefits more effective in spreading employment. Higher overtime premiums, and overtime premiums paid as tax to the government rather than as income to the employee, would dis-courage overtime. Instead of overtime, Sweden uses pools of perma-nent, full-time relief staff to cover absences of regular employees; such pools make up about 4% of Sweden's workforce.

Stronger impediments to overtime would also have the valuable side effect of discouraging workaholism.

Work Options

Job sharing, phased retirement, banked overtime, permanent part-time, V-time, and deferred salary leaves are voluntary, individual arrangements to reduce work hours.

JOB SHARING is an arrangement in which two workers share the hours, duties, salary, and benefits of one position.

PHASED RETIREMENT is an arrangement in which workers can cut back their workweeks in the years before retirement, without reducing their eventual pensions.

BANKED OVERTIME is an arrangement whereby workers can take extra time-off in lieu of overtime pay.

PERMANENT PART-TIME is less than full-time work, with benefit and seniority rights comparable to full-time.

V-TIME is a payroll system in which employees can sign on for small reductions in work time (typically 2.5%, 5%, 10%, 20% or 40%), and take the time off as a shorter workday, shorter workweek, or extended vacation.

DEFERRED SALARY LEAVES are saving plans where, typically, 20% of employees' salaries are held in trust for four years, after which they can take a year off, with pay.

Survey results indicate that almost one-third of full-time workers in Canada would prefer to be working less—even if it meant earning less. Economist Frank Reid has estimated that if everyone in Canada who wants to work less were allowed to do so, it would open up 250,000 new jobs.

Work options have clear, beneficial side effects in that they remove us from the one-size-fits-all straitjacket of the 40-hour workweek. They make more balanced lifestyles possible for some, and open up new jobs for others.

If flexible work schedules received more support from the union movement and the federal government, their spread could make a significant dent in Canadian unemployment. (Work Well currently receives no government funding to promote work options.)

An additional limit on the use of flexible work schedules is that they are more popular in a healthy economy than in a sick economy like our own. This is a function of three factors:

- The depressed wages that accompany prolonged unemployment mean that in a sick economy, fewer workers can afford to work less;

- When unemployment is high, employers are often more rigid and inflexible about alternative work schedules than when unemployment is low;

♦* When business is poor, employees tend to be afraid to ask for reductions in work hours.

For these reasons, alternative work schedules cannot be looked at as the main solution to the problem of unemployment. However, if unemployment were lower and wages higher, increased use of work options could easily take us that last step to full employment.

THE ELEGANT SOLUTIONS

Reductions in the length of the workweek, longer vacations, impediments to overtime, paid educational leave, and flexible work schedules are all potent strategies to bring production and consumption back into balance, painlessly. They offer clear social benefits in the form of increased leisure and reduced stress.

Why, you may ask, haven't reductions in work hours been used in recent years? That's an excellent question. The long answer covers the whole of Part IV of *Working Harder Isn't Working*. The short answer forms the introduction to the next chapter.

12

Consuming Addictions

Growth for growth's sake is the ideology of
the cancer cell.
EDWARD ABBEY

For the past 40 years, we have abandoned controls on the size of the workforce in favour of measures to expand consumption. To a large degree, this is an unintended result of the post-war 1950s.

After World War II, North America lacked so many consumer goods that it took years to fill the backlog. And as fast as the economy grew, we produced more babies, who in turn had more needs. North America had almost 20 years in which to develop the fantasy of a permanently expanding economy.

When we began to hit the limits of our real needs somewhere in the 1960s, we couldn't consciously address the situation. Too many sacred cows were involved:

- We were in a Cold War with the Reds. Suggesting that our market economy had any limitations would have been tantamount to treason.

- We were the Free World. The idea that we might need to limit how many hours a person could work, or who could work — that would be totalitarian!

- Technological progress was our secular religion. To suggest that it could lead to harm was political heresy. How could we speak ill of our plastic, fantastic lover?

In this political context we couldn't take steps to restrict the labour supply. We couldn't even admit there was a problem. Instead, we developed unconscious and unstated strategies to expand consumption.

Advertising, disposable products, military spending, government spending, and debt have been the primary strategies to expand our economy's capacity for consumption.

The Big Sell

The most prominent way we've tried to expand our ability to consume is through advertising. Every day we are subjected to hundreds of advertising messages designed to persuade us to need and buy more. Advertisers talk explicitly about "creating needs." That's the hidden agenda of all advertising: to get us to buy more.

If the Soviets had conducted the degree of psychological manipulation the advertising industry has inflicted upon us, we'd have called it brainwashing.

Advertisers often maintain their intent is not to increase consumption but merely to increase the sales of a particular brand of product. In point of fact, most advertising tries to do both. Particularly in areas of new technology, the consumer must be sold on a product as much as on a particular brand. Potential customers must first be sold on the value of fax machines per se, before they can be sold on the virtues of Panasonic versus Sony.

Advertising promotes a specific set of values connected with high consumption. New, bigger, faster, and more expensive are better. It wants us to measure our self-worth in the dollar value of the toys we own. The underlying message of advertising is that things will make us happy. If you want to be successful, important, sexy and happy: buy X, Y and Z.

Advertising is built around selling sizzle, not steak. If people bought automobiles only as dependable transportation, they would buy fewer and less expensive cars. Instead, we are sold on images that the right car will bring us public adulation and sexual prowess.

Where sizzle isn't enough, advertisers rely on shame. "Ring around the collar," "jungle mouth," and endless vignettes on the life-threatening embarrassment of dandruff all try to manipulate us with shame.

Advertising can even persuade us to follow behaviour counter to our physical wellbeing. Canadian consumption of alcohol and tobacco fell off faster after advertising restrictions were placed on those products. How many drunks still live in the fantasy world of advertising, imagining they are sophisticated and worldly wise, when their behaviour is loud, crude, and boorish?

Advertising has been very successful at getting North Americans to consume. It is in fact a double-effect expansion of consumption, as advertising itself requires labour and resources in its production. Whole forests of trees have given their lives to become advertising flyers.

■ SIDE EFFECTS OF ADVERTISING

Unfortunately, advertising must also be considered the most toxic of strategies in the side effects it brings. Let's quickly itemize the negative impacts of advertising.

First, advertising confuses us about our real needs, causing us to buy items that don't really serve us. People don't need to be persuaded to buy what suits their real needs; the need itself is motivation. The constant repetition of advertising, and the continual pairing of products with evocative images of success and sexual allure, are not about rational choices; they are manipulation. In William Wordsworth's words: "Getting and spending, we lay waste to our powers . . . We have given our hearts away, a sordid boon!"

Advertising manipulates us into wasting time, money, and resources on products that won't make us happy. By placing so much attention on getting and having *things*, advertising takes energy and attention away from spheres of life which are better able to generate satisfaction. The real juice in life comes from loving relationships, personal challenges, the appreciation of nature's beauty, and acts of service. Self-worth is found in the open and giving heart, not the all-consuming mouth.

The end result of the orgy of consumption brought on by advertising is the ongoing depletion and poisoning of the planet.

Advertising has shown considerable success in expanding consumption, enabling it to grow almost as quickly as production. This having been said, advertising has little further potential as an economic solution. At both personal and planetary levels, we need to get off the treadmill of artificially inflated consumption.

The Throw-Away Line

A second strategy to increase consumption has been to produce a multitude of items designed to be thrown away: disposable lighters, disposable diapers, now even disposable cameras.

The trend to disposables is so strong that many disposables have become, at some level, invisible as disposables (the daily newspaper, Kleenex, and ballpoint pens all fall into this category). The strategy has been extremely effective at stimulating consumption. Disposable diapers alone are a multi-billion-dollar-a-year business in North America.

Disposables do offer the positive side effect of personal convenience. Nonetheless, their most robust side effect is that we are drowning in our own wastes.

Another strategy of deliberate waste is excessive packaging. It is the packaging industry itself which has most actively encouraged over-packaging.

The Ultimate Disposable

Military hardware is the ultimate disposable: products designed to be destroyed. As long as the Reds matched our weapons production (or as long as we could pretend they did), we had a pretext for a never-ending economic expansion.

The world is now spending a trillion dollars a year on equipment whose purpose is to hurt human beings. And we're hooked on it; Wall Street breaks into a cold sweat if we're threatened with an outbreak of peace.

Both here and south of the border, military expenditures are judged not on national security value but as job-creation prizes. Military contracts are a prime way that governments have rewarded their friends.

Military expenditures are cost-ineffective on a dollars-per-job basis when compared to alternatives like expanded public transit. However, spending on public transit reduces the number of cars people buy, so such purchases do not increase overall consumption. Because military spending creates a useless product, it is more effective in expanding consumption than are socially advantageous alternatives.

Military expenses siphoned off much of the increase in productivity in the North American economy in both the 1960s and the 1980s. Expanding military production creates jobs but does not create a higher standard of living. Much of the extra wealth created by recent improvements in productivity has ended up channelled into the production of tanks, missiles, bombs, and bullets. It has not been converted into goods and services which improve the quality of our lives.

Here we see what Hazel Henderson describes as the folly of the gross national product. Traditional wisdom says that when the GNP is increasing, it reflects a rise in our standard of living. However, a missile in every silo is a very different prosperity from a chicken in every pot.

The negative side effects of military spending need little amplification. Military expenditures represent a massive waste of energy and resources which could have gone to more positive uses. Although much of Canada's arms production is sold to the U.S., Canada has been under constant American pressure to raise defence spending if it wants continued access to U.S. arms sales, with the result that about 11% of your federal taxes go to feed Canada's war machine.

A second, more serious problem is that our military hardware is almost as dangerous to us as it is to our supposed enemies. The accidental explosion of one nuclear warhead on Canadian soil would cause thousands, perhaps hundreds of thousands, of deaths.

An inherent danger in having our economy so dependent on defence monies is that a huge armaments industry has a strong self-interest in promoting rather than resolving international conflicts. It does not help the cause of peace when powerful interests have an economic stake in finding military solutions to international problems.

With the collapse of Soviet communism, we have a huge

opportunity to transfer resources from destructive to constructive purposes. Yet so long as we structure our economy to need the "fix" of military spending, we are unlikely to be able to turn swords into ploughshares.

Government Spending

There are many who would maintain that it is increased government spending which has undermined our economy. They fail to understand the demands of a permanent-growth economy. While government has not always made the wisest use of tax dollars, massive expansion of the public sector in the staffing of schools, hospitals, colleges, libraries, and government offices has been essential to restraining the growth of unemployment.

More than 22% of employed Canadians work directly or indirectly for government. Think what unemployment would be like if we tried to close down the public sector!

Government also provides indirect employment through purchases of everything from highway maintenance to paper clips to firetrucks to military hardware to computer consulting.

Government payments for welfare, unemployment insurance, child benefits, and pensions have been essential to insure that the unemployed have the means to be somewhat effective as consumers. We often justify such payments in terms of social justice. The fact is, the economy would be in big trouble if groups excluded from the workforce were also lost as consumers.

■ THE ESSENTIAL ROLE OF TAXATION

We have been inundated with the right-wing political philosophy that all government is bad, and that "government spending drains the economy." We have lost sight of the role of government in recirculating wealth.

An increasing proportion of the wealth in our economy is not generated by human labours or entrepreneurial brilliance, but simply reflects the relentless power of the machine. Without adequate taxation, wealth gravitates towards those who own the technology.

The ecology of the economy requires that money continues to circulate through the economy. Taxing the owners of the machines and, to a lesser extent, high-wage workers within highly mechanized industries, insures that money continues to circulate.

We have tended to see taxes in a negative light, without recognizing the extent to which they are essential to the functioning of our economy. Taxation and government spending are essential mechanisms for recirculating wealth in a high-tech economy.

Much of the expansion of government has been positive. Few of us want to give up our parks, libraries, schools, and hospitals. We might want to find ways to spend less for those services, and perhaps to get rid of some parts of the bureaucracy. Overall, however, government services are of major benefit to us all.

■ LIMITS ON THE EXPANSION OF GOVERNMENT

Taxes on the rich help recirculate wealth within the economy, yet only minimally hurt the ability of the rich to consume. Taxes on middle and lower classes, however, are a double-edged sword. On the one hand, tax monies create new employment, either directly as public sector jobs or indirectly through government purchases. On the other hand, high taxes make these groups less effective consumers, eliminating jobs elsewhere in the economy.

A second limit on government spending is that we are operating in an open economic system. We fund the public sector of our economy through taxes on the private sector. Products coming in from countries where the public sector is small have fewer taxes included in their production costs. Whenever we raise taxes, it becomes harder to sell exports to such countries and harder not to be undercut by their imports. Transnational corporations are skilled at rigging their account books to shelter their profits outside Canada, in countries where taxes are low.

A third limit is that public sector programs which are efficient in their use of resources create less consumption than private sector alternatives. The free services of Agriculture Canada reduce the opportunities for private sector consultants. Our publicly funded health care system offers us lower per capita costs than the U.S. system, but the inefficiency of American health care creates more jobs.

A final curb on the expansion of the public sector is the limits on what services we may want from government. It serves all of us to have hospitals, schools, libraries, parks, weather reports, and automobile safety standards. However, there is a limit to the number of services which we can agree serve the common good, and serve it efficiently. To have the expansion of the public sector driven by the need to create employment is to have the tail wagging the dog. Tax revolt movements of the past decade indicate that we may have reached the limits of our collective interest in having the public sector expand.

Much has been made of the degree to which the U.S. public sector is smaller than the Canadian public sector. However, the U.S. has been under similar pressures to raise government spending to expand consumption. Where Canada's increased spending has gone into schools, hospitals, and public service, the U.S. government's has gone into a massive expansion of the military. I think we got the better deal!

Buying Time

Unfortunately, despite all the frantic consumption, the waste, the madness of the arms race, and the rapid growth of the public sector, we've still outstripped our ability to keep everyone working. High unemployment has so damaged our wage structure that workers don't have the money to buy all of what they can produce.

Debt is a stopgap solution to the design flaw in the economy created by high unemployment. Workers can be loaned money to make up the difference between what they produce and what they can afford to buy. Loans can be direct, in the form of credit cards or bank loans, or indirect, in the form of government debt.

Government debt serves an identical function to individual debt, but in a covert form. The working population is advanced funds in the form of lower taxes, against the credit of federal, provincial, and municipal debt.

In the past decade we've had to resort to this most desperate of patch-up strategies. Government debt, corporate debt, high mortgages, and personal credit cards were all designed to help us maintain a feeding frenzy of consumption in a sick economy.

The full picture of our indebtedness is horrifying:

Type of debt	Cost per household
Federal debt	$45,000
Provincial & municipal debts	$21,000
Corporate debt	$34,000
Mortgage debt	$32,000
Consumer loans & credit cards	$11,000
Total Debts	$143,000

The total of government, corporate, and consumer debts is over $140,000 for each Canadian household!

The prosperity of the Reagan years in the U.S., and the early Mulroney years, was a false prosperity built on credit. Germany's recent and brief prosperity in the face of global recession had similar roots; the immense costs of reunification were all being financed on credit.

■ DEBT TRAPS

Unfortunately, debt is, at best, a temporary solution that ends up making the underlying problem worse, even while it is covering up the symptoms. The obvious problem with borrowing is that each of us ends up owing what we borrowed, plus interest payments as well. The process further concentrates money in the hands of those who already have too much. We can avoid facing the underlying problem by borrowing even more money — but eventually a credit limit will be reached.

Initially debt creates a stimulus for consumption, helping to ease problems of overcapacity. As debt builds, interest charges begin to sap consumer spending. When debts grow as large as they have in recent years, demand for credit begins to outstrip the supply. The law of supply and demand causes real (i.e., corrected for inflation) interest rates to rise. Rising interest charges further sap consumer spending. Each Canadian household's share of interest charges on public, corporate, and consumer debts is now about $14,000 per year:

one-quarter of the average family's income! Debt is no longer an economic stimulus, but a huge drain on consumer spending.

It is easy to blame governments for their irresponsibility in running up such a huge tab. But here's the dilemma: if government had paid for all its expenses through taxes, problems of overproduction would have soared. At best, there would have been a huge increase in unemployment; at worst, a repeat of the 1930s.

BANKRUPTCY!

Step back for a minute to consider the lunacy of the past 30 years: all the energy we've wasted trying to get people to buy things they don't need with money they don't have, all the wasteful and destructive products we've created. Consider the damage that has been done to the environment, and the debt with which we've saddled our offspring.

It is important that we be careful in assigning responsibility for what has happened. It is not appropriate to blame the advertising industry, the producers of disposables, defense industries, or the public service. In an economic configuration which requires constantly expanding consumption to maintain balance, those groups were only doing their jobs. If they hadn't done what they did, unemployment would easily be two or three times current levels. The problem is an economic structure where the tail wags the dog; instead of producing only what we need, we are pushed into increased perversity trying to create artificial demands. Much of the energy of today's economy goes into activities which damage the quality of our lives, even though they increase the gross national product.

> The Four Horsemen of the Modern Apocalypse — Materialism, Waste, Militarism, and Debt — are all functions of an economic structure that has to go faster and faster all the time, or crash.

13

Producing Solutions

*The part played by orthodox economists, whose common
sense has been insufficient to check their faulty logic, has
been disastrous up to the latest act.*

JOHN MAYNARD KEYNES

Despite the extreme lengths to which we have gone in our attempts
to increase consumption, our ability to produce has grown faster
than our ability to consume. We have needed to find ways to curtail
production as well.

High interest rates, production controls, and productivity controls
have all been used to curb the growth of production.

The Interesting Solution

To talk about interest rates as a tool to curtail productive capacity, it
is necessary to take a slight detour into the realm of Keynesian economics. For many years, sleepwalking government officials justified
Canada's high interest rates with the theories of John Maynard
Keynes. This is a gross misrepresentation of Keynes's ideas, but the
argument has been made so often it must be challenged.

■ KEYNESIAN ECONOMICS

It was John Maynard Keynes who first clearly articulated how and
why a market economy tends to oscillate between rapid growth and

recession. What Keynes observed is that a market economy tends to *overreact* to a surplus of either demand or supply.

When an economy is growing, growth feeds on growth: that is, as new factories and stores are built they, in turn, generate demand for building supplies, machine tools, etc. In this heady atmosphere, new businesses will continue to open even as the market reaches saturation.

Once all those new factories start producing, the market becomes flooded. New construction stops, and the demand for construction materials and industrial equipment shrinks abruptly.

What happens then is the flip side of the cycle. Profits tumble and consumer confidence falters. Individuals and businesses get scared and cut purchases to a minimum. Companies lay off workers, which reduces consumer demand further. Because demand has been reduced, the market will remain flooded even when production has dropped *below* previous levels. Companies continue to go out of business until demand has shrunk far below what it was.

Having overshot in the opposite direction, the cycle is now ready to repeat, yo-yoing back and forth between rapid growth and recession.

Keynes's contribution to economics was to suggest that government can smooth out the swings in the economic cycle with judicious control of the money supply. When economists talk about an economy "overheating," they mean the economy is growing so quickly it will soon overshoot demand. Higher interest rates can be used to curb economic growth by making it expensive to borrow funds for a new or expanded business. They also curb inflation, as described in Chapter 8.

Keynes further suggested that governments could curb growth by raising taxes, and by cutting government spending. (Most governments are too concerned with popularity to take such measures, so that part of Keynes's prescription is rarely used.) The combined set of strategies is known as "tight money" in economic jargon.

When an economy is falling towards recession, government can stimulate demand by lowering interest rates, or by running a large deficit. When government spends more than it takes from the economy in taxes, it artificially augments consumption — "jump-starting the economy" in economic jargon.

Since Keynes's theory has been in use, growth and contraction cycles of the economy have been much gentler. John Maynard deserves our thanks.

■ KEYNESIAN ECONOMICS ON ITS EAR

In Keynes's model, changes in the money supply were to be used as temporary and periodic measures to fine-tune economic growth.

A reasonable analogy can be made to driving along a hilly highway, and trying to stay exactly at the speed limit. Much of the time the driver can maintain speed with only minor adjustments of the gas pedal. Occasionally the road will go down a steep hill and the driver needs to touch the brakes to keep from going too fast. Going up a steep hill, the driver may have to drop down to a lower gear to maintain speed.

That's how Keynesian measures were intended to be used. From time to time a light touch of the brake of higher interest rates will be needed to slow the economy. Sometimes a short burst on the accelerator of deficit spending will help get the economy back up to speed. In between, the economy should purr along, neither too fast nor too slow, all on its own.

When supply and demand are kept roughly in balance, periodic adjustments of money supply can be effective in smoothing the bumps and dips out of the economic cycle. In recent years, however, productive capacity has so outstripped our ability to consume that we have been using Keynesian tools in a very different manner from what he intended.

For years at a time we've had to keep interest rates at high levels to choke back growth in the productive capacity of the economy and rein in the inflationary growth of real estate prices. Simultaneously, we've needed to stimulate consumption with huge government deficits.

In terms of our metaphor, we have one foot hard on the brakes of our economic car, while the other foot is pushing the gas pedal to the floor — all the time.

■ THE WOUNDED DRAGON

I can remember a fairy tale in which a princess came upon a dragon that had been very badly wounded. She fell immediately in love with the beast, captivated by its whirling eyes and the iridescent glow of its scaly skin.

Each morning she fed the dragon huge kettles of chicken soup, and tenderly bathed and rebandaged its wounds. She scratched it lovingly behind its huge scaly ears and endlessly praised its beauty.

However, the princess was not so lovestruck as to forget that a healthy dragon likes nothing better than a princess or two as a morning snack. Each night, while the dragon slept, she would creep back and reopen its wounds, so that each morning the dragon would awaken alive, but near death.

Needless to say, this was a difficult balancing act. I don't remember how the story ended. It may have been that the princess fed the dragon too much soup for breakfast, and became lunch herself. Or perhaps one night she bled the dragon too long and it died, leaving her with a broken heart. At any rate it was a GOOD TRAGIC TALE.

Our economy is like the dragon. Our technological economy is so potent in its ability to produce that if it were at all healthy it would quickly flood the marketplace and drive us into a severe recession. We have to use high interest rates to constantly bleed the economy, to keep it sick enough that it doesn't grow. Unfortunately, the economy is so sick that we must also constantly nourish it with deficit spending, so it doesn't die.

■ SIDE EFFECTS OF HIGH INTEREST RATES

High interest rates make everything bought on credit more expensive. They inhibit sales of such big-ticket items as houses, cars, and furniture, choking off consumption as well as production. The raising of interest rates has often created recessions in the attempt to avoid a full-scale depression.

Higher interest rates also mean that capital makes more money than labour. The rich do well and the poor do badly when interest rates are high. The working public sees a disproportionate amount of their incomes disappear in interest payments on their home mortgages. There is also evidence that high interest rates contribute to inflation, even while purporting to fight the inflationary cycle.

■ END OF THE LINE

The Canadian government finds itself increasingly limited in the use of Keynesian interventions. The public debt is now so high that the government dares not stimulate demand through larger deficits. Those same debts have pushed up the cost of credit, limiting government's ability to stimulate the economy with lower interest rates. If the economy begins to slide into a depression, there's little the government can do to prevent a crash.

Similar difficulties exist in trying to moderate economic growth spurts with higher interest rates. Today's economy has developed such deep structural problems that even modest increases in interest rates can tip the economy into recession, as was clearly demonstrated in 1989. High interest rates have always been a blunt tool for curbing production; as the economy grows sicker and sicker, they are a tool which is increasingly too dangerous to use.

Production Controls

Wage and price controls, and production quotas, are controls on production which represent a decision to suspend the free market. Such steps are sometimes necessary in emergencies; we've already mentioned how such measures were imposed during World War II in response to across-the-board *under*-production.

Wage and price controls have sometimes been used to put a temporary brake on inflation. By stabilizing prices, they also act to curb explosive growth in the economy, providing a short-term restraint that prevents production from overshooting consumption.

Production quotas have some value in protecting or allocating scarce resources. The federal government, by restricting the number of boats which are given commercial fishing licenses, curbs the total "production" of fish, and thus helps protect fish stocks. In a similar

way, when the British coal miners' strike in 1973 reduced the availability of electrical power, restricting British factories to three-day-a-
week operation allocated scarce electricity in a reasonably equitable
fashion.

Wage/price controls and production quotas have never been seen
as a long-term, across-the-board solution to our economic problems.
The reason for this is quite simple. Either intervention represents a
suspension of the free market. In the absence of free market
incentives, small imbalances in the economy tend to grow. The
longer that production controls are in place, the more the economy
develops the kind of surpluses and shortages the Soviet Union was
famous for. When production controls are removed, free market
forces will quickly shift energies to eliminate shortages and
surpluses, but the economic adjustment is often painful — and more
painful the longer production controls have been in place.

The Luddite Response

The Luddites were a group of textile workers in England in the early
nineteenth century. They realized that labour-saving machinery was
creating massive unemployment and harming the interests of
working people — so they went on rampages to try to destroy that
machinery.

Unions which try to prevent computerization and automation
provide modern echoes of the Luddite theme. The refusal to allow
the installation of labour-saving equipment is clearly an inelegant
solution. However, in the absence of arrangements to share the
benefits of new technology and/or to share employment, it may well
serve workers' interests to restrict technological change until more
effective solutions are implemented.

NO GOOD ANSWERS HERE!

Aside from technical problems, high interest rates and controls on
production have a more basic drawback as economic strategies. If

we reduce the amount of work to be done without reducing the supply of labour, the immediate result is unemployment on a massive scale.

The Luddite response is little better: it is painful to forego opportunities for increased leisure simply because we haven't found ways to share the work.

> **Strategies to reduce production do not offer effective solutions to our economic dilemma.**

14

Solutions for Some

Are you in favour of big business, or free enterprise?
PAUL SAMUELSON

Several other strategies are worthy of note, though they protect only specific sectors of the economy. Corporate concentration and marketing boards have been used to protect certain industries from overcapacity. Unions and professional associations have shown comparable effectiveness in shielding parts of the labour force. Minimum wage laws have partly shielded the working poor.

Corporate Safety Zones

The corporate concentration we have seen over the past 30 years is business's way of protecting itself from the inefficiency and unprofitability of a crowded marketplace.

Unlike other strategies discussed so far, corporate concentration does not protect the economy as a whole from a surplus of supply over demand. However, it does protect specific business sectors. How does it work?

In much of the small business sector, access to a particular market niche is not expensive. There are thousands of Canadians with enough savings to open up a corner store, hair salon, restaurant, or video arcade. It would be hard to exercise control over markets so porous that there are thousand of possible entrants.

However, while it's possible to open a small janitorial business for

121

under $50,000, it would be hard to open a modern factory to produce laundry detergent for less than $50 million. Access is not nearly so democratic. Suddenly it seems possible for a few players to exercise control of the market.

If there were 20 detergent companies, all competing for your laundry detergent dollar, they would so oversupply the soap market that none could make a profit. The reader's immediate response might be to note that there are at least 20 brands of laundry detergent on the market. However, if you look more closely at those 20 brands, you'll find that almost all of them are made by just three companies: Colgate-Palmolive, Proctor & Gamble, and Unilever. Most of the brand names you see are artifacts of past competitors in the soap business. (Double-barrel names are also often a clue to past mergers.)

The process goes like this. In a crowded market niche, all players operate at less than full capacity, and all suffer from low profitability. The two or three biggest firms buy out the smaller or less profitable firms. Alternatively, smaller firms merge to avoid being "eaten" by large ones.

The combined units then, in the jargon of takeovers, *rationalize* their business. Rationalization means that the merged company keeps only its most efficient factories; the others are shut down. Brand names that have developed strong customer loyalty are retained. Every time a factory is closed down it means that those factories remaining operate closer to capacity, and more profitably.

■ CONTROLLED COMPETITION

Once corporate concentration has proceeded to the point where only a few companies remain, those companies can act in concert to see that they operate at full capacity and high profitability.

When a particular market is dominated by a few companies, what we might call "controlled competition" becomes possible. In such situations, the tendency will be to compete on areas other than price. Companies will compete on advertising, promotional gimmicks, even on product quality, before they will compete on price. Prices might be dropped for temporary sales promotions, but not as an ongoing strategy to gain an increased market share.

Price-fixing legislation can prevent companies from explicitly agreeing on prices or production levels, but it cannot prevent informal practices which amount to the same result.

If one of the companies breaks ranks by building new plants or cutting prices, profitability quickly disappears. In such situations the corporate world quickly discovers the importance of cooperation!

Once a few large firms dominate the national market for a particular commodity, they often act in concert to prevent newcomers from gaining a toehold. If a new corporation is foolish enough to build a competing factory, a price war will ensue until the newcomer goes under or agrees to be bought out. Prices can then return to normal.

Corporate concentration enables certain market sectors to be profitable even when the economy as a whole is doing badly. When high unemployment has driven wages down, it makes for high profits in market niches where corporate concentration has restricted overcapacity.

■ THE EXTENT OF CORPORATE CONCENTRATION

It is a mistake to think that all big businesses operate in protected markets. Airlines are very large businesses, but corporate concentration has not protected them. Many nations (Canada included) have made it a point of pride to establish and support national airlines. Lacking the control of concentrated ownership, the airline industry has suffered from overcapacity for years.

National pride has also restricted corporate concentration within the auto industry, with similar, though less severe, results. This being said, industries lacking high corporate concentration should probably be looked at as hold-outs rather than exceptions. In the past few years, the trend towards corporate concentration has shown itself with a vengeance within the airline industry. Takeovers of Wardair and PWA have left Canada with only two national airlines. Analysts predict that within a few years, a half dozen international carriers will dominate world air travel. The extent of corporate concentration in Canada is chilling: StatsCan reports that one tenth of 1% of Canadian corporations control 75% of all corporate assets in Canada.

■ SIDE EFFECTS OF CORPORATE CONCENTRATION

Corporate concentration clearly undermines the competitiveness we think of as essential in a market economy. However, in an economy which has built-in surpluses, at least part of the economy functions. Profit is the goal of any business, and in an economy as sick as Canada's, only in those niches where overcapacity has been controlled are profits consistently high.

A more important criticism of corporate concentration is that large corporations have had undue influence in maintaining the status quo. Political contributions from large corporations have helped conservative political parties maintain power. Corporations have kept in place an economic perspective which neither acknowledges nor addresses our economic problems.

Another unfortunate side effect of corporate concentration is that the relative profitability of big business has obscured the underlying ill health of the economy. We need to recognize that what is good for big business is not always good for the country.

Marketing Boards

Agricultural marketing boards control the supply of various farming commodities through restrictions on production. In the dairy industry, for instance, only farmers who have milk quotas are allowed to sell milk. Because the amount of quota is controlled, production can be balanced with consumption. Prices can be kept consistent, and at profitable levels.

A quick survey of Canadian agriculture gives immediate validation to the economic importance of marketing boards. Farmers in supply-managed commodities in Canada have consistently made fairly good incomes. Farmers in non-managed commodities have been taken on a roller coaster ride. Most are slowly or quickly growing broke.

Commodities managed by marketing boards are marginally more expensive than non-managed commodities. On the other hand, prices for managed commodities are more stable.

Marketing boards have considerable power to set monopoly prices, which makes public supervision advisable. Agricultural marketing boards are closely monitored by government, which has helped keep their prices fair. Within the real estate industry, marketing boards have controlled prices in a less salutary way.

The major trade bodies within the real estate industry are the Multiple Listing Service Real Estate Marketing Boards. How MLS works is that any agent for any member company can sell any home listed by any other agent in the MLS system. The selling agent then splits the commission with the original agent who first listed the house for sale.

Real estate agents make wonderful sales pitches for the Multiple Listing approach: "With MLS, every agent and company in the MLS network is trying to sell your home." This misses the point, which is that MLS Boards can effectively set commission rates for the whole real estate industry.

Housing prices have risen faster than inflation, but rising commissions have not been enough to keep a rapidly increasing supply of real estate agents solvent. Over the past 30 years, real estate boards have had to raise dramatically the rate of commission paid to agents, from 4% to 5%, and finally to 7% of the sale price of a house. In real dollars, it costs almost three times as much to sell your home now as it did a generation ago.

The power of real estate boards to set prices makes OPEC look clumsy and ineffectual. On the one hand, MLS Boards will proclaim loudly that they are firm believers in free enterprise, and that they do not have a monopoly on commission rates. On the other hand, all agent members of the MLS Board must charge the MLS rate on all house sales. And any independent agent or company foolish enough to try to undercut the MLS rate is shunned, harassed, and bad-mouthed unmercifully until they fall into line.

Marketing boards protect certain sectors of the economy from overcrowding, and have obvious value for those protected sectors because they create relative stability. However, as with corporate concentration, marketing boards do not solve the underlying problem of the crowded marketplace.

■ SIDE EFFECTS OF MARKETING BOARDS

Marketing boards have some important drawbacks. The first and most profound is that they suspend the operation of the free market and institute a "managed economy model" within various sectors of the economy. As managed economies, they tend to show the same problems as the managed economies of traditional communism. Managed economies lack the self-correcting feedback of a free market.

Managed economies work only so far as the management boards successfully predict demand and, when necessary, curtail production so as not to exceed consumption. A number of years ago the Canadian Egg Marketing Association accumulated a huge surplus of eggs, which then spoiled. Fixed prices mean that supply and demand must be accurately predicted by marketing boards.

The real estate industry demonstrates another problem with marketing boards. Real estate sales is one of the few professions which hasn't tried to restrict access through educational barriers. Unfortunately, the result of this is that too many people have become real estate agents. Rather than addressing the problem of an oversupply of real estate agents, the real estate industry has simply upped its fees. From the consumer's point of view this is a rather expensive and inelegant solution.

Unions and Professional Associations

Unions and professional associations function much like marketing boards, but are usually more subtle in their approach.

When a professional association has a legal or *de facto* monopoly over a particular trade or occupation, it will often restrict membership access to the professional association as a way of guarding against oversupply.

A less obvious form of this technique is to assign jobs in a particular trade according to seniority, as does the carpenters union. Anyone with a valid carpenter's ticket can join the union — but those below a certain point on the seniority list are not going to get work. Assigning work within a particular trade by seniority discourages growth of the profession beyond the available work.

Professional associations that have a legal or practical monopoly on a particular occupation's services can also control prices. Even when professional associations lack the legal clout to control prices by fiat, they can influence prices by establishing a scale of suggested rates for particular services. Such rate scales are always rationalized in terms of making sure prices are "fair and equitable" and that "professional standards" are maintained. However, as far as the members of such associations voluntarily "work to scale," it amounts to a form of price control. If manufacturers' associations were to take identical steps, they could be charged with price fixing and sent to jail!

The power to strike is the crudest weapon that unions and professional associations have to fight the effects of an oversupply of labour. Unionized workers have seen minor erosion of their wages over the past 15 years, but the threat of expensive strikes means union members have been more successful holding the line against falling wages than non-unionized labour.

As implements to control overproduction, unions and professional associations have the same basic problem as marketing boards: they protect only part of the economy.

■ THE ERECTION OF EDUCATIONAL BARRIERS

One other supply-management technique deserves special mention. Professional associations and unions frequently restrict access to their particular occupations with barriers of high educational qualifications. Such barriers are always erected under the high-minded rubric of maintaining professional standards.

Take psychologists, for example. Until 1978, a master's degree in psychology was adequate to become registered as a professional psychologist in British Columbia. However, psychology was popular at universities and soon the field was in danger of being flooded.

The B.C. College of Psychologists became preoccupied with professional standards. It expressed grave concern that under-qualified practitioners of psychology would harm the unsuspecting public. The qualifications for a registered psychologist were raised from a master's degree to a doctoral degree, which involves two or more additional years of full-time study.

When the educational requirements were raised, hundreds of practising psychologists (including new graduates) were "grand-fathered"; it was okay for them to be psychologists without a PhD because they had qualified under the old rules.

Research on counselling skills suggests that PhD graduates show no greater skills and no better outcome with clients than those with master's degrees. The requirement for a PhD may be rationalized under the ideal of professional standards, but clearly the real reason is the need to limit the supply of psychologists.

We have seen this same process in teaching and nursing. The trades are setting up longer apprenticeships and requiring high school or college diplomas.

The obvious side effect of educational barriers is higher educational costs for the individual and for society. While such barriers protect specific professions from the effects of an oversupply of labour, they do nothing towards solving that oversupply.

During World War II, when most of the trained professionals were off at the front, jobs which, on paper, required years of training were learned by young housewives in a matter of weeks. How different would it be today? Schooling is an inefficient way to learn most jobs.

One can argue that new education requirements have improved the levels of competence in various trades. However these same improvements could have been made via expanded in-service training or expanded peer review processes at far less cost.

Our current preoccupation with education has more to do with keeping people out of jobs than with making sure they are competent in their jobs. With education costs eating up somewhere around one third of all Canadian tax dollars, the strategy of erecting educational barriers, however popular, must be considered a very inelegant solution to the oversupply of labour.

Minimum Wage Laws

Employment standards legislation has functioned as a union of last resort by setting a legal minimum wage. Such standards have marginally protected those with the lowest incomes from the worst effects of an oversupply of labour.

Governments are limited in the use of such standards in a free trade economy. If the minimum wage were raised even to the poverty line, many businesses would no longer be viable and would shut down; unemployment would rise. A higher minimum wage also accelerates the number of companies moving to Mexico.

INELEGANT SOLUTIONS

Corporate concentration, marketing boards, unions and professional associations, and minimum-wage legislation all mitigate the effects of overcapacity for certain subgroups. Unfortunately, they also cause financial inequity, and undercut change. They don't help the economy as a whole to bring production and consumption into balance.

> **Solutions which protect only part of the economy create inequity and inaction.**

15

Non-Solutions I:
Canada's Trade Policies

*All that would happen with that kind of concept [Free
Trade] would be the boys cranking up their plants
throughout the United States in bad times, and shutting
down their entire branch plants in Canada.*

BRIAN MULRONEY (1983 VERSION)

Free trade and foreign investment have been touted as solutions for
Canada; in reality, they are problems.

Export Promotion

Canada's government has made increased exports the cornerstone
of its economic policy. Initiatives include:

- Canada's protective tariffs cut from an average of 30% in
  1947, to just 3.3% today;

- Implementation of the Canada-U.S. Free Trade Agreement,
  and proposal of a North American Free Trade Agreement;

- Creation of trade shows, trade missions, and an array of
  incentives and supports for Canadian exporters.

Canada, like many countries, is deeply enamoured of the strategy of selling its surpluses somewhere else. The logical incongruity of all the world's nations simultaneously dumping excess production into the black hole of increased exports has a certain grim irony. The fantasy is that exports will grow by leaps and bounds, while imports will creep up slowly. It doesn't happen, at least not more than temporarily, because of a basic flaw in the strategy: currency exchange fluctuations automatically push exports and imports towards a rough balance.

If Canada has more exports than imports, it will accumulate foreign currency, driving down the currencies of our trading partners. Meanwhile Canada's trading partners will suffer a shortage of Canadian funds, causing our dollar to rise in value. Those changes will make imports to Canada cheaper, and exports more costly, until exports and imports are roughly equal in value.

When exports and imports are in balance, every job we gain selling new exports is offset by a job lost because of new imports. For every Canadian company that expands to fill a foreign market, there is a corresponding Canadian firm downsizing due to import competition. International trade is a revolving door, with jobs coming in one side and going out the other. Extensive and expensive promotion of Canadian exports has inevitably led to increased imports to Canada, with no net gain in employment.

Export enthusiasts will often point to Japan, with its $100 billion trade surplus, as a model of how a nation can relieve overcapacity by exporting more than it imports. For a number of years, Japan was able to delay the counteracting effects of currency fluctuations because its foreign investments roughly equalled its trade surplus. However, these investments in turn created increasing amounts of foreign income (as well as creating direct competition for Japanese exports!), which eventually made it impossible to hold down the value of the yen. The yen has nearly doubled in value in recent years —making Japanese exports dear and foreign imports to Japan cheap. The 1991 meltdown of the Tokyo Stock Exchange gives a clear signal of how counterbalancing currency fluctuations have affected the Japanese economy. Over the long term, every nation must import as much as it exports, so exports cannot and should not be seen as a cure for overproduction.

Currency manipulations can also be employed to create a temporary surge in exports — but this should not be seen as a long-term solution to the problem of overproduction. In 1993, the Conservative government dropped interest rates sharply, causing our dollar to tumble in value. This in turn made our exports cheaper and imports more expensive, causing a boom in exports and a strong trade surplus just prior to the federal election. By 1994, this same trade surplus will have caused Canada to amass a large surplus in the currencies of our trading partners, and our trading partners will be short of Canadian funds. This will drive the Canadian dollar up, making our exports expensive and imports to Canada cheap. Exports will then slide and imports will boom until an overall balance is restored. In the second half of the cycle, we'll lose as many jobs as were gained in 1993 — and more. The Conservatives' temporary "fix" made them look better at election time — but it won't solve our economic problems.

The promotion of exports has hurt Canadian self-sufficiency. When most Canadian trade was internal to Canada, the Canadian economy was relatively autonomous. As an independent economic unit, Canada had the power to make whatever changes it needed to put its own house in order.

The effect of exports promotion has been to move us from a relatively self-sufficient economy to a specialist economy dependent on world trade. We are now importing many of the products we used to make here. Food production is a key concern; Canada stands to lose much of its fruit and vegetable production over the next few years. When the world economy collapses, we may find our ability to take care of ourselves has been compromised.

■ FREE TRADE

In *Parcel of Rogues: How Free Trade is Failing Canada*, Maude Barlow eloquently documents the many flaws of the Canada-U.S. Free Trade Agreement. Two issues deserve special attention here: a lack of community standards, and the potential for American bullying.

The Free Trade Agreement lacks the means to establish common standards for social welfare, employment rights, occupational safety, and environmental protection. The result is that Canada is under pressure to lower its standards to those of the U.S. In those

few cases where Canada has lower standards, the U.S. is under pressure to lower its standards to match those of Canada. The political
buzzword for this process is *harmonization*. Under the rubric of
harmonizing our system with that of the U.S., a wholesale dismantling
of Canadian social programs is under way. As an example, the recent
tightening of our unemployment insurance qualification rules is
designed to harmonize our unemployment insurance with the
American model; far fewer Canadians now qualify for UIC.

Within free trade, the U.S. is in a perfect situation to bully Canada.
How so? Consider what happens when we have factories on both
sides of the border that produce for the North American market. If
the border is closed, American firms lose 10% of their market, a
painful but manageable loss. Canadian firms, on the other hand,
would lose 90% of their market when the border is closed, a
devastating loss. This differential makes Canada highly vulnerable
to U.S. bullying. Exchange rate fluctuations can whipsaw Canadian
manufacturers in a similar fashion; if our dollar rises in value (or has
been manipulated to rise) Canadian manufacturers in a North
American market find themselves priced out of 90% of their market.
Canadian businesses realize how vulnerable they are under free
trade: one quarter of Canadian manufacturing jobs have moved
south since the free trade deal was signed.

Free trade is a sellout of Canadian sovereignty. Former U.S. Trade
Representative Clayton Yeutter, who helped draft the deal, has said:
"The Canadians don't understand what they have signed. In 20 years
they will be sucked into the U.S. economy." Free trade has not even
helped our trade balance. Duncan Cameron reports: "Since the FTA
came into being, U.S. exports to Canada have grown by $22.6 billion
more than Canadian exports to the U.S. That's 340,000 jobs less for
Canada."

The Promotion of Foreign Investment

The Conservative government has promoted foreign investment in
Canada as part and parcel of developing an export economy. The
theory was that foreign investment would create new production
facilities, which in turn would create thousands of new jobs.

The reality is far different. Maude Barlow reports that, in recent years, 96% of foreign investment in Canada has gone not into new facilities, but into purchasing existing Canadian firms. Typically, when a Canadian firm is bought out, upper management, research and development, marketing, and (sometimes) accounting are all transferred to the foreign parent. Canadian workers who had performed those functions are laid off.

Americans can be remarkably candid about the costs of a branch-plant economy when they forget we are listening. Here's Lester Thurow: "The nature of the problem can be seen in the case of Canada, where the majority of manufacturers are owned by foreigners. Canadians have a good standard of living, but they can never have the best. The best jobs (CEO, CFO, head of research, etc.) are back at headquarters, and that is somewhere else. Even if Canadians were to get the best jobs, and they don't, they would have to live abroad."

StatsCan reports that Canadian-owned firms create 330 times as many jobs for each billion dollars in profits as do American-owned subsidiaries. In contrast to the government's rhetoric, foreign investment in Canada has created thousands of job losses.

Once a Canadian firm has been taken over, the new foreign owner will carefully manipulate prices in interchanges with its Canadian subsidiary so as to reduce on-paper profits, and thereby minimize Canadian taxes. The process, called *transfer pricing*, works like this: any raw materials or services the Canadian subsidiary buys from the foreign parent are priced artificially high, while finished products are sold to the parent at artificially low prices. As a result, the Canadian subsidiary makes very little profit on paper, and pays little or no corporate tax. The foreign corporation then conducts the same operation in reverse with a shell corporation in a tax haven like Bermuda — arranging to make most of its on-paper profits in a low-tax jurisdiction. More than half of Canada's imports and exports may be affected by transfer pricing; the tax loss has been estimated at $17 billion.

When free trade is combined with foreign ownership, the effects are even more devastating. Mel Hurtig says it well: "When times get tough and cutbacks are in order, more jobs end up back at head office or in a plant in the U.S. that is operating at less than capacity.

Canadians get to do some assembly at 'screwdriver plants' but, more and more, Canada becomes simply a distributing centre for goods that are researched, designed and produced in other countries — where the jobs are."

NON-SOLUTIONS!

At a time when the world economy is out of control, and failing, our government has been pursuing a policy which amounts to chaining ourselves to the deck rail of the Titanic.

> **The promotion of free trade and foreign investment has undercut Canadian autonomy and self-sufficiency, and created job losses in the hundreds of thousands.**

16

Non-Solutions II: Canada's Job Policies

The current Canadian government is hamstrung by its position that nothing is seriously wrong with Canada's economy. This stance restricts official policies to interventions which are little more than window-dressing. Official federal initiatives include the encouragement of entrepreneurship, immigration, and investment, plus the job-creation programs of the Labour Force Development Strategy. Government's denial of our economic problems means that its real responses to our difficulties are also covert: institutionalized unemployment, and the doctrine of competitiveness.

Encouraging Entrepreneurship

Among the ways the Canadian government has promoted entrepreneurship are:

- Subsidized workshops and conferences on how to start and run a small business;

- Low-interest start-up loans and loan guarantees through the Federal Business Development Bank;

- Income subsidies during business start-up, through the Self-Employment Incentives program;

- Advice on business planning from experienced business-persons, via Counselling Assistance to Small Enterprises.

Federal government programs offer useful aid and expertise which make it easier to start a small business. It is also true, as the government's glossy pamphlets are fond of telling us, that the small business sector is the source of most new jobs in Canada. On the surface, the promotion of entrepreneurship looks like a potent strategy to reduce joblessness. Looking deeper, we find it isn't so.

The small business sector earns its title as the source of most new jobs by default, and at great cost to itself. In Chapter 14 we saw how, in areas of corporate concentration, big business voluntarily restricts its growth to maintain profitability. As a result, big business does very little in the way of creating new jobs. In similar fashion, professional associations actively restrict the growth of the professional sector. The small business sector has no mechanism to prevent over-capacity, so it expands willy-nilly, creating a lot of new jobs.

Unfortunately, the encouragement of small business does nothing to address our most basic economic problem, i.e., that we are able to produce more than we can consume. Within a context of over-capacity, the promotion of small business becomes a painful trade-off. Jobs are created, but as the small business sector becomes overcrowded, it displays all the symptoms of the crowded market-place: lower efficiency, higher prices, lower profitability, and a rising number of bankruptcies.

The upbeat theory behind the promotion of entrepreneurship proclaims that budding capitalists will find underutilized market niches and exploit them, or come up with brand new ideas involving whole new markets.

Unfortunately, new business niches that don't have any competition, and don't threaten existing businesses, exist more in theory than in practice. This can be seen most easily with an example.

When the first video rental stores appeared they had no *direct* competition. However, people who watched videos went to the movies less often. Theatres were restructured to be smaller, with more screens, so as to offer more choices. Theatres also offered discount nights to lure back customers they had lost — so even early video stores had competition. Furthermore, most of the new jobs in video stores were offset by layoffs at cinemas.

In a crowded marketplace there are only a few market niches which are temporarily underserviced. Most new businesses must try to make a go of it in markets that range from comfortably full to badly overcrowded — a difficult, if not impossible, task.

Nonetheless, there are legions of talented Canadians who are fed up with unemployment, dead-end jobs, or welfare, and many of them have shown the initiative to open new businesses. In an overcrowded marketplace, many of them fail. Those who survive often do so by driving established businesses into bankruptcy.

The promotion of entrepreneurship is an irresponsible act when the small business sector is already overcrowded. It sets up a lot of hard-working, gutsy people to fail in new business ventures, and pushes many existing businesses into bankruptcy. There are a lot of Canadians who have put heart and soul (and life savings) into small businesses. They have worked long, hard, and well, and still ended up in bankruptcy court.

In recent years, Canada has seen more business and personal bankruptcies than ever before: 76,000 bankruptcies in 1992 alone. These job losses must be subtracted from the apparent successes of entrepreneurship. Small business promotion creates a revolving door, with job gains being offset by job losses at every turn.

Encouraging Investment

A second cornerstone of Canada's economic policy has been to encourage investment, both domestic and foreign. Among initiatives to encourage investment are:

- The $100,000 lifetime exemption on capital gains;

- Investment promotion offices and trade fairs at Canadian embassies abroad;

- Provisions which allow foreign investors to immigrate here;

- A wide array of tax incentives for investors;

- A tax structure which keeps taxes on corporations and the rich low to promote investment.

Canada's investment policies are loosely based on *supply-side economic theory.* Supply-side theory is a carefully crafted political agenda which masquerades as an economic strategy; a cynical cover story which the rich have used to evade their fair share of the tax burden. Supply-side theory emerged from richly endowed right-wing think tanks. Professional economists in pinstripes and Guccis have served as shameless pimps for the interests of the wealthy.

The gist of supply-side economic theory is simple:

❶ **The source of our economic problems is that other nations have invested more in labour-saving equipment than we in North America have, making their products cheaper and causing us to lose out in global trade.**

❷ **Heavy investment in new plant and equipment, and in labour-saving technology, is required if North America is to recover its competitive advantage.**

❸ **Only the wealthy have the resources for that level of capital input, so the rich must be given tax cuts and incentives to make the required investments.**

❹ **Once the new, highly efficient infrastructure is in place, export sales will boom, creating a massive economic expansion which will put everyone to work.**

❺ **Each worker will produce more wealth once more efficient technology is in place, which will lead to higher wages for the working population too.**

Supply-side theory draws a careful and tight little box around our economic problems. It looks like a very workable solution — until we look beyond the box.

What would happen if the supply-siders were successful? First of all, if new technology enabled each worker to produce twice as much, the economy as a whole would have to produce twice as much to keep everyone working: an immediate environmental nightmare.

Also, what happens when the flood of cheap exports hits the global economy? Will overproduction push global trade into an outright depression, or just a severe recession? We can only be grateful that supply-side economics has not achieved its ostensible goals!

Supply-side theory was not designed as an economic platform. The wealthy used it as a rationale to push through huge tax cuts for the rich. These cuts and exemptions often translate to tax savings of $50,000 a year on a $250,000 annual income.

Supply-side theory was sold in a cunningly crafted package. Big tax cuts for the rich were combined with modest tax cuts for everyone else. (These tax cuts were rationalized under the rubric that excessive government spending hurts North America's international competitiveness — despite the obvious and indisputable fact that North America's major trading partners spend more on government services than we do.) It was politically easy to get tax cuts approved when most of the population could see its tax bill drop, never mind that the rich won tax savings that were a hundred times as large.

The beauty of supply-side theory was that it did create a temporary boost for the economy. In the early Reagan and Mulroney years, it did look like supply-side theory had revitalized the economy. On closer examination however, all that really happened was that we *looked* richer; we were living on the credit of the public debt.

Even taken on their own terms, Canada's current investment policies are poorly designed. The Conservative government has made little differentiation between productive and speculative investment, and has rewarded land and real estate speculators with the same incentives and tax breaks it gives those who make a legitimate investment in new production facilities. In rewarding speculation, our government has foregone a great deal of tax revenue and actively encouraged inflation. This from a government which has claimed that fighting inflation is one of its priorities!

Encouraging investment has had some legitimate value only in the area of regional economic development; that is, moving jobs to where the people are.

Encouraging Large-Scale Immigration

The federal government has tried to create growth in the Canadian economy by the promotion of large-scale immigration. Immigrants need new homes, cars, and appliances, and create some economic stimulation in these areas. Unfortunately, immigrants also need jobs in comparable numbers, so while immigration may increase the number of employed Canadians, it does not decrease unemployment: another non-solution.

The purpose behind massive immigration is not economic, but political. The gross national product grows as the population increases, which makes it look like the economy is growing, even when it is shrinking. Per capita GNP — each Canadian's share of the national income — has been falling, almost without interruption, since 1989. Per capita GNP has shrunk by a full 6%; the pie may be getting bigger, but your slice is getting smaller!

The Labour Force Development Strategy

The final thrust of Canada's official policies is the patchwork of programs in the Labour Force Development Strategy, formerly known as the Canada Jobs Strategy. LFDS includes four streams: skills training, job-search training, employment grants, and adjustment services.

■ SKILLS TRAINING

The **SKILLS TRAINING** program involves two main streams. One approach involves paying tuition and living allowance for short university, college, or technical school programs. The other involves subsidized wages for new workers during specified training or apprenticeship.

Skills training has value as a retraining tool. Many workers are being laid off from resource or manufacturing jobs, and must make major career shifts. Unfortunately, skills training has been promoted as a cure-all for unemployment despite three obvious facts:

❶ **Every job vacancy in Canada could be filled tomorrow, and most unemployed Canadians would still be without a job.**

❷ **Many of the jobs vacant because of a difficulty finding qualified applicants are in remote and inhospitable places. Canada may have job openings for physicians in Inuvik but there is no shortage of trained doctors.**

❸ **Many vacancies have inflated educational requirements. The problem often is with the process of setting qualifications — not with a lack of trained workers.**

Skills training can have a minor impact on reducing unemployment. On the other hand, it is fallacious to blame Canadian unemployment on a lack of skilled workers.

■ JOB-SEARCH TRAINING

JOB CLUBS are short (three-week) programs that teach resumé-writing and interview skills, and arrange a blitz of calls and information interviews with employers.

Longer job-search training programs cross over into a grey area with skills training. In addition to career counselling, interviewing, and resumé skills, such programs may also include communication skills training, computer training, and a work experience placement.

(In a work experience placement, the government pays a small allowance to the participant, and the employer gets a free trial of a new employee for several weeks.)

Job-search training has some limited value. It is targeted to what the government calls "employment-disadvantaged groups." Job-search training gives a leg up for the young, the old, natives, handicapped people, re-entry women, and the long-term unemployed. It helps soften the damage of unemployment by attempting to spread unemployment around, making sure that no group has outrageously high unemployment, and that fewer people are unemployed for a long time.

Job-search training has some impact on who gets the available jobs. Unfortunately, it does nothing to change the total number of Canadian unemployed.

■ EMPLOYMENT GRANT PROGRAMS

Over the years, the federal government has offered a variety of grant programs designed to create short-term employment. Some were designed to enable unemployed persons to work enough weeks to qualify for unemployment insurance. Others, like the long-lived Section 38, were meant to supplement UIC income.

The intent of such grant programs has been to ease the financial burden of unemployment, particularly among "employment-disadvantaged groups," and to a certain extent, they have done so.

The short-term nature of grant programs, their constantly changing rules, and the haphazardness with which programs are changed or abandoned, have all undercut their ability to fund socially useful work.

Nonetheless, grant programs have had a very real usefulness to the community, underwriting important environmental and social service activities that would not otherwise have been funded. Grant programs are also superior to UIC or welfare as income supports, in that they are supportive of the self-esteem of recipients.

■ ADJUSTMENT PROGRAMS

INDUSTRIAL ADJUSTMENT SERVICES help individual companies manage plant closures and layoffs. IAS will fund retraining and job-search programs for laid-off employees, and can underwrite the costs of researching alternatives to layoffs.

COMMUNITY FUTURES is a program to help communities which have been hit hard by layoffs. Local Community Futures committees have the mandate to fund virtually any of the approaches listed so far: the encouragement of entrepreneurship and investment, retraining, job-search programs, and employment grants.

As tools of regional development, IAS and Community Futures have shown both imagination and some limited usefulness. The Labour Force Development Strategy as a whole has shown some usefulness in helping minority groups and disadvantaged regions, and as a tool for retraining. These are modest accomplishments, a far cry from the hype which has accompanied the LFDS.

Institutionalized Unemployment

Unemployment is the default solution to overcapacity. Successive federal governments have allowed unemployment to rise, and institutionalized it with income support programs.

It's strange to talk about unemployment as a "solution" to overcapacity, but in a way it is. If we were to put all the unemployed back to work tomorrow, it would create such overproduction that Canada would find itself in a major crisis. Income supports for the jobless are essential; in our sick economy, overcapacity can only be eliminated when a large proportion of the workforce consumes without producing.

Recently, the Conservative government floated a trial balloon for a guaranteed annual income program. We must not forget a guaranteed income is just welfare by another name. As with current welfare programs, it will undoubtedly provide income levels far below the poverty line, under the rationale that a livable income would "reduce the incentive to work." At best, a guaranteed income will be a cosmetic change; at worst, it will be an attempt to off-load the costs of unemployment onto the provinces.

Institutionalized unemployment results in the long-term effects described in Chapter 7: declining wages, and built-in overcapacity. It's a non-solution par excellence.

The Doctrine of Competitiveness

The rhetoric of conservative politicians sounds bold and progressive: Canadians must "compete" in a "new global economy." It is less appealing when we look at the specifics:

🔥 Wages must fall to compete with those in Mexico;

🔥 Unions must be weakened;

- 🌢 Our social programs must be slashed to American levels;

- 🌢 Environmental standards must be lowered to attract foreign investors;

- 🌢 Transnational corporations must be given *carte blanche* to do as they see fit; and

- 🌢 Canadians must work longer and harder — for less.

The doctrine of competitiveness is no more, and no less, than an attempt to transform Canada into a Third World economy.

BEYOND NON-SOLUTIONS

Canada's best economic strategies have been almost useless, while our worst policies have been unmitigated disasters. No matter how brilliant an economic policy appears to be, unless it reduces production or increases consumption it is a non sequitur.

> The obvious but ignored solution to our economic problems is a shorter workweek. Why have we clung so tenaciously to the 40-hour workweek when it has cost us so much to do so?

It is that question to which we now turn.

PART IV

WHY ARE WE DOING THIS TO OURSELVES?

Why are we clinging so desperately to the 40-hour workweek? To answer this question requires the exploration of four issues:

❶ Historical forces have pushed our culture into an unprecedented obsession with work. This work obsession has been aggravated by a stand-off between the genders.

❷ A culturally sanctioned pattern of work addiction, and a lifestyle built on an obsessive relationship to work, have created a need for expanding, rather than shrinking, work hours.

❸ A work-obsessed culture creates toxic values, which in turn further our obsession with work.

❹ Leaders in both government and the union movement have chosen politically expedient policies which create few enemies but offer no opportunity to solve our economic problems.

In the next four chapters we will explore these issues. Then, before moving on to Part V and a positive vision for the future, we will ask an important question: Where are we headed if we don't change course?

17

A Short History
of Work

Our crazy and contradictory attitudes to work make more sense when we look at the history of work. Each economic era of the past has left some legacy to our current relationship with work.

Work in the Stone Age

For the first million years of our history, human beings lived in small, nomadic tribes that hunted and foraged for food.

Such tribes had few possessions because each possession was an extra weight to be carried as people moved from place to place in search of food. Property tended to be communal, as sharing reduced the amount that had to be carried between camp sites.

Though a hunting and gathering economy was inefficient in terms of people it would support per acre, it was very efficient as a lifestyle. In *Stone Age Economics*, anthropologist Marshall Sahlins estimates that stone age peoples spent about 25 hours per week on activities we would describe as work. In other words, the stone age equivalents of job and housework *combined* required only 25 hours of labour per week.

Although by no means fixed, there appears to have been a widespread pattern that men were the zoologists — hunters of game — and women were the botanists — gatherers of fruit, roots, and seeds. Periodically, either game or vegetable foodstuffs would be in short supply, which meant that both genders' food contributions were crucial for survival. This interdependence usually resulted in a fairly even distribution of power between the sexes.

Because the tribe was more viable as a unit than was a collection of isolated individuals, there was a strong incentive for democratic decision making. If irreconcilable conflicts arose within a group, it was easier and safer to go separate ways than to fight. (Before antiseptics, even a small battle wound might prove fatal.)

The hunter/gatherer lifestyle involved an intimate relationship with nature. Even today, "primitive" peoples show a deep sensitivity to the needs of their environment, and a reverence for nature.

For more than 99% of our history on the planet, human beings lived this way. Evolution proceeds slowly; our current genetic make-up derives from the hunter/gatherer lifestyle. So if by Wednesday afternoon you feel fed up with work, your genes may be sending you a message.

Work in the Agricultural Age

About ten thousand years ago, a major economic transformation took place. Instead of subsisting on nature's freely given bounty, humanity began actively planting and tending food crops.

Farming first grew up in fertile deltas and river valleys. While it took more work to plant and tend crops than to forage, there were advantages. Agriculture was a more dependable supply of food than hunting or gathering in that seed crops could be stored against hard times. Staying in one place meant that more substantial homes could be built, and saved a great deal of time in packing and moving. Labour-saving tools previously too heavy to pack around now became practical. The workweek was roughly what it had been before: 28 hours per week.

In *The Chalice and the Blade*, Riane Eisler provides a wealth of information on this period of our history. The archaeological record indicates that the first 5000 years of the age of agriculture were peaceful. The earliest European settlements were built in the middle of open valleys rather than on hilltops or other defended sites. These archaeological sites are almost devoid of weapons; we can only presume that warfare was not a major preoccupation.

The period from 8000 to 3000 B.C. was also a period of strong ascendancy for women. Women's historical expertise in botany meant they also became the experts on farming. Deities were more often goddesses than gods; priestesses were more common than priests. What cultural material remains from that time shows a playful, creative society. There was a strong reverence for the fecundity of life. Social organization in this period appears to have been relatively equitable, democratic, and decentralized.

An emphasis on fertility seems to have been the undoing of this idyllic way of life. Population grew rapidly in the period before 3000 B.C., and people eventually began to crowd one another. As agriculture became more efficient, surpluses of food resulted. This surplus freed a growing portion of the population for the making of clothes, tools, jewellery, pottery, and metals.

A rapid expansion in stored human wealth made warfare economically viable. Roving bands of brigands could steal food and property more easily than they could grow or make it. Such thugs quickly found that it took less effort and bloodshed to stay in one community and exact periodic tribute than it did to pillage successive villages. As Thomas Paine observed in *The Rights of Man*: "It would have been no difficulty in the early and solitary ages of the world, while the chief employment of men was that of attending flocks and herds, for a banditti of ruffians to overrun a country and lay it under contributions. Their power thus being established, the chief of the band contrived to lose the name of Robber in that of Monarch; and hence the origin of Monarchy and Kings."

Brute force and expertise in the use of weaponry made men the new leaders. The skills of the soldier became social virtues. (Jehovah was originally the Hebrew god of war.) Society became centralized and more hierarchical. Women lost status and power.

The need to support an overclass somewhat increased the workload of the general population — but not to an extent that was onerous. As recently as the Middle Ages there were 180 Christian holy days per year, on which most of the population did not work.

Many of our sentimental or nostalgic values about religion, family life, and work come from the age of agriculture. In an agrarian economy, work was not the only, or even the most central, sphere in people's lives.

Work time was also family time. Most of the population worked on family farms or in family businesses; artisans passed on their trades to their offspring.

Religion was a collective, communal web of activities requiring daily participation. Extended family structure meant that nurturing the young, caring for the old, and tending the sick all took place within the family. Celebration, sport, and self-expression were public, participatory activities. Work was only one of several activities out of which people developed a sense of identity and worth.

Our strong sentimental attachments to family and church may seem out of proportion to the time we spend on these activities today. However, they are not disproportionate if seen as a hungering for a balanced lifestyle we once had, and lost.

Work in the Industrial Age

Around 1800, several changes heralded the death of rural culture.

The use of the scientific method in agriculture meant that far fewer farmers were required to meet the population's food needs.

The growth of Protestantism championed individual salvation over community well-being. Protestant churches also sanctioned interest-bearing loans. Prior to this time, loaning money at interest was considered to be the sin of usury; capitalism grew rapidly once it was accepted that wealth could be used to generate more wealth.

The invention of steam power, combined with the introduction of the factory model, transformed the economic base of society. By 1825, the average workweek had shot up to more than 75 hours. Even young children worked 12 hours a day, 6.5 days a week.

Work so dominated daily life that all other activities were trivialized or pushed aside. Families no longer worked together and there was little time for family life. Religious life was confined to an hour on Sunday morning. The working population had neither the time nor the energy for sport, song, or dance.

Social historians have a rule of thumb that a culture's deepest values will be centred 100 to 150 years in its past. Today's virtues are the central life lessons and moral prescriptions adopted by our great-great-grandparents. Their lives were dominated by labour; work was, of necessity, the paramount virtue.

North America was more strongly affected by the nineteenth century obsession with work than was Europe. America was a frontier continent. What few traditions we have came from the homesteading pioneers. The endless task of settling a new land prepared us to accept industrial-strength overwork as normal. This perhaps explains why Europe has longer vacation times, more work time flexibility, and fewer dual-earner households — Europe never fully lost the traditions of a balanced lifestyle. North America's deepest moral values were formed during the most overworked century in all of humanity's million-year tenure on Earth.

Work in the Service Economy

Throughout the nineteenth century, the actions of democratic governments and the union movement softened the effects of industrialism. The abolition of child labour and the introduction of shorter working hours reduced unemployment, causing wages to rise. That, in turn, made even shorter hours affordable. The workweek progressively shortened towards the 40-hour level we think of as normal, and married women left the workforce. By the beginning of this century, some semblance of balance had been restored to the lives of working people. However, higher wage levels initiated another transformation in the workplace.

Rising labour costs led to the increasing use of machines to replace human labour in agriculture and manufacturing. Because fewer workers were needed in these areas, more and more of the workforce was shifted to providing services: advertising, retail sales, hospitality, education, banking, entertainment, tourism and health care. The growth of the public sector has been responsible for much of the increase in new employment.

Service sector expansion completed the curtailment of family and community life. The specialized nature of work meant that workers often had to move to find jobs; the nuclear family increasingly supplanted the extended family as the social norm.

The care of children became the province of professional teachers, and caring for the infirm, the domain of the medical profession. Entertainment became an industry for consumption more than participation. Sport was largely given over to professional athletes. Unpaid activities lost status; people became "just" housewives, or "just" volunteers.

As the service economy developed, so did a fundamental split between the genders. Men were to be the breadwinners, women the caregivers. Men's work was clearly more important, though it contained the "dirty" element of grubbing for money. Women's work in the home was sentimentally elevated; mother was the most saintly of beings. Women became the custodians of society's morals, but the trade-off was that they were increasingly denied both economic and political power. Strong differences in gender roles were rationalized as being based on biological and innate character differences between the sexes. The church even entered into the fray, giving God's stamp of approval to the new gender roles.

Perhaps the strongest legacy of work in the early twentieth century has been this strident ideology of gender. We must recognize that the gender roles we think of as normal are recent inventions, whose roots are economic rather than biologically or divinely ordained.

The Era of the Gender Stand-Off

Several factors made women's re-entry into the workforce inevitable.

As housewives, married women had little political or economic power, and low status. The expansion of the service sector increasingly nibbled away at territories which had once been women's sphere of influence. What remained of the housewife's role was undervalued. Since much of the growth of new employment in the service sector was in areas of female expertise, women wondered why they should spend their days in unpaid activities of low status, when they had the skills and temperament for paid work of higher status.

By enforcing rigid full-time work schedules, a predominantly male workplace made it difficult for married women to re-enter the workforce, but it did not stop them.

At first, women tried to lead double lives. At work they did their best to pretend they didn't have a family. At home they tried to see that nothing had changed. The house was still clean and hubby's work shirts neatly ironed. Dinner was still on the table when the man of the house arrived home. Women of the 1970s tried to "have it all." By the 1980s, women had just plain had it.

By then a deteriorating economy had left women trapped. Initially women's income may have gone for discretionary spending. By the 1980s, more and more families needed two full-time incomes to survive. Even if part-time work were available, few women could afford it.

Men's unwillingness to accommodate women's legitimate demands for an equitable division of economic power and social status has created an economic and social nightmare. A massive increase in the number of workers, without a corresponding decrease in the workweek, has made a shambles of our economy.

Families with two full-time breadwinners are placed under incredible stress; there just aren't enough hours in the day for work, domestic chores, parenting, and marriage. The result has been a huge increase in family and marriage breakdown.

An unresolved stand-off between the genders has greatly aggravated our economic difficulties. Any return to economic health must therefore also include a more workable social contract between men and women.

As a man, I feel a need to address other men briefly: *Under the old system, as a gender, men coerced and exploited women, and undervalued their contributions. You may not have done it personally, but it happened. It happened too often, to too many women, for women to be willing to go back to the way things were. Even when the old system wasn't exploitive, it left both genders with too few choices. Women are not going to leave the workplace just because it's designed to be difficult for them. If you haven't noticed, at this point it's difficult for almost everyone. Men, we need to push for workplace change too, rather than sullenly resisting it. Issues like shorter hours, work options, wage equity, sexual harassment, daycare, and family leave are not "women's issues." They are* sanity *issues — for all of us.*

Our 40-hour workweek was designed for men with stay-at-home wives. It wasn't designed for men whose partners are employed, and it certainly wasn't designed for women, or for single parents of either sex. It hurts everyone to leave the stand-off unresolved.

THE LEGACIES OF THE PAST

Human history exerts several forces upon us:

- Our genetic heritage equips us for a 25-hour workweek;

- Wistful values from the age of agriculture direct us towards a more balanced lifestyle;

- Moral virtues carried over from the industrial age program us to be compulsive about work;

- The gender ideology of the service economy bequeaths us an unworkable relationship between the sexes;

- The gender stand-off of the past two decades has aggravated our economic problems and increased the employment burden of the average Canadian family.

18

The Addiction to Busyness

Work-and-spend has become a mutually reinforcing and powerful syndrome — a seamless web we somehow keep choosing, without ever meaning to.

JULIET SCHOR

North America suffers from an epidemic of workaholism rivalling in size and severity the problem of alcoholism. The epidemic is largely invisible and is actively aided and abetted by the culture.

Before exploring the dynamics of work addiction, try the following self-test (after all, this chapter may be about you).

Work Addiction Diagnostic Test

INSTRUCTIONS: *Mark the number of the answer of the most accurate response to each statement below. When you're done, go back and total those numbers to get your score.*

1. I make lists, and leave piles of work where they'll nag me.
   Sometimes or never (0)   Frequently (1)   Almost always (3)   ___

2. I think or obsess about work issues when not at work.
   Sometimes or never (0)   Frequently (1)   Almost always (3)   ___

3. When people ask "How are you?" I respond by telling them what I've been doing.
   Sometimes or never (0)   Frequently (1)   Almost always (3)   __

4. When I have been compulsive or obsessive about work I rationalize it or make excuses for myself.
   Sometimes or never (0)   Frequently (1)   Almost always (3)   __

5. I work more than I want because the organization would fall apart otherwise.
   The statement is false (0)   I act as if statement were true (1)   __
   The statement is true (3)
   I make sure my organization can't function without me (5)

6. I feel guilty.
   Sometimes (0)   Frequently (1)   Instantly (3)   Always (5)   __

7. I work to escape uncomfortable feelings or situations.
   Rarely (0)   Sometimes (1)   Frequently (3)   Almost always (5)   __

8. I like to work myself into overdrive for the high it creates.
   Occasionally or never (0)   Frequently (1)   __
   I'm always on overdrive (3)

9. I have stress-related health problems.
   No (0)   Occasional or minor (1)   Chronic or major (3)   __

10. I am perfectionistic.
    Sometimes or never (0)   Frequently (1)   Almost always (3)   __
    Even on matters that are trivial (5)

11. I have trouble saying "no" to work requests.
    Sometimes or never (0)   Frequently (1)   Almost always (3)   __

12. I make time to relax and do nothing.
    Regularly (0)   At least once a week (1)   __
    Rarely (3)   I climb the walls if I'm not busy (5)

13. I turn my play into work.
    Sometimes or never (0)   Frequently (1)   Almost always (3)   __

14. I find it hard to relax.
    Sometimes or never (0)   Frequently (1)   Almost always (3)   __

15. When I'm not busy I drink or smoke more.
   False (0)   Sometimes or frequently (1)   Almost always (3) ____

16. When family or fun activities conflict with work:
   Work usually comes second (0)   Work predominates (1)
   Work comes first (3) ____

17. I feel like I haven't done enough.
   Sometimes or never (0)   Frequently (1)   Almost always (3) ____

18. When I make "Do Lists" I do the high priority items first.
   Almost always (0)   Frequently (1)   Sometimes or never (3) ____

19. I feel a strong need to be in control.
   Sometimes or never (0)   Frequently (1)   Almost always (3) ____

20. How would you feel if your supervisor came into your office
   and threw out all your files?
   Relieved (0)   Disoriented or angry (1)   Panicked(3) ____

21. On vacations I am:
   Involved and/or relaxed quickly (0)
   Fretful and a little lost the first few days (1)
   Fretful and agitated or depressed for a week or more (3)
   What's a vacation? (5) ____

22. I forget social engagements and work right through.
   Rarely or never (0)   Sometimes (1)   Frequently (3)
   What social engagements? (5) ____

23. When I'm in the middle of a job that's too big to get done
   today, I stop:
   At the normal quitting hour (0)
   An hour or more after quitting time (1)
   When I'm exhausted (3)
   When the job is done (5) ____

24. I continue to work even after my productivity has fallen off.
   Sometimes or never (0)   Frequently (1)   Almost always (3) ____

25. At least some of my activities have a compulsive or driven feel.
   Sometimes or never (0)   Frequently (1)   Almost always (3) ____

26. My partner (or friends) tell me I work too much.
Seldom (0) Sometimes (1) Frequently (3)
They've given up talking to me about it (5) ____

27. I work holidays or weekends.
Sometimes or never (0) Frequently (1) Almost always (3) ____

28. I sneak work home, and do it surreptitiously.
Never (0) Sometimes (1) Frequently (3)
I sleep at the office (5) ____

29. I would respond to a high score on this test:
Seriously (0) Dismissively (1) Jokingly (3)
I won't total the score, so I won't know!(5) ____

Scores:

0-15	Relatively healthy
15-25	Addictive tendencies
25-50	Strong addictive tendencies
Over 50	Get help now!

If you scored 25 or more, you should pay close attention to what follows.

Workaholism: The Respectable Addiction

Most people falsely identify workaholism as an addiction to one's job. Workaholism is actually the addiction to being busy. While the most common focus for busyness is job-related activities, a confirmed workaholic is like a hardcore alcoholic: bottles hidden everywhere. Compulsive busyness can be expressed in relation to housework, volunteer activities, building projects, hobbies, computers, shopping, or obsessive parenting.

Never go on vacation with an active workaholic; she'll take you to Europe for 10 days — and tour 28 cities. Another sign of a hardcore workaholic: he can't eat dinner without simultaneously reading the paper and listening to the radio.

Part of the difficulty in recognizing workaholism is that the addiction to busyness can be satisfied in so many ways that it's easy to deny the underlying pattern. There are workaholics in part-time jobs and at home. To live with a workaholic retiree is to spend time in hell.

An addiction is a compulsive relationship with any substance or process which is designed to take us away from intimacy with self. It may take us away by distracting us or by creating a euphoric mental state. What characterizes an addiction is that the underlying purpose of the compulsive act is to distract or numb us as a way to hide from problematic situations. The addictive process is the same whether the addiction is to a substance — alcohol, drugs, cigarettes, or food — or a process — gambling, work, or sex.

Addiction is a learned coping strategy: we try to deal with problems by ignoring them. The basic bankruptcy of addiction is that few problems go away on their own. Most problematic situations fester when we try to ignore them.

How does a healthy enjoyment of work differ from work addiction? Our relationship to work is healthy when it does not have an underlying function of avoidance. Work is not used to escape negative emotions, to suppress parts of ourselves, or to avoid problematic situations and relationships in our personal lives.

The fact that a person enjoys his work, or finds satisfaction in it, does not protect him from workaholism. If anything, those side benefits will make work a particularly attractive focus of addiction. A person who says, "I just like my work so much that's all I ever want to do" — is an addict. There simply isn't room for a whole person in such a life. It's like the alcoholic who claims she really enjoys drinking. The statement may be true but it's not the whole truth. No real change happens so long as denial persists.

Burnout is often confused with work addiction. Burnout is the end result of work addiction. It is to the workaholic what skid row is to the alcoholic. A person can be a workaholic without being burned out. In the same way, an individual can recover from the symptoms of burnout without healing the underlying addiction to work.

■ DIFFERENT STROKES: PATTERNS OF WORK ADDICTION

Four distinct patterns of overwork are common.

COMPULSIVE WORKERS are generic workaholics — people

who are simply driven to work all the time. Usually they are perfectionists, and super-responsible.

BINGE WORKERS tend periodically to get high on benders of overwork. It is a cruel fate to have a binge worker for a manager; they can manufacture crises which will throw a whole department into bedlam for days.

CLOSET WORKERS have some awareness their relationship to work is unhealthy. They've learned to be sneaky. They'll hide a work report behind the cover of a steamy novel. Even at the beach, in the back of their minds they're gnawing at a work project.

WORK ANOREXICS oscillate between binge working and heavy-duty procrastination. The pattern is not a common one and most often shows itself as an interim stage in the recovery from work addiction.

■ HOW WORK ADDICTION WORKS

Four forces create workaholism: denial, boundary confusion, co-dependence, and self-aggravating cycles.

DENIAL operates at two levels. The first level is the avoidance of some situation or emotion the addict doesn't want to face. The most common emotions addicts seek to avoid are pain and fear. Grief, guilt, loneliness, emptiness, anger, or frustration may also be denied.

Aspects of self may be denied: childhood trauma, the person's creative or unique aspects, sexuality. Any part of self that the conscious ego has trouble embracing may be denied through overwork.

Difficult situations beyond a person's ability to cope invite denial: troubles in the relationship with a spouse or a child, even troubles in the relationship to co-workers.

Always there is something an addict doesn't want to face, and an obsessive relationship with busyness is used to deny or ignore that aspect of life.

The second level of denial is to deny that overwork is being used as an escape. Overwork is always rationalized: "I work so much because we're so far in debt," "I work so much because my clients need me," "I work so much because I love my work," "I work so much because my boss is a workaholic" — anything but the real truth.

BOUNDARY CONFUSION is another way of saying that addicts have a hard time setting limits. Addicts don't know their place on the Great Chain of Being.

The Great Chain of Being is a life spectrum that has God at one end, slimy worms at the other, and human beings in the middle. Boundary problems happen either when humans demand of themselves god-like powers, or think they have no more rights than a worm.

As human beings, we all have certain basic rights: the right to have feelings, needs, and desires, and the right to self-expression. Addicts are forced into denial when they believe they have no more rights than a worm.

WORMS	HUMANS	GOD
No rights or privileges	Have rights to: - Feel - Change - Need - Make Errors - Want - Have Limits - Express - Be Sexual - Be Responsible for Self	- No Change - No Errors - No Limits - Responsible for Everything

Low self-esteem is linked with a worm-like lack of boundaries. Non-intimate families train us in the idea that some parts of ourselves are unacceptable and unworthy.

An example would be the woman who works obsessively to avoid feeling sexual. It's a normal human right to have sexual feelings but she believes she doesn't have a right to any urges which might upset mom or dad.

At the other extreme, addicts can get into trouble by not accepting their limits. As humans, we change, make mistakes, have limited powers and limited responsibilities. Growing up in demanding or perfectionist families, addicts do not learn a healthy humility — if they don't complete every task with God-like perfection, they feel worthless.

At one point in my history with Work Well, I found myself being obsessive about work. I had created a dynamic organization to promote flexible work schedules, and after five years my interest had shifted — I wanted to write *this* book. But I hadn't given myself permission to change. I had started the organization and I felt I owed it to all the people who had supported me to continue it forever. Once

I released myself from the God-like demand of unchangeability, my compulsiveness disappeared and I was able to devote my energies to writing.

CO-DEPENDENCE is the technical term for the ways in which the people closest to an addict consciously or unconsciously support the addiction. An alcoholic's spouse often colludes with a partner's drinking, seeing no alternative but to cover for the addict. Work addicts are usually supported in their addiction by their spouses, friends, co-workers, and the media. In our society, breaking free of an addiction to work requires swimming upstream!

Spouses of work addicts have little social support for setting strong and healthy boundaries. As with spouses of alcoholics, the unwillingness to leave an intolerable marriage helps to keep the addiction in place.

SELF-AGGRAVATING CYCLES are an inevitable part of work-aholism in that the more I work to avoid dealing with something, the more that situation will spiral out of control. If I work to suppress my anger, more anger is likely to be pent up inside. The more anger builds, the greater the chance it will explode destructively.

The addictive behaviour itself will often aggravate the problem. As an example, let's say you have a spouse who is cold and angry because you don't spend enough time with her. It can be uncomfortable to hang around an angry person. It's tempting to find more and more that you simply must do at the office. The more time you spend at work, the colder and angrier your partner will become.

The more I suppress my emotions with obsessive activity, the less likely I am to know my true needs when it comes time to make the next decision. It's a little like the situation alcoholics face — after each drink it becomes harder and harder to say "no" to the next one.

The final hook to work addiction is that it hurts to change. If you've been an activity machine for a while, there's hell to pay when you finally stop. At first you'll feel exhausted and numb, and not know what you want. Then the feelings you've been trying to avoid will start to surface. You'll begin to notice what a mess your private life has become while you were off on another planet.

Remember the alcoholic's bumper sticker "Avoid Hangovers — Stay Drunk All the Time"? Most work addicts adopt a similar strategy. Like alcoholics, most work addicts think they are happy when they are feeling no pain.

Addictive Organizations

Work addicts are made, not born. Few people's boundaries are so healthy that the right organization can't make them workaholics, at least for a time.

In *The Addictive Organization*, Anne Wilson Schaef presents the thesis that most organizations function, to one degree or another, like dysfunctional families. Indeed, organizations themselves can display many of the behaviours and personality traits that we would normally associate with an active alcoholic or workaholic.

We live in a society so addicted to work that many people feel guilty about not being workaholics (survivor guilt!). They feel it would be disloyal to take active steps to make their organizations healthier, assuming that organizations get more from workaholics than from healthy staff.

I'd like to dispute that assumption. Productivity tends to be low in workaholic organizations because of staff burnout.

The standard situation in the early stages of workaholism is for addicts to have very high productivity. However, as they become more dysfunctional, their productivity falls below normal. Once they hit the burnout stage their output hits the skids. They may spend a lot of hours at work, but they accomplish little. Eventually they must be given time off to recover, or be fired and replaced. In either case, there's a further period of low productivity.

The graph on the next page shows the difference in productivity between a healthy worker and a workaholic staff member. Actively discouraging workaholism will increase the productivity of most organizations. The reduced productivity of workaholics is even more obvious if quality of work is considered. Work addicts create lots of sound and fury, but much of their activity is off-purpose and ineffective.

Organizations can display addictive behaviour at four levels:

❶ **Addicts are in key organizational roles;**

❷ **Co-dependents enable and cover for them;**

❸ **The organization itself becomes an addiction;**

❹ **The organization itself functions like an active addict.**

These four levels are mutually supportive.

■ ADDICT IN CHARGE!

An active addict in a key role will often set the emotional tone for an
organization and determine its communication patterns. In their
book *The Neurotic Organization*, Manfred DeVries and Danny Miller
found that organizations take on the personality of key personnel,
becoming dramatic, depressive, paranoid, compulsive, or schizoid
in keeping with the character of the senior managers.

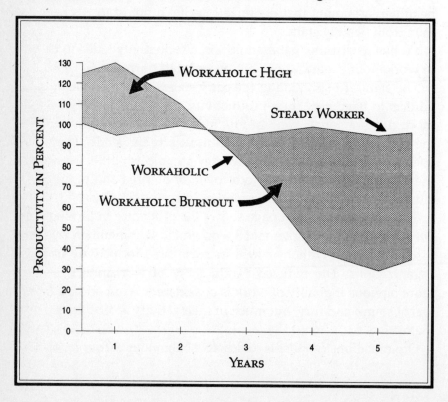

When an active addict is involved in an organization, he brings the traits and strategies of his addiction into the organization. These traits are similar for all addictions.

Addicts are isolated from normal feedback; they don't receive early warning signals of problems. The result is organizations that lurch from crisis to crisis. Dishonesty about the addiction itself means the addiction can become severe without corrective action taking place.

The perfectionism of the addict wastes excessive energy on low-priority items and pushes the whole agency to do the same. The grandiosity of the addict leads her to push the organization to take on more than it can handle.

A workaholic in a key position becomes the role model for the organization. Co-dependents will take on extra work to try to "protect" the workaholic, which does no good at all because the workaholic then immediately takes on even more tasks for the organization. Healthy people tend to leave such organizations, or are driven out.

■ THE CO-DEPENDENCE DANCE

People will often repeat in organizations what they learned in addictive families. The perfectionism and self-criticism of the adult children of addicts helps set them up to fit right into perfectionist organizations. Feelings of insecurity or inferiority can often be assuaged by overwork. Work may appear safer than intimate relationships.

Co-dependents have a high tolerance for confusion and are practised mind-readers. Often, they will not demand the clarity they need to do their job properly. They may have excessive loyalty, making excuses or keeping secrets for an addict rather than confronting him.

■ HOOKED ON THE ORGANIZATION

In the late 1960s, the term "company man" was used to describe someone who had become totally identified with the company for which he worked.

Companies may actively support such over-identification with promises like: stick with us and you'll get ahead, you'll be important, you'll belong.

Some organizations will try to become the staff's whole social life, to further tie them into the organization. Sometimes organizations try to "hook" people with security promises: stay long enough and you'll get a longer vacation, a pension, or a bigger office. Some agencies try to hook people with a rah-rah cheerleader approach, getting everyone revved up for the "big game." Within such an atmosphere, it's easy for employees to forget that their needs and the organization's are not necessarily the same.

Paycheques which are based on a fixed salary, as opposed to an hourly wage, tend to slide staff into ever-increasing workloads in organizations which are growing.

All of these techniques create shaky boundaries for staff, who can easily slip into workaholism.

■ ADDICTION WRIT LARGE

The less healthy an organization is, the more it will display the behaviour and characteristics of an addict. As an organization deteriorates, it loses the communication and decision-making practices that would otherwise prevent small problems from growing. The best staff are likely to leave and be replaced by people who are attracted to the addictive pattern.

Communication becomes vague, confusing, and indirect. Messages are transferred by memos and gossip. There are secrets. Not only will there be much that can't be talked about, but even the undiscussibility of the secrets will be undiscussible. The mundane will get more attention than the important. There will be an excessive concern with appearances over substance.

The expression of feelings will be muted or absent. Decision processes will be overly rational, without sufficient inclusion of the emotional and the intuitive. The agency will not learn from its mistakes. The mission or purpose of the organization will get lost in crisis management.

Denial and dishonesty will be built into the management process. There will often be an unstated set of procedures and priorities for the organization that is very different from the official mission statement.

In structure, the agency will try to engender competition rather than cooperation, to heighten control, to apply punishment, and to guarantee predictability. There will be more rules and structures as the organization gets sicker. Staff will be seen as untrustworthy. The organization will become inward-looking, isolated, and self-centred rather than actively connected to the larger community. Such agencies breed workaholics in large numbers.

The Addictive Society

In *When Society Becomes an Addict*, Anne Wilson Schaef goes even further, suggesting that addiction is the basic motif of our culture. Addictions to drugs, alcohol, cigarettes, over-eating, gambling, and work are not separate problems, but symptoms of an underlying pattern.

Our culture actively aids and abets attempts to distract and numb ourselves. Addictive family patterns repeat themselves generation after generation. Our failure to admit the extent of addiction means we make only token attempts at treatment. (In the next chapter, we will explore how the moral values of popular culture support addiction.)

Worked Over: The Work-Obsessed Lifestyle

A lifestyle dominated by work tends to perpetuate itself. If I work more than is healthy for me, it is tempting to reward myself with expensive treats — a fancy car, an expensive restaurant meal, or an exotic vacation. Paying the bills for today's treats will push me to overwork again tomorrow: "I owe, I owe, it's off to work I go."

If I work long hours, I won't have enough energy to enjoy my leisure time. Rather than doing something interesting or engaging, I'll "veg out" in front of the TV. If I allow work to take over my life, there's nothing left that's important enough to pull me back to balance. If I have active and satisfying friendships, for example, I will have a strong incentive to protect my private time. On the other hand, if I have allowed my friendships to wither, I don't have the same motivation to protect my free time.

If I work too much at a job which is sedentary, I may grow overweight and unfit. This, in turn, may inhibit my willingness to enjoy myself in sports, dancing, or sex.

If I consistently work too much, I will feel exhausted and lost when I do stop working. I may find that my spouse and my children have become strangers to me. I won't feel this discomfort if I keep running at top speed.

If I'm always running on empty and in overdrive, I will have neither the time nor the energy to know my true needs. I will be easily manipulated into spending most of my life in activities that will make someone else richer, but which won't make me happier. Many people need a heart attack to slow them down enough to realize when they are not happy.

Living in a sick economy has pushed many Canadians into workaholism. Ironically, they may then be too busy to notice that the economy is becoming sicker still.

THE POWER OF ADDICTION

The tenacity with which we have resisted shorter work hours says much about the power of work addiction.

Recognition of our social pattern of addiction, and more active support of recovery programs, are essential pre-requisites to reclaiming a future of abundant leisure.

19

Work and Self-Worth

*Our politics, religion, news, athletics, education and
commerce have been translated into congenial adjuncts
of show business, largely without protest or even much
popular notice. The result is that we are a people on the
verge of amusing ourselves to death.*

NEIL POSTMAN

Our underlying problems are not economic, but spiritual. Moral
values are expressions of the spirit in which we live. Addictive
values are both a cause and a result of our culture's obsession with
work.

Popular culture in North America surrounds us with values
which promote addiction. In popular sayings, in oft-repeated themes
in the media, in school curricula, church sermons, news programs,
at work and at play, our values are massaged at every turn. Sometimes toxic values are explicit; sometimes they are assumed. In either
case, it's a bit like flu season: it's hard not to get infected when the
germs are all around you.

One of the ways we can protect ourselves from addictive values
is to identify them, and to sensitize ourselves to popular clichés
which express them.

In this chapter, we will look at five characteristics of addiction
which have embedded themselves in the larger culture: self-worth
which is relative and conditional; shame; a failure to value uniqueness and diversity; obsessive busyness; and a worldview of scarcity.

Relative Self-Worth

Healthy self-worth is based on the awareness of myself as a unique being. I am worthwhile by the simple act of having been born, and because I have a one-of-a-kind perspective on the world — my own thoughts, feelings, gifts, and insights. External references, such as grades or the opinions of others, provide only a secondary back-stop for an intrinsic sense of worth.

For the addict, personal worth is relative: I have value only insofar as I am measurably better than someone else. My worth comes from external sources: more money, a fancier home, a job with status, a more attractive spouse. My worth, perhaps even my identity, comes from career and possessions. Self-worth is also conditional. If I'm not able to keep up with the Joneses, my worth disappears.

■ 'I'M BETTER THAN YOU ARE!'

Self-worth which is based on winning requires the presence of losers. The Ku Klux Klan is populated by the poorest whites; if the only way to be worthy is to be better than someone else, someone must be made a "nigger." The stars of *Lifestyles of the Rich and Famous* are attention junkies; they need the adulation of the poor and the anonymous to feel okay about themselves.

Part of the intractability of poverty in North America is that many of the rich *need* the poor. Sexism, ageism, and racism will be hard to eradicate so long as people measure their worth by their position in a social pecking order.

■ 'WINNING IS EVERYTHING'

An attitude that winning is the goal follows right along from the belief that we need to be better than others. Winning becomes more important than fair play, more important even than the game itself. Winning is essential when your self-worth rides on it.

When winning is everything, there is no point in doing anything unless you can be the best; the result is a culture of spectators. Sport is no longer a vehicle for exercise, play, and challenge. Sport becomes a passive activity, more likely to promote a beer belly than physical well-being. It is no longer a game, but serious work.

Art ceases to be an opportunity for self-expression for all. Instead, it is a source of fame for the artist and a speculative investment for the art connoisseur.

■ 'WHOEVER HAS THE MOST TOYS . . . '

When a person's self-worth is centred in her personal integrity, her feelings, and her spirituality, she is difficult to manipulate. When a person's worth is tied up in possessions, he is an easy mark for the advertiser's hooks. "Buy a new and improved whatzit and you'll be a Very Important Person." Wealth becomes not a practical instrument for creating comfort and pleasure, but a yardstick of personal worth. Even our language has come to express this confusion: is my personal net worth really a financial balance sheet?

Erich Fromm, in *The Sane Society*, suggests that it is a mistake to refer to North Americans as materialists. Rather, he maintains, we are *abstractionists*, more concerned with commodities as symbols of success than with their capacity to bring us satisfaction.

■ 'THE JOB COMES FIRST'

When worth is tied to social position, career assumes an exaggerated importance; other relationships get short shrift. Family, community life, and spirituality are neglected. When a person's basic sense of worth (perhaps even her very identity) becomes synonymous with her job, it is easy to blackmail that person with veiled threats of firing, or entice her to superhuman efforts with dangled promises of promotion.

Shame

For most addicts, relative self-worth is a patch-up job, a cover-up for a deep sense of shame. Shame is the experience of feeling fundamentally flawed and irreparably broken — the I-just-want-to-hide-so-nobody-sees-me feeling.

It is virtually impossible to build a happy and constructive life if my foundation is the belief that I am fundamentally inadequate and unworthy. Yet our culture actively promotes shame, in schools, in churches, and in the workplace, as a means of social control.

Shame-based individuals use shame to control others. After all, how can I trust others to behave with goodwill and integrity if I cannot experience and validate those qualities in myself? Shame begets shame.

Shame has created a culture obsessively concerned with outward appearances, and with looking "normal." The vain hope is that if I look good on the outside, no-one will notice that I am broken on the inside.

■ THE DOCTRINE OF ORIGINAL SIN

As a counsellor, I received training in the use of hypnotic suggestion. The hypnotists who offered that training placed hypnosis in an everyday context: "If you think people only go into trance in hypnosis, watch more closely the next time your teenager plays Nintendo!"

Professional hypnotists will tell you that the most powerful hypnotist in your life is you. Any statements you make about yourself repeatedly and sincerely will unconsciously draw forth that kind of behaviour from you.

If you are constantly churched in a theology that says, as a human being, you are inherently selfish, weak, and sinful, you will draw forth that very behaviour from yourself. Shame draws forth "shameful" behaviour.

Churches often claim to be teaching humility when they instill shame, though the two are very different. Humility is the recognition that I am limited and that that's okay. Shame is the belief that I am unworthy or evil.

Promoting the idea that human beings are inherently evil and sinful enables Christian churches to control their flocks with shame. Such attitudes torpedo the development of a healthy sense of self-worth. They bring out an individual's worst, rather than supporting what is best in the human spirit.

Failure to Value Uniqueness and Diversity

How can you measure a rose against a sunset, a poem against a text-book, a musician against an engineer, or a shrimp omelette against cologne? Part of the miracle of life is the uniqueness of its pleasures. It is this abundance of unique pleasures and attributes which creates a universe of fullness and joyful cooperation.

In the same way that addicts diminish their own unique worth (and that of others) by measuring everyone against a single imaginary scale of value, so does the addict diminish the richness and diversity of life by trying to make money the measure of all things. Instead of seeing "a time for every purpose under heaven," the addict will ask, "What's the bottom line?"

■ THE VALUE OF A THING IS ITS PRICE TAG

At a party, George Bernard Shaw is said to have asked an attractive young woman, "Would you sleep with me for a million dollars?"

When the woman replied in the affirmative, Shaw then asked, "Will you sleep with me for 10 dollars?"

"What do you think I am!" she replied, indignantly.

"We've already established that," observed Shaw. "Now we're just haggling about the price."

An economy in which everything has a dollar value, in which most social relations are trades or bargains, turns us into all into prostitutes. A life where every act is but a means towards an end, where a person "gives" only in order to get, is a life without authenticity, a life without love.

Friendships and marriages work badly as bargain-based relationships. There can never be a free flow of love in relationship when the partners are busy keeping score.

In a culture where everything has a price tag, intangibles escape public attention. Part of the reason our environment has been so badly damaged is that it's not included in our financial balance sheets. It is in exactly this context that a British Columbia minister of forests once claimed that a tree has no value until it is cut down.

■ WOMEN'S WORK DOESN'T MATTER

In a society where the value of an item is considered to be its price tag, the value of unpaid work is discounted, almost invisible. Since most of women's duties in this century have been unpaid, this has translated into undervaluing women's work and the skills and characteristics of women. Women often internalize these skewed values, speaking of themselves as "just" housewives or "just" volunteers.

Because parenting, family life, and domestic chores were all unpaid women's work, these activities got little respect. The resulting values, that failed to reflect the real importance of the home arena, have had severe consequences. Family life atrophied in the 1980s; many marriages died of neglect.

When asked in surveys to name characteristics of the "ideal man," the "ideal woman," and the "ideal human being," both men and women assign traits to the ideal human that strongly resemble the pattern chosen for the ideal man. As a result of such faulty valuing, skills and characteristics which have been labelled "feminine" are often underdeveloped in both men and women.

Obsessive Busyness

Denial is one of the central characteristics of addiction. The addict secretly hopes, "If I keep myself busy enough, distracted enough, or high enough, maybe I won't notice the pain and emptiness inside me." This frenetic avoidance of intimacy with self is supported broadly in our culture, both at work and at play.

Obsessive busyness gives life a shallow, sleep-walking quality. In the words of John Bradshaw, it turns us into "human doings" instead of human beings. Denial creates a mindless busyness that usually bears no resemblance to a person's deeper needs and desires. After all, how many people on their deathbeds are likely to say, "I wish I'd spent more time at the office"?

■ 'AN IDLE MIND IS THE DEVIL'S WORKSHOP'

The extent to which Protestantism was co-opted by the capitalist elite is obvious in its attitude to work. We might expect that a tradition concerned with spiritual growth would put a priority on spiritual activities. Instead, early Protestantism let the people who paid the piper call the tune. To support the rich, the Protestant churches made unremitting work a moral virtue. To distract attention from the avarice of the wealthy, it made sexual sins the focus of moral scruples.

We live with the legacy of this sell-out. We have created a culture in which people who stop to consider the nature of God, who want more time with their children or spouse, are made to feel guilty and lazy. People who live lives of selfishness, so long as they are driven by acquisitiveness and unrelenting labour, can bask in moral smugness.

■ 'WORK HARD, PLAY HARD'

Neil Postman's book *Amusing Ourselves To Death* provides a detailed account of the way obsessive busyness has become a cultural model. What is perhaps most subversive about this busyness is that it is relentlessly packaged as entertainment.

Entertainment is designed to be light, diverting, easily digestible. It is meant to amuse, to keep us "occupied." Entertainment is the perfect "fix" for the addict.

A culture of entertainment skips along the surface of issues. It makes little distinction between the profound and the banal; the destruction of the ozone layer must fight for its three minutes of public attention on an equal footing with teenage acne cures and the discovery of the world's largest cockroach. A culture of entertainment doesn't so much ignore crucial issues as it trivializes and overwhelms them.

As an example of the shallowness of the entertainment model, Postman compares political debate today with that in the time of Abraham Lincoln. Lincoln and his presidential opponents engaged in public debates where each candidate would speak for three hours at a time. Debate was detailed and probing. By contrast, in the culture of entertainment, George Bush and Bill Clinton are reduced to trading sound bites: "Read my lips: no new taxes" and "It's the economy, stupid."

The culture of entertainment is the ethos of the addict writ large: keep me amused, keep me occupied, keep me busy, so that I don't have to face my problems. As with all addiction, problems which are ignored tend to fester. We may, indeed, be amusing ourselves to death.

■ 'SHOP 'TIL YOU DROP'

Shopping is the other great escape. North Americans spend three times as much time shopping as do Europeans. Advertising constantly reassures us that things will make us happy. We have created a culture where, as the bumper sticker says, "When the going gets tough, the tough go shopping."

A Worldview of Scarcity and Struggle

The inner world of the hard-core addict is a harsh one. The individual feels alone and isolated. Life is a struggle for scarce resources — every man for himself; every woman for herself. Love is in short supply.

This worldview comes from the addict's experience of life. It also creates the addict's experience of life: it is hard to experience community, abundance, and goodwill when they don't have a place in your picture of the world.

The larger culture, in stressing the individual over the community, competition over cooperation, and hoarding rather than sharing, promotes this worldview of isolation, struggle, and scarcity.

■ 'LOOKING OUT FOR NUMBER ONE'

Prior to the Reformation, spiritual life was a community activity; God was honoured in collective worship. Repentance and the forgiveness of sin took place in community. Penitents would serve God by helping the poor and the infirm.

Protestantism made salvation an individual affair and helped break down the sense of loyalty and responsibility to the community. The accumulation of great wealth was no longer the sin of avarice, but earthly evidence that God looked kindly on the rich person's soul.

The breakdown of community created the lonely crowd. Lacking the solace of human friendship, isolated individuals find consolation in shopping binges. Lacking trust, they reassure themselves with chain-link fences.

When the commandment to "love one another" loses its force, community starts to die. When self-love is the only love, the anomie of unfettered individualism breaks down both the social order and the environment.

The discipline of economics bears some responsibility for the elevation of selfishness to a quasi-virtue, with its doctrine that the "invisible hand" of the free market will turn all acts of free-market selfishness to the public good. We do not yet have "a system so perfect that no-one needs to be good" — and economists have done us all a disservice by pretending otherwise.

■ 'NICE GUYS FINISH LAST'

The scientific correlate of individual salvation was the doctrine of evolution, as framed by Charles Darwin. Sociologist Herbert Spencer extended the doctrine of survival of the fittest into social relationships.

These doctrines painted unrestrained competition as the natural order. If my neighbour starves, it is not my responsibility, merely the natural order of things. If I step on others on my way to the top, that's just how life is.

The modern science of ecology makes it clear that natural systems are not so much a series of battles as an intricately orchestrated dance. Unfortunately, the lessons of ecology have not yet penetrated the public consciousness. We still live in the mental world of Charles Darwin.

■ DOMINION OVER THE EARTH

In earlier centuries, the biblical concept that human beings had God-given "dominion over the earth" was interpreted as a stewardship or caretaking role. Human beings had a responsibility to cherish and honour the Creator's handiwork. Protestantism reinterpreted human dominion over nature to align with the capitalist doctrine of private property. The earth and everything on it were the private property of humanity, to do with as they pleased.

Assigning ownership of the earth to humanity has obscured our dependence on natural systems for our survival. Our relationship with the environment still suffers from this mindset, which sees nature as a commodity to be exploited. More often than we like to imagine, humanity is like the cartoon logger, busily sawing through the very branch upon which he sits.

Until humanity sees itself as a member of the larger community of life, we will continue to exploit the natural world — much as the addict exploits his family and friends.

VALUES THAT POISON

The values of addiction poison our social climate in much the same way that chemical pollutants contaminate the natural environment, invisibly and insidiously.

- ❧ Self-worth is defined in relation to position and possession;

- ❧ Shame is taught in church and at school;

- ❧ Money is made the measure of all things;

- ❧ Obsessive busyness is promoted at work and at play;

- ❧ A toxic worldview turns life into a contest where isolated individuals must struggle for survival in a world of scarcity.

20

The Politics of Scarcity

*Millions sense the pathology that pervades the air, but
fail to understand its roots. These roots lie not in this or
that political doctrine, still less in some mythical core of
despair or isolation presumed to inhere in the "human
condition." Nor do they lie in science, technology, or
legitimate demands for social change. They are traceable
instead to the uncontrolled, non-selective nature of our
lunge into the future. They lie in our failure to direct,
consciously and imaginatively, the advance into
super-industrialism.*

ALVIN TOFFLER

Why has public debate on employment issues been so sterile? When
we begin to look at this question, we see that Canada's major interest
groups have chosen policies of expediency over those of courage and
vision.

The Mindset of Scarcity

It may be a legacy of our long past as hunters and gatherers that the
human species is cued to react to scarcity and ignore surpluses.
(After all, surpluses weren't a problem, while food scarcities were a
survival threat.) In the case of employment, this perceptual block is
so strong that a wonderful *opportunity* for abundant leisure is seen
instead as the *problem* of a scarcity of employment.

Hoarding is our automatic response to fears of scarcity. The University of Arizona once had a research program in garbology — the study of garbage. Researchers found, to their surprise, that whenever a food item was in short supply, people threw out more of it. What happened was that as soon as it appeared some foodstuff might become unattainable, people bought as much of it as they could. As often as not, they would buy more than they could immediately use, and it would spoil.

We see the same self-fulfilling cycle around work. Fearful of not getting enough work, we have millions of Canadians working more than is necessary or healthy for them. Higher expenses eat up much of the higher income that results, so they are no more secure than if they worked less, and unemployment is made worse.

The fear of scarcity acts as a self-fulfilling prophecy, creating scarcity at several levels. Fearful and driven people are largely numb to pleasure, so they feel a dearth of pleasure in their lives. Compulsive individuals lack time for family and friends, so love also becomes scarce in their world. Finally, high unemployment creates low wages and a sluggish economy, so there's a scarcity of income and a scarcity of business opportunities.

We have forgotten what our tribal ancestors knew clearly and without equivocation: without collective security, there can be no real security for the individual.

The Framework of 'Not Enough Jobs'

It has been politically expedient to discuss our economic problems within a framework of "there aren't enough jobs," as if jobs existed only in 40-hour packages.

The framework of "not enough jobs" lets everyone who is employed off the hook. Those with jobs aren't asked to make any personal contribution towards solving the unemployment problem; the problem of unemployment isn't their responsibility.

The problem with this framework is that we have exhausted all of the solutions it can generate. Our environment won't let us expand consumption further, and we are in debt as far as we can go.

The framework of "not enough jobs" makes our economic difficulties mysterious and offers no viable solutions. All we can do is watch while our economic ship steadily sinks. Individuals are powerless, as the "experts" claim the general public can't even understand our economic problems, let alone solve them.

Political Expediency

All of Canada's political parties (with the exception of the Green Party) have ducked the unemployment issue.

Any talk about a shorter workweek is attacked as a retreat from full employment. There seems to be an almost schizophrenic machismo among Canadian politicians: on the one hand most claim to be environmentalists, while on the other they press us to believe that the solution to our economic woes is to grow, grow, grow.

The strategy of creating more jobs is designed to please all and offend none. The stance asks nothing of employed Canadians, while appearing to promise jobs to the unemployed. Who could oppose more jobs?

Conservative politicians claim that creating a "healthy climate" for big business will create jobs — despite the fact that big business has been cutting, not creating, jobs. They claim that free trade will create jobs — despite evidence that we have lost one quarter of our manufacturing jobs since free trade was introduced. The government has put more effort into public relations than into economic policy.

What is perhaps more surprising is that no major opposition leader has had the courage to tell the truth about our economic problems. Only by taking the risk to tell the truth, and then developing a clear vision of how it could be different, can opposition parties hope to generate widespread support.

Union Expediency

In the past century, most of the progressive changes which created a healthy and dynamic balance between production and consumption originated with the labour movement. Today, unions more often protect than challenge the status quo. What happened?

Originally, unionists *had* to think about the big picture. In the early 1800s it was obvious there could be no individual security without collective security. The principle of *solidarity* was not idealism, but rather intelligent self-interest. Most union leaders were unpaid, so even though they may have represented a particular union, they were not beholden to it.

Unfortunately, as unions grew more powerful and the economic climate more benign, unions felt less need to campaign on behalf of all workers. Instead they concentrated their efforts on their own membership. Many union leaders began to see themselves as advocates not for all workers, but for their specific sub-groups.

As times began to get tougher in the 1970s, such unions failed to address the problem of growing unemployment as a collective issue. Instead they focused their efforts on protecting the jobs of the established membership of their unions through seniority lists, restricted access, barriers of educational qualification, work rules, restrictions on contracting out, and resisting automation.

This type of narrowly defined self-interest has cost the unions much public support. Insofar as people see unions serving only a specific membership rather than the interests of all workers, they are less willing to make sacrifices for unions and more willing to cross picket lines, ignore boycotts, and work as strikebreakers.

Unions have exacerbated this process by sticking to policies which aggravate unemployment. Union policies restricting the hiring of relief staff and the availability of part-time work, and preventing the spread of job sharing, have alienated the support of the unemployed. In opposing such measures, unions were responding to legitimate fears that, in the absence of strong contract and employment standards protections, relief staffing and part-time work would be misused by employers. However, by not making a strong public fight for such protections, unions *appeared* to be hoarding work for their own members.

The official policy of the union movement as regards working hours is to campaign for a shorter workweek with no loss in pay. This is a classic stance of political expediency in that it offends no one. The policy pays lip service to the ideal of solidarity, while asking union members to contribute nothing whatsoever towards helping their unemployed brothers and sisters.

Even when it apparently succeeds, this policy fails. When shorter workweeks are negotiated with no loss in pay, the workweek reduction is typically only an hour or two. Research from economist Frank Reid suggests that small reductions in work time are handled through job speed-up, attrition, or task elimination — not by new hiring!

With this politically safe policy, the union movement also abandons the deeper interests of its membership. Fighting unemployment deserves more energy, more attention, and a more realistic policy. Individual unions will not be able to bargain from strength so long as unemployment is high.

Corporate Myopia

My favourite Eric Kierans maxim is: To understand why things are as they are, ask: "Who does it serve?"

A worsening economy has not been without benefits for big business. A sick economy means a lower wage bill. The open system of global trade means that big corporations can hide their profits wherever taxes are lowest.

Corporate concentration shelters big companies from most of the ill effects of an overcrowded marketplace. High unemployment leads governments to woo corporations with extravagant promises of grants and incentives.

Given these factors, Canada's corporate elite can be forgiven for thinking that high unemployment and global competition work to their benefit. Our corporate elite has offered huge financial support to free trade and the do-nothing policies of the federal Progressive Conservatives, based on the idea that such policies serve their interest.

Looking at the larger picture, such support is clearly shortsighted. The discrepancy between wages and prices has created a chronic imbalance in our economy. Rising debt loads have offered only a temporary respite.

Corporations are already having to cope with a business climate which is less stable and less healthy. Is it necessary to conduct a replay of the 1930s before the corporate world realizes that it too is threatened? Olympia & York, Bramalea, and Central Guaranty Trust are only the advance casualties of a major corporate bloodbath to come if our economy continues to deteriorate. Perhaps the corporate elite of Canada have been so comfortably insulated from painful realities they have forgotten the obvious: they have the most to lose if the economy melts down completely.

In discussing the business reaction to shorter working hours, we should perhaps remember that famous Murphy's Law: "Never attribute to malice that which can be adequately explained by stupidity." Having worked with business for years around the issue of flexible work schedules, I came to see that its major objections to shorter hours are more mundane. They include:

- The fear by supervisors that shorter hours would lead to more work for them, personally;

- The fear that if employees worked shorter hours they would be less committed to the organization;

- The belief that if employees didn't "give their all to the company," the firm would lose out somehow;

- The fear that shorter or more flexible hours would cause the employer to lose control in some undefined way;

- The fear that if hourly employees worked less, with a corresponding drop in wages, salaried employees would expect to work less for the same money;

- The fear that shorter hours would make them "less competitive" in the "global marketplace";

- The belief that by working all their employees as much as was humanly possible, they saved on training and benefit costs.

Not all businesses had objections. Innovative companies tended to look upon flexible hours as a win/win situation. Up-and-coming businesses saw that flexible hours helped them retain good people, and that employees who worked schedules which suited their needs were happier and more productive. Unfortunately, many of Canada's major corporations are led by what one Work Well board member has labelled "dinosaur businessmen" (and they almost always are *men*). These executives see all workweek changes as win/lose: if employees are better off, their companies must be losing out. They also begin with an assumption that any government regulation must be bad.

Within the more reflective parts of the business community, there is a recognition of the problem of individual versus collective good. Employers are aware that replacing employee overtime hours with relief staffing would reduce unemployment in their communities. But they also know that if they did so on their own, they would bear all of the costs of that change, and receive only a minuscule share of the benefit. They can see that if all employers simultaneously did the same, everyone would benefit. While business is not likely to initiate a push for shorter working hours, there is a large segment of the business community which recognizes that across-the-board changes to working hours could help business too, by creating a healthier economy.

In summary, while business has been the major practical roadblock to shorter working hours on a case-by-case basis, it is not as clear what its reaction would be to a reduction in the standard workweek.

Selling Ourselves Short

In his book *Surplus Powerlessness*, Michael Lerner suggests that, although big government, big business, and big unions reduce the power of individuals to control their own lives, the greatest obstacle to change is the individual's belief in her or his powerlessness.

Lerner's awareness of this issue emerged in the 1960s while he was working in the peace movement. As the anti-war movement began to achieve a high public profile and public sentiment turned strongly against the war in Vietnam, Lerner was amazed to find how many of his colleagues in the peace movement were unprepared for success. They distrusted new recruits and dismissed or discounted both small and large victories in the struggle to end the war. In talking with many activists, Lerner often found an underlying belief that their efforts didn't matter and wouldn't make a difference. When it became obvious that their efforts were having an impact, they would go out of their way to dismiss their successes, or sabotage them. Non-activists were even more convinced of their own power-lessness; so much so that they weren't even willing to go through the motions of working for change.

Lerner found an awful paradox in his studies: when individuals believed themselves powerless, they behaved in ways that made them powerless. He went on to suggest that it is this self-imposed help-lessness, this surplus powerlessness, which is the biggest obstacle to changing the world in which we live.

Lerner also found that the central dynamic of surplus power-lessness was that individuals looked at their actions and needs in isolation. He saw that the first step for individuals to recover their personal power is to recognize that they are not alone.

I have talked with enough people to know that most Canadians are very concerned about unemployment. Many Canadians recog-nize that the only way to significantly reduce unemployment is to share the work. Most Canadians would welcome shorter working hours for themselves, and would be willing to make some degree of financial sacrifice to achieve that goal. Together we represent the voting majority in a democratic country; clearly the power to change is ours. The biggest single obstacle we face in implementing shorter working hours is the belief that we can't do it.

I have wrestled with this issue myself. I knew, three years ago, that I wanted to write the book you now hold. I knew the issue was important. I was also aware this book would not be new information and would not be a brilliant or deep analysis. What I have to say is obvious, common sense: The Emperor is naked! What gave *me* the right to say it? Who would listen? Would it make a difference? After three years, I decided that the issue is important enough for me to be willing to take the risk that my actions won't matter.

I invite each and every reader to make that same decision. A shorter workweek is important enough to the future of all of us that it is worth the risk of failure. The only authority you need for your actions is that you live in and care about this country. To do otherwise is to give up on ourselves, and give up on the future.

TURNING IT AROUND

For shamanic healers, the first step in coping with mental illness is to help distressed persons to name their "demons." The simple act of attaching a name to what is wrong confers power.

We have now named the demons confronting us:

- ✒ **An accident of history which has made work a moral virtue instead of a means to provide for needs;**

- ✒ **A cultural pattern of addiction, particularly workaholism;**

- ✒ **Values that define self-worth on the basis of position and possession;**

- ✒ **A political arena in which debate has been subverted by the disempowering framework of "not enough jobs."**

Understanding better what has gone wrong, we can now move on to the positive task of envisioning the future of our dreams. But first we must ask: where are we headed if we don't change course?

21

The Default Future:
Where Are We Headed?

*Debt cannot go on compounding faster than output
forever. At the rate it expanded in the United States in
the 1980s, interest payments would consume 100% of
GNP by the year 2015. No such thing will happen. Long
before debt reaches that extreme, it will be wiped away.
Either an economic deflation will cause the financial
system to implode, or a political inflation of an extreme
kind will obliterate much of the value of debts
denominated in dollars. One way or the other, we expect
a great reckoning.*

JAMES DALE DAVIDSON

We didn't consciously choose to have 20% of Canadians out of work
while the other 80% flirt with burnout; we merely failed to take any
action which would have diverted us from that all-too-predictable
result. Where will we go next if we continue to let inertia be the
central guiding force behind Canadian economic policy?

The End of the Long Economic Cycle?

In Chapter 8 we talked briefly about how speculation in real estate
creates 50-year boom-and-bust cycles in the economy. How does the
long cycle work?

A depression marks the beginning of the long cycle. Depression wipes the economic slate clean: a collapse in real estate prices makes housing affordable, and bankruptcies liquidate most outstanding debt. Once something (usually a war) kicks the economy into gear again, the combination of low prices and low debt makes for decades of sustained economic growth.

Growth continues despite occasional setbacks. Speculation in real estate may push house prices so high that the economy stalls; mismanagement of interest rates may choke back growth; the economy may overheat and stall.

At some point in the cycle, the balance between production and consumption is lost. Unemployment builds and wages then decline despite increases in productivity. Speculation increases the upward pressure on real estate prices. Debt accumulates rapidly. Eventually debt charges and housing costs start to drain the economy.

In the last years of the cycle, a final explosion of debt creates a short burst of false prosperity — much as we saw in the 1920s or the 1980s. This false prosperity ends when debt charges spiral out of control. Lenders become reluctant to expand credit further; as the stimulus of debt is removed, the economy collapses.

The situation is analogous to a poker game where one player has won all the chips: the big winner can keep the game going for a while by advancing credit to the other players — but only to a certain point. Once the winner loses faith that the IOUs will be repaid, the game stops.

Where in the cycle are we now? Real estate prices, despite their recent slide, are at historical highs. Debt loads are higher than ever before in history.

A good case can be made that the economic malaise of the 1990s is the run-up to a 1930s-style depression. In *The Great Reckoning*, James Dale Davidson asserts that the world has seen five long economic cycles in the past 200 years, and that each cycle has followed a similar pattern. Most scary about Davidson's analysis is his checklist of the events that preceded each of the past five depressions:

❶ **Depressions are preceded by a long slide in raw material commodity prices. North American commodity prices have fallen 40% since 1973;**

❷ In the decade prior to the depression there is a major run-up of both stock and real estate prices — such as was seen in the 1920s and the 1980s;

❸ This is followed by a real estate crash, which results in widespread bank failures — much as we have seen in the past five years;

❹ The stock market of the world's emergent power then crashes — as did the New York Stock Exchange in 1929 and the Tokyo Stock Exchange in 1991;

❺ As the economy slides into a depression, interest rates go into free-fall without creating recovery — as seen in the early 1930s and again in the 1990s.

Are you nervous yet? Unbridled speculation has pushed our economy to the brink of collapse. The huge fall in interest rates in the early 1990s may yet result in a minor recovery, but this may be no more than a short-term respite.

As early as 1974, some economists were predicting that a major crash was imminent, and at least once every few years since we have seen books like *How to Profit From the Next Great Depression*. Michael Harrington has suggested that instead of abrupt economic collapse, what is more likely in the 1990s is a "slow 1929."

Why is this so? In the 1930s, when workers lost their jobs, they were almost immediately lost to the economy as consumers. This set off a chain reaction, with layoffs leading to more layoffs. Today, income supports for the unemployed mean that layoffs reduce demand only a little, and slowly, which helps keep recession from escalating into depression.

Also, prior to the spread of Keynesian theory, governments responded to downturns in the economy by slashing spending, which created further layoffs until widespread panic took over. Today, government use of Keynesian principles has reversed this trend; when the economy enters a downturn, governments increase spending so as to moderate the contraction.

There was no deposit insurance program for the banking system during the 1930s. Then, unlike today, if a bank went bankrupt, its depositors lost everything. A single rumour that a bank was in trouble could cause a panic and create such a run on its reserves that it would in fact go under — setting off a domino chain of business and bank failures.

Better understanding of the economy has (so far) enabled modern governments to prevent the kind of wholesale panic and loss of consumer confidence which, in years past, would have created an economic crash. Lester Thurow has suggested that the U.S. stock market crash of 1987, the real estate crash of 1989, and the collapse of hundreds of Savings & Loan banks in the late 1980s, each could have triggered the kind of panic which marked the onset of the Great Depression — if governments had not intervened firmly and forcefully.

While such interventions do prevent the downward spiral of panic, they do not prevent the gradual build-up of debt, unemployment, and inefficiency. Ballooning increases in the public debt now limit the ability of the government to cushion future downturns with deficit spending.

If we continue on our current course, the most likely scenario is that the economy will slowly deteriorate, with periodic short upturns in which economists will busy themselves arguing about whether the recession is over. At some point (exactly when, we do not know) the imbalance between production and consumption will grow too great, and the economy will go into a 1930s-style collapse.

The Current Status of Corrective Strategies

In Part III we looked at two dozen macroeconomic interventions which are being used, have been used, or could be used to restore the balance between production and consumption. What is the current impact of these various strategies? Is help on the way?

The table on the next page lists all of the strategies we have discussed. The column on the right gives a summary of their current impact on the problem of overproduction: happy faces mean changes are helping to restore balance to the economy; sad faces mean changes are causing the economy to worsen; neutral faces mean the strategies have no measurable effect.

STRATEGY	CURRENT USE AND/OR EFFECTIVENESS	IMPACT ☺=positive ☹=negative 😐=neutral
Restrictions on the size of the workforce		
Exclusion of women, children & seniors	Women re-entering workforce in large numbers	☹☹☹
Shorter workweek	Not used	😐
Time-off benefits	Not used	😐
Impediments to overtime	Eroding in effect	☹
Flexible work schedules	Minor usage only	☺
Expansions of consumption		
Advertising/ consumerism	Must be reversed for environment	☹☹☹
Waste	Must be reversed for environment	☹☹
Military production	Reversing with end of Cold War	☹☹
Government spending	Limited by debt	☹
Debt	Debt charges draining economy	☹
Curtailments of production		
High interest rates	Falling rates create temporary boost	☺☺☺
Production controls	Not Used	😐
Luddite response	Minimal Use	😐
Corporate concentration	No positive effect on system	😐
Marketing boards	No systemic effect	😐
Professional assoc. & unions	No positive effect on system	😐
Minimum wages	Minimal impact	😐
Current policies		
Export promotion	No systemic effect	😐
Entrepreneurship	No systemic effect	😐
Encouraging investment	No positive effect on system	😐
Immigration	No systemic effect	😐
Training/job search	Little positive effect on system	☺
Unemployment	Growing in impact	☹☹
CUMULATIVE EFFECT	**RECESSION / DEPRESSION**	☹☹☹☹☹ ☹☹☹☹☹

The picture which emerges from this table is very clear: most of the recent changes in the structure of our economy are aggravating rather than solving the gap between production and consumption. If we do nothing, the Canadian economy will continue to deteriorate. Our economic outlook need not be bleak — but a happy future will require a profound change in course.

The Future of Work

What are the long-term workforce trends? Historically, only part of the increase in productivity resulting from technological change has been offset by shorter working hours. The rest has been made up by opening up new sectors of economic activity. Our workforce history is shown graphically in the chart below.

Technology has already created two major shifts in the workplace. We now find ourselves in the midst of a third. As technological pro-

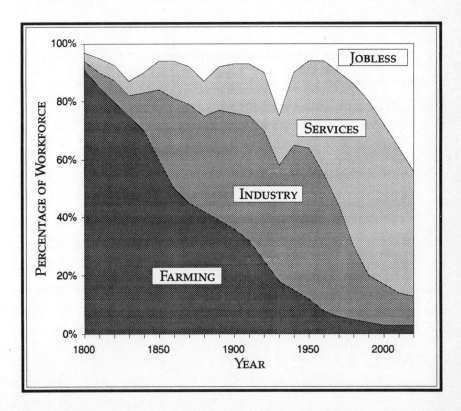

gress eliminated jobs in agriculture, manufacturing jobs opened up to fill the gap. As mechanization eliminated manufacturing jobs, workers transferred to service and information sector jobs. Computerization is now rapidly eliminating white-collar jobs. Where will displaced workers go?

Some have suggested that the information sector will be the fourth wave in the workplace. This seems unlikely, given that information jobs are prone to automation. Others have suggested that government employment is the wave of the future — despite evidence that most taxpayers want less, rather than more, government. For those willing to see it, the fourth wave is already visible: joblessness.

THE DEAD-STICK ALTERNATIVE

If we continue on our present course, we can expect the following:

✒ Increasing automation and computerization;

✒ Increasing corporate concentration;

✒ Erosion of safety and environmental standards;

✒ Increasing unemployment and decreasing wages;

✒ Continued high levels of family stress;

✒ An increasing gap between rich and poor;

✒ A further slide in real estate prices;

✒ Economic collapse in the not-too-distant future.

PERHAPS A CHANGE OF COURSE IS IN ORDER?

22

How Do We Fix It?

The problem is similar to what happens at a football game. Suppose an exciting play takes place. To get a better view individual spectators stand up; but if everyone stands up no one gets a better view and now everyone is uncomfortable since they have to stand rather than sit. But the first one to stand up gets a better view until everyone else stands up. Only collective action can keep everyone seated; individual actions will lead to everyone standing. But what about the process of sitting down? The first person to sit down gets the worst view, and the last person to sit down gets the best view. Everyone wants to be last and everyone stands.

LESTER THUROW

If left unattended, our economic problems will grow more severe: the gap between rising productivity and environmental constraints becomes larger with each passing year. Clearly, some sort of action is required. But what is to be done?

The modern conservative position is that the free market would work just fine if governments got out of the way; if individuals were free to pursue their own self-interest unfettered, the economy would heal itself. I maintain that the opposite is true: when individuals try to protect themselves from the consequences of inefficiency, unemployment, and inflation, their actions make those very problems worse.

Lester Thurow's words at the top of the page give us a perfect metaphor for this economic conundrum. A quick review of the vicious circles we have already seen will give several examples of the unhappy dynamic he describes:

- 🖙 When individual companies respond to the low profits created by overcapacity by installing labour-saving equipment, they make overcapacity worse;

- 🖙 When individuals respond to the insecurity created by unemployment and overcapacity by spending less, they make overcapacity worse;

- 🖙 When individuals try to protect themselves from the falling wages created by high unemployment by working more, they make unemployment worse;

- 🖙 When individuals try to protect themselves from soaring house prices by rushing to buy a home, they push house prices up further.

Everywhere we look the message is clear: individuals acting alone cannot, and will not, solve our economic problems. Anything that I can do to protect myself from the consequences of inefficiency, unemployment, and inflation will have the long-term result of aggravating those problems.

Sources of Collective Action

If we can't fix our economic problems separately, how can we take collective action to solve them? Organized labour, employer groups, social change movements, and governments are the four main players. What are the resources and limitations of each?

The **LABOUR MOVEMENT** in Canada has limited direct power due to its size — only about one-third of the Canadian labour force is unionized. Organized labour in Canada has been under strong attack in recent years, and most of its energy has gone into defending itself rather than into pro-active or outward-looking action. In Europe and Japan, organized labour represents a much larger proportion of the population; there it has the power to be the prime agent of change. If European or Japanese labour congresses were to intervene in the economy in major ways, with positive results, it could provide strong leadership for Canadian labour's efforts.

Organized labour has been a strong catalyst for change in years past, negotiating into collective agreements new workplace arrangements which have proven to be so effective that they were later adopted throughout the economy. (Pensions, maternity leave, and paid vacations are three examples of many that could be named.) Establishing prototypes of new workplace structures, followed by concerted political lobbying to see those new structures written into law, remains the best use of labour's limited powers for collective change.

EMPLOYER GROUPS in Canada also have limited power, due to the voluntary nature of their membership. Corporations in Europe and Japan have much stronger ties between them, through central banks and interlinked share ownership, which make employer groups more able to impose rules and policies which all businesses must follow. As with labour, a strong and effective lead from Europe or Japan could perhaps give Canadian business groups the necessary impetus to take positive steps.

A more fundamental limitation is the reality that an economy which is mildly unhealthy is not necessarily bad for big business. As we saw in Chapter 14, big business is often able to protect itself from the problem of excess capacity. High unemployment benefits large corporations by driving down wages. Wealthy corporate owners also benefit, more than suffer, from real estate speculation and high interest rates. For all these reasons, big business, until recently, has tended to work against positive changes in our economic direction.

Of late, Canada's economy has become so unbalanced that even big business is suffering: corporate profits in 1991 were at the lowest levels since the 1930s. Corporate Canada could become a force for change; at the very least, big business may mute its opposition.

SOCIAL CHANGE MOVEMENTS are limited in the type of role they can be expected to play. Voluntary movements to institute economic change have poor prospects for success — the rewards for breaking ranks are too great. As an example, let's imagine a voluntary movement to institute a four-day week. This is exactly the situation Lester Thurow describes in the quote at the chapter head: the first people to cut back their hours pay the highest price, while the last people to work less receive the most benefit. (This same dynamic has undercut the labour movement's ability to negotiate shorter workweeks on a union-by-union basis; only when all workers cut back their work hours at once are the benefits of reduced workweeks greater than the costs.)

The best role that social movements can hope to play is to inspire labour, business, and government to action. A strong and concrete vision of a positive future is the most potent tool available to such groups. Raising public awareness of the true nature of our economic plight can also set the stage for change.

GOVERNMENT, particularly the federal government, is the one sector which has the ability to make rules that all players in the economy must follow. It also has the power to set collective economic policies. By taking a strong leadership role, it can coordinate the activities of business, labour, and social change movements so that they all pull together.

It is for this reason that government must bear the prime responsibility for restoring balance to the economy, and past governments must carry the major share of the blame for our current economic difficulties.

This is not to say that the task facing Canada's major political parties is an easy one; the kind of changes we need are politically risky. As an example, a shorter standard workweek, though it would greatly benefit the unemployed and would be in the long-term self-interest of all workers, would demand a short-term sacrifice by the majority of voters. As well, the financial power of big business to influence the media (and election campaigns) means that reactionary voices are likely to have more money, and more air-time, than positive voices for change. Even after being elected, any party which made changes that big business perceived as threatening its interests would face powerful opposition.

This being said, any political party which clearly identified why and how the economy isn't working, and presented a positive and concrete vision for the future, could undoubtedly garner the enthusiasm of the voting majority. If elected, such a party would need to show courage to institute change in the face of well-funded opposition. Nonetheless, if the changes it introduced brought renewed prosperity, re-election should not prove impossible.

The fact that we haven't had a federal government with vision (or courage) for many years doesn't mean that it couldn't happen. A change in government economic strategies, whether by lobbying or by election, remains our best hope for reclaiming the future.

You and I are not let off the hook: after all, collectively, we have elected a long string of economic incompetents. The individual's prime responsibility for fixing the economy is to be politically active. Only by supporting and electing leaders who display vision and courage can we hope to find a way out of our economic mess.

Options for Intervention

In Part III we examined and rated two dozen strategies which can be used to restore the balance between production and consumption. Let's review those ratings quickly:

- In Chapter 10 we saw that excluding some groups from the workforce is effective, but creates economic inequity, stereotyping, and discrimination, so is not a recommended solution.

- ✔ In Chapter 11 we saw that reductions in the workweek, time-off benefits, impediments to overtime, and work options all were effective — and had the positive side-effect of increasing leisure.

- In Chapter 12 we examined the frenetic fantasy of a permanently expanding economy, and the damage that has ensued from addictive consumption, waste, militarism, and debt. Any "solutions" along this path would be fatal!

- In Chapter 13 we saw how the blunt instrument of high interest rates has become a very dangerous solution, and production controls offer only emergency help.

- In Chapter 14 we explored how specific sub-groups can protect themselves from the worst effects of a sick economy.

None of these strategies protects the economy as a whole, and all create inequity.

✒ In Chapters 15 and 16 we examined Canada's current economic policies and found that none of them affects the problem of overproduction: non-solutions all.

Clearly, shorter working hours are the only viable solution to the problem of overproduction, and any program to restore balance to the economy must be built around them. In designing a program to restore the economy to health we must also consider ways to undo some of the damage which has been created by living for so long in a dysfunctional economy. In Part V we shall look at one vision of how this could be done.

WE SINK OR SWIM TOGETHER!

Action is needed to restore a healthy balance between production and consumption, yet individual isolated responses to inefficiency, unemployment, and inflation tend to make those problems worse rather than better. Only by working together can we fix what is wrong. Furthermore, government is the only player on the economic stage with the power to make the necessary interventions. The tool we need to restore the economy to health is clear: shorter working hours. What's missing is the political will to implement a solution.

✔ **Collective action, particularly action by government, is essential if we are to restore a balance between production and consumption, and make the Canadian economy effective and healthy again.**

✔ **The individual's best hope for a happier economic future is through political action to change Canada's federal government.**

✔ **Shorter working hours are the only effective tool available to restore balance to the economy.**

PART V

RECLAIMING THE FUTURE OF OUR DREAMS

Six steps will reclaim the future of our dreams:

❶ We must solve the problems of overcapacity and unemployment through the mechanism of a shorter workweek. The change must be smooth, efficient, and affordable.

❷ We must reclaim our national sovereignty.

❸ We must undo the damage the past 30 years has wrought on the democratic process, health care, housing, education, the national debt, and national security.

❹ We must protect the environment.

❺ We must promote healthy values and a healthy lifestyle to overcome the distorted values and work addiction of the past.

❻ To bring about the above changes, we must build a grassroots coalition for a *politics of abundance*.

These steps are explored in the final chapters.

23

The Four-Day Workweek

Without great plans, it is hard, and often self-defeating,
to make little ones.
DAVID RIESMAN

If we are lucky, we may be able to eke one more (weak) recovery out of our stressed economy — a window of perhaps two or three years. During that period we must make major changes or risk a 1930s-style depression.

Restoring a healthy balance between production and consumption will require careful planning and step-by-step change. Our current economy is built around the consumption patterns resulting from a 40-hour workweek. A shorter workweek will create large changes in labour force needs, tax revenues, consumer spending, and transport patterns. Change must be designed to be non-inflationary and affordable for the individual.

Reducing the workweek in a series of steps will minimize disruptions. As unemployment falls, wages will once again rise in step with productivity. This, in turn, means that living standards can be maintained through several successive reductions in work time.

I propose, as an initial social policy target, the implementation of a four-day, 32-hour workweek. In this chapter I lay out one specific plan for how that could be done. The specifics of when and how a four-day workweek is to be implemented should be established through a full debate in the public arena; what I've written here is meant only to point us in the right direction.

The plan which follows assumes that we will show the foresight to act before the economy crashes. If we dawdle too long, we may need to jump immediately to a 28-hour workweek in order to resuscitate the economy.

Preparatory Steps

Changes to employment standards legislation are central to the implementation of shorter working hours. Unfortunately, such changes now straddle the boundary between the federally administered Canada Labour Code and provincial employment standards legislation. To put new rules in force across Canada will require that all provinces come to an agreement setting up similar rules, or (better yet) that the provinces cede control of employment standards to the federal government. In either case, agreement on this matter is a prerequisite to other changes.

The following changes to employment standards legislation would lay the groundwork for a reduction in the standard workweek, while making a preliminary cut in unemployment:

❶ **Employers would pay a tax on all overtime wages paid to employees: 50% in the first year and 100% thereafter;**

❷ **Businesses would be allowed to institute annual hours programs, in which employees could work extra hours at some time in the year so long as they were given compensatory time off at other times. Within an annual hours program, businesses would pay overtime tax only on employee hours in excess of 2000 hours per year;**

❸ **Employers would be required to convert all salaried positions to hourly wage positions;**

❹ **Employers would be required to pay prorated benefits, or cash in lieu, to all part-time employees. Employers would also be required to alter pension plans so that staff in their**

final five years before retirement could reduce their work hours without reducing the pension they will receive on retirement.

Employers should be given six months' notice before these new rules came into force. At the same time they would receive detailed kits explaining how to change their payroll accounting systems. Employers would also be given 24 months' notice that legislation implementing a 32-hour workweek was on its way.

These initial steps have the disadvantage that they will place most of the first burden of sharing the work on those who normally work large amounts of overtime. On the other hand, that may have its own rough justice; those who have traditionally hoarded work will be asked to make the opening contribution towards sharing it.

Phasing in the overtime tax over two years will give both employers and employees some time to adjust. When the overtime tax hits 100% in the second year, it will virtually eliminate overtime. Restrictions on the amount of unpaid overtime by salaried staff will also result in new hiring. These two steps can be expected to result in a 4% increase in staff numbers in most organizations.

Guaranteed benefits for part-timers should unblock union opposition to part-time work. This, plus pension protection for older workers, will result in companies facing a rush of applications for job sharing and phased retirement. Most companies, knowing they will soon have to adjust to a four-day week for all staff, will welcome requests for reduced work time. Increased use of voluntary work options can be expected to result in most companies' expanding staff numbers by a further 2%, bringing the average number of new hires to 6% of staff size.

Upgrading of casual and part-time workers will absorb some of the new employment. Nonetheless, the drop in unemployment should be substantial.

Implementing the Four-Day Workweek

Two years after the preparatory steps were announced, the shift would be made to a four-day workweek running from Tuesday through Friday. Four changes in employment standards legislation are required to implement a 32-hour workweek:

❶ **The 100% overtime tax would apply on work hours over 32 hours per week or 1600 hours per year (50 weeks x 32 hours = 1600 hours);**

❷ **The minimum wage would be raised by 20%;**

❸ **All statutory holidays would be cancelled as paid time-off benefits (holidays would be celebrated on Mondays as part of a normal three-day weekend);**

❹ **Employers would be required, on a one-time basis, to raise the hourly wages of all employees by 15%, effective the date of implementation of the new rules.**

At the same time these changes took effect, the federal government would stop collecting unemployment insurance contributions from both employers and employees. A four-day workweek will so reduce unemployment levels that income supports for the unemployed can be funded from general revenues.

Basing the overtime tax on 1600 hours per year, rather than on a straight 32 hours per week, will enable individuals and companies to work less in whatever way best suits their needs and wishes. Perhaps some employees would prefer to work five eight-hour days each week all winter in return for 12 weeks of holidays in the summer. Others might prefer to work nine hours per day, four days a week, to earn seven weeks of holidays. Post Office employees might want to work extra hours at Christmas in return for more holiday time in summer.

■ **MANAGEABLE COSTS**

What effect will this new arrangement have on employees' take-home pay? Employees would get paid for 80% as many hours, at 115% of their former hourly pay, for gross pay levels 92% of previous earnings. Employees would no longer pay 3% of their income to UIC, and would pay slightly lower taxes, so take-home pay would be about 95% of what it had been on a five-day week. A higher minimum wage insures that those at low wages will not suffer any income loss at all.

In this way, the workforce could drop back from a five-day to a four-day workweek, yet take-home pay will drop by only 5%. Think about that for a minute. Wouldn't it be worth trimming your living costs by 5% to get 52 long weekends a year? You may recoup much or all of that 5% loss through savings on the costs of commuting, lunches out, and childcare.

What will be the effect on an employer's wage bill? There is considerable case-study evidence that employees on a shortened workweek show an increase in productivity of about 5%. Employers will no longer be required to make a contribution to UIC equivalent to 3% of employees' incomes. Employers will no longer be paying for statutory holidays — which will reduce the employers' wage bills by almost 4%. When these three savings are factored in, a 15% hourly wage increase will increase employers' unit labour costs by about 3%. Increased benefit costs can be expected to add a further 2% to the employers' wage bill, for a total of 5%. While this is a significant cost, it is not unmanageable.

Structured in this manner, a four-day workweek will increase aggregate consumer demand by about 4%. This is enough to take some of the excess capacity out of our economy — which will make Canadian business more efficient and profitable — but not enough to create major inflation.

■ THE IMPACT ON UNEMPLOYMENT

How will these measures impact on unemployment? Several factors will influence the number of new hires:

- A 5% increase in productivity will cut the number of new hires by one-third;

- The approximately 20% of the workforce already working part-time would not reduce their work hours;

- Less than full compliance could be expected among the self-employed (one seventh of the workforce);

- Some individuals will leave marginal self-employment situations as more jobs become available;

- Some businesses are over-staffed, and won't need as many new hires as otherwise expected;

- Many businesses will hire in new staff on three-day weekend shifts working only 24 hours per week — which means they will need to hire one-third more workers than for a 32-hour workweek.

Together these various factors mean that a 16% reduction in work hours could be expected to create only about an 8% increase in the number of jobs available.

Will companies actually hire in new workers to make up for shorter staff hours? Economist Frank Reid has examined numerous situations in which working hours were shortened. The only times when shorter hours did not translate into new hires was when the reduction in work hours was very small. (If the standard workweek was shortened by only one hour, for instance, companies would usually not hire additional staff. Instead, the reduction was handled through some combination of staff speed-up and the elimination of unnecessary tasks.) Whenever the reduction in work hours was significant — say a half day or a full day per week — Reid found that new staff were hired equivalent to at least 50% of the reduction in hours — confirming my projection above, that a 16% decrease in work hours will generate 8% more jobs.

■ THE BEGINNING OF DOUBLE-SHIFTING

I expect that most factories, and businesses which serve the public, will hire in new staff on three-day weekend shifts. For factories and hospitals, weekend shifting will make seven-day operation easier. In offices and stores, weekend shifting will extend hours of service — and new hires can use existing space and equipment.

Because many of the new employees will be hired in on three-day weekend shifts, they will only be working three-quarter time. These new hires will receive gross pay of about 74% of the old full-time rate, or take-home pay 80% of the old full-time rate. While not perfect, this is more than UIC pays — and a huge improvement on welfare!

When the weekday shift is four days and weekend shift only three, the 25% pay differential this creates will limit the popularity of the weekend shift. However, in addition to the 8% new hires, perhaps an additional 4% of current weekday workers will shift to the weekend. Some will be the spouses of new hires wanting to be on the same shift as their partner. Others will find a three-day workweek itself to be a major incentive.

Companies will want to equalize the two shifts to save on office space, equipment, and phone lines — and to provide extended hours of service. Some companies will opt to have three 10-hour days on the weekend in order to encourage staff to shift over to the weekend shift. Weekday and weekend shifts would then receive similar paycheques; the prospect of four days off each week would be strong incentive to work the weekend shift.

Schools will be under pressure to provide a weekend stream so that whole families can be on parallel timetables. Seven-day-a-week operations like hospitals, airports, and factories will probably elect to move to a simple two-shift system with weekday and weekend shifts. Workers in such facilities, rather than being on strange 9-day or 16-day rotations, will be on straightforward weekday or weekend shifts matching those of their spouses.

With even a minority of the workforce on a second shift, weekday pressures on commuter roads will be less, and weekend pressures on recreation facilities eased.

■ **SUPPORTING INITIATIVES**

Several companion programs could ease the transition to a shorter workweek.

ADEQUATE LEAD TIME AND SUPPORT MATERIALS: Adequate lead time will make it easier for companies to hire and train new staff, make renovations, change their advertising to reflect new service hours, and update payroll accounting.

New employment standard regulations, recommended payroll guidelines, and support materials for such changes as an annual hours accounting system, could all go out to employers as a kit.

Citizens could be sent packages outlining their rights under the new system. A grievance tribunal could be set up to handle complaints from employees who feel their employer is abusing the change in work hours. The tribunal would have the power to police employers who bend or break new standards. It would also monitor abuses or legal loopholes in the regulations and make recommendations for corrections. Employment T4 forms could be amended to include a box to list the number of hours worked, to enable government to track (and if necessary, tax) moonlighting.

CRASH COURSE JOB TRAINING: Shorter working hours will open up new employment across the entire occupational spectrum. New jobs will be created in almost every field and for every level of training. During the two years when overtime is being phased out, most of the new positions which require advanced education can be filled by unemployed Canadians who have the necessary training. By the time the shift is made to a four-day week, most of those who already have adequate training will have been absorbed. If the remaining jobless are to be employable, many will need retraining.

Planning and projection of training needs must be done carefully. Some fields will have enough qualified candidates among the unemployed to fill all job vacancies. In other trades, huge training programs designed to get participants into new positions as quickly as possible will be needed. Such programs could combine classroom time with extensive on-the-job training and active trainee supervision. In some fields, government may reduce inflated qualification requirements. In either case, most of these changes should be initiated during the two years when overtime is being phased out, not once a four-day workweek is already in place.

BUSINESS BUY-OUTS: Many market niches are badly overcrowded, particularly in the small business sector. Rather than allow market forces to effect a shake-out, government could ease the transition by buying out businesses in overcrowded markets — a euthanasia program for terminally ill businesses, in which overcapacity would be reduced more quickly and gently than through bankruptcies and business failures. Such businesses would be able to pay off their creditors before shutting down, and make at least partial recompense to investors. Areas of environmental concern should be given special attention: a major buy-out of the fish boats on both coasts could make that industry more sustainable.

INFRASTRUCTURE REBUILDING: Construction is the industry that will be hardest hit by the change to a four-day week. More efficient use of space in a two-shift economy will result in major savings for businesses and taxpayers, but will mean that fewer new expressways, bridges, schools, and government buildings will be needed. Construction of new office space will slow down. To soften the blow faced by the construction industry, governments could undertake to refurbish Canada's infrastructure.

Many of our bridges, sewer systems, and highways are old and falling apart. They need to be repaired and rebuilt; government can put the money it will save on new capital projects into rebuilding infrastructure. In addition, many of the buildings of businesses bought out to reduce overcapacity could be converted to other uses.

These measures would simply ease the inevitable shrinking of the construction industry, which should be targeted for major retraining of personnel and a buy-out of overcapacity.

UNEMPLOYMENT INSURANCE CLAIMS: The shift to a four-day workweek will result in all sorts of adjustments in the economy. Some organizations may increase the number of staff by a full third. Other businesses will hesitate to hire new staff immediately. Some businesses will shut down entirely. It is probable that it will take eight to twelve months for the economy to stabilize and for most of the unemployed to find jobs. To ease this transition, UIC should continue to pay out claims for the first twelve months after shorter hours are introduced.

■ **ISSUES TO BE MONITORED**

A shorter workweek could go astray in several ways.

Not all the workforce is covered by employment standards legislation. Self-employed professionals, freelancers, and contract workers might continue working five days a week, undercutting the effectiveness of a reduction in hours. However, given that these individuals' spouses and children will be on four-day or three-day shifts, as will most of their business contacts, the push to shift to a parallel workweek will be strong. Governments could also exert some control over self-employed professionals who are indirectly employed by government. Doctors' incomes could be capped, for instance, and the government could restrict its purchases of legal services to law firms with staff on a 32-hour workweek.

Moonlighting may become more of a problem, and this too would undercut the spreading of employment that shorter hours would otherwise bring. Government must monitor moonlighting and put tax disincentives on moonlighting income, if necessary.

Salaried staff will also be under pressure to do more in less time. For this reason, regulations requiring that all salaried positions be converted to hourly wages should be enforced and monitored. Doing so will provide salaried employees with a bulwark to limit their work hours to reasonable levels. If fewer managers are workaholics, more companies will show flexibility and compassion regarding the non-work lives of their staff.

Some companies will try to skimp on hiring new staff and enforce a work speed-up on employees. Grievance tribunals must be given the power to force employers to hire adequate staff. In addition, such tribunals should have the power to fine heavily any employer who fails to do so — to discourage other employers from dragging their feet on new hiring.

Rules alone cannot insure a smooth transition to shorter hours; public recognition that shorter hours benefit everyone in the long run, and a shared willingness to pull together for the common good, will be essential.

■ THE IMPACT ON GOVERNMENT REVENUES AND EXPENSES

Government will see a multitude of changes in its revenue patterns. It will receive less tax revenue from those who were previously employed 40 hours per week, but this will be offset by increased tax revenue from the newly hired. The tax on overtime will generate some new income. Retraining programs, restorative buy-outs, infrastructure rebuilding, and the 12-month unfunded extension of unemployment insurance will be a heavy drain on the government purse in the first year of shorter work hours.

Once these initial costs have been absorbed, the long term impacts on the economy are highly salutary. With unemployment lower, wages will start to rise to reflect increases in productivity. Within two years, most workers' real net income will rise to equal their former incomes from a 40-hour workweek. As workers' incomes begin to reflect productivity, chronic problems of oversupply will dissipate. Canada's economy will show an unaccustomed dynamism.

Within two years, government will have had time to recoup most of the transition costs associated with the move to a four-day workweek. Governments will begin to reap large cost savings:

✔ Reduced health costs, as both the formerly unemployed and the formerly overworked move to more balanced lives;

✔ Reduced welfare costs;

✔ Reduced crime costs;

✔ Reduced education costs as the number of involuntary students decreases and unnecessary educational qualifications are removed;

✔ Reduced capital costs for transportation and the building of offices and schools as a result of moving towards a two-shift workplace.

Such savings should reduce government expenses by roughly 20%. Tax revenues will also rise as wages rise and unemployment falls.

THE KEY STEP

A 32-hour workweek is the first step towards reclaiming the future of our dreams. It will set the stage for rising wages, stronger family life, and a sustainable relationship with the environment.

24

Going All The Way

We could now reproduce our 1948 standard of living (measured in terms of marketed goods and services) in less than half the time it took in 1948. We actually could have chosen the four-hour day. Or a working year of six months. Or imagine this: every worker . . . could now be taking every other year off from work, with pay.

JULIET SCHOR

If the move to a four-day workweek is not seen in the context of an ongoing program for shorter hours, its success could be its undoing. The steps outlined in the previous chapter will increase total employment by about 14%. The official unemployment rate should drop to about 3%, and the true unemployment rate to about 6%.

We can expect, at that point, that strutting government officials will announce the unemployment problem has been solved, and that the remaining unemployed are either unemployable or temporarily between jobs. If this happens, it will soon lead to a repeat of the economic malaise of the past decade.

Technology continues to eliminate about 1.5% of current jobs every year. As well, if we are to reduce consumption to environmentally sustainable levels, we will need to cut employment further. Unless we want a repeat of today's economic crisis, we must plan on making a significant reduction in work hours every three or four years.

Interim Steps

Vacation times are a flexible tool for contracting the supply of labour between major reductions to the workweek. Each week which is added to the legal vacation allotment cuts work hours by about 2%.

Conversely, if cutting back the workweek by half a day will create too sharp a drop in the labour supply, decreasing the vacation allotment by a couple of weeks will make overall cuts in work time smaller. A few years later, vacation allotments can be put back up again as technology continues to raise productivity.

Another approach is to cut the standard workday by 30 minutes to effect smaller reductions in the labour supply in the interval between major cuts to the workweek—remembering, of course, that smaller cuts do not translate as directly into new jobs. Conversely, reductions in the workweek can be made more moderate by increasing the length of the workday slightly whenever the number of workdays is reduced.

Double-Shifting

Once wages have reached or exceeded former levels and government expenses have begun to drop, conditions will be in place for a 3.5-day workweek. Within five years of the introduction of the 32-hour workweek, unemployment will be inching back up to the 7 or 8% range — enough to provide all the incentive needed for a further reduction.

The 28-hour workweek is tailor-made for a workplace designed around two complementary shifts covering a seven-day schedule. One shift works Tuesday, Wednesday, Thursday, and every second Friday; the other shift works alternate Fridays and every Saturday, Sunday, and Monday.

Institutions which must operate seven days per week will probably begin moving to double-shift staffing of their own accord. Airports, hospitals, nursing homes, and factories will find it more efficient and cost effective. Having models of a more efficient work schedule already in place will make the government's task of selling the 28-hour workweek easier.

Three changes will then be required in employment standards legislation to institute a 28-hour workweek:

❶ **Overtime tax would begin after 28 hours per week or 1400 hours per year;**

❷ **Employers would be mandated to increase hourly wages by 5% when the new schedule took effect;**

❸ **The minimum wage would be raised by 10%.**

Simultaneously with the implementation of the new schedules, federal and provincial taxes for individuals would be dropped by an average of 20%.

For individuals, these changes would mean take-home pay would once again be 95% of what it had been on a five-day, 40-hour workweek. This time a 5% loss in income will give workers a *four-day weekend* every second week; another excellent trade-off! Raising the minimum wage will again insure that incomes of the lowest-paid do not fall.

For businesses, increases in productivity and efficiency will partly offset the increase in per-unit labour costs. Labour productivity can be expected to rise by perhaps a further 3%. With two identical shifts of 28 hours, businesses could channel growth into the "B" or weekend shift, which would mean most business growth would not entail increases in office size: another saving.

Part of the time I was executive director at Work Well, I worked alternating three- and four-day weeks. I found it created a really good flow in my life. Weeks when I worked four days were when I scheduled my biggest and most demanding projects. Four-day weekends were like mini-vacations, and I always looked forward to them. It was a schedule which kept me in good balance. I tried to go back onto a five-day workweek in order to finish writing *Put Work In Its Place* — but my productivity per hour fell so much it just wasn't worth it. Shorter workweeks are more efficient — and more fun!

■ THE EFFICIENCY OF DOUBLE-SHIFTING

Our current system, with most everyone working the same five days on, two days off, is very inefficient. It means many schools, offices, stores, and factories stand empty two days a week. Parks and golf courses, on the other hand, are nearly empty five days a week and burst at the seams on weekends. Highways and public transit suffer from the same pattern of overload and underuse. Workers must scramble to complete errands at lunch hour because many services are unavailable on the weekend.

A 3.5-day workweek offers us a perfect opportunity to restructure the workplace around two complementary shifts of roughly equal size. Schools, offices, and factories can be smaller when the same space serves two sets of workers. Commuter traffic on roads and highways will be spread out over seven days, easing traffic and saving on road-building costs. Golf courses, resorts, and recreation centres will benefit strongly from more even usage throughout the week. Workers can do errands any time on their days off, knowing that a full range of services is always available.

Doctors, dentists, lawyers, and real estate agents will also be able to make seven-day-a-week use of their offices and equipment through job partnering.

Parents will have the option of working opposing shifts, taking turns in the active parent role if they don't want to put very young children into daycare.

Schools will be far less crowded once double-shifting is widespread. Most portable classrooms can be retired and fewer new schools will be needed.

Some people may initially resist the idea of children going to school on the "weekend," but as it becomes clearer that such families have merely traded which days are weekdays and which are weekend, I expect this resistance will subside. We can expect popular clichés to reflect the new reality: workers on the weekend shift will probably say TGIM — thank God it's Monday!

In offices, most workers will have a "job partner," someone on the opposing shift with whom they share a desk and phone number. A whole job-partnering etiquette will be developed for passing on messages, leaving the desk clear when you go off shift, not stealing your desk partner's pens, and so on.

People will likely find play partners as well as job partners. Increasingly, it will make sense for families to share the use of cottages, sail boats, and RVs with families scheduled on the opposite shift.

The move to two-shift operation will not be without its problems. Undoubtedly there will be instances where partners find themselves stranded on opposing shifts. Many of these glitches will be straightened out fairly quickly, and within a few years the number of mismatched schedules will probably be fewer than we have now.

■ A NEW LEVEL OF ECONOMIC HEALTH

A 3.5-day workweek will represent a 12% reduction in the standard workweek. This reduction will nibble away at some of the remaining problem areas in the economy. Weekend staff on three-day shifts will add a half day to bring them into equity with weekday staff. Unemployment would get knocked back to the 2% range again. Companies at the low end of the service sector will find staff leaving for better-paying jobs, and will need to raise wage rates or shut down. All of these changes will, bit by bit, restore health to the economy. The economy will show a dynamism such as we haven't seen since the 1960s.

Leisure industries will do well, particularly those catering to active rather than passive leisure. This will create shifts in the economy — not growth — as people's lifestyles change. Instead of one expensive two-week holiday in Hawaii, for instance, many couples will opt to buy a camper or sailboat for regular use. It's likely that people will do more of their own cooking, dress-making, and wine-making, and less eating at restaurants, shopping for clothes, and buying ready-made wines. We might expect to see more music lessons and fewer CDs purchased, more "little theatre" and less TV-watching.

Over the next few years, rising productivity combined with low unemployment will push wage increases ahead of inflation. The small business sector will show healthy profits again. We'll be closer to the future we once imagined.

Extended Vacation Time

The next time unemployment exceeds 5%, we could increase the minimum vacation time, first to five and later to seven weeks per year. Such a measure is not farfetched; in France the legal minimum is already six weeks of vacation per year. A permanent relief staffing pool would cover for vacationing staff, much as locums are now used to cover temporary absences of professional staff.

Another alternative is that workers could accumulate five weeks per year in credits towards sabbatical time, in the same way that vacation allotments now accrue. Once every five years, workers could take six months off with pay. They could use that time to write a book, go to school, take a long trip, or goof off and lie in the sun. (This option would create a work-time reduction with a time delay; the logistics would need careful attention.)

A third possibility would apportion part of the extra time off work to paid educational leave. This would help insure that our workforce develops the skills needed to cope with new technologies.

With any of these approaches, unemployment could be knocked back to very low levels. Labour would be in short enough supply that more part-time employment would open up for teenagers, students, and seniors.

The Three-Day Workweek

From where we are now, a three-day workweek seems almost incomprehensible. However, by the time we reach a 3.5-day work-week, much of the workforce will have grown to expect shorter hours and will actively seek the improved quality of life that reduced work time brings. By that point, a three-day workweek may simply be seen as the next logical step. Annual vacation allotments could get bumped back to four or five weeks per year, if necessary, to prevent labour shortages.

Triple-Shifting

The future really arrives with the 20-hour workweek. One shift might work Monday, Tuesday, and every second Wednesday; another shift, alternate Wednesdays, and every Thursday and Friday; the third shift, Saturdays and Sundays.

Triple-shifting offers us the first real opportunity for an equal relationship between the genders. Spouses could take turns working and caring for the home, and still have at least two days per week off work together.

Triple-shifting will also make it much easier to combine school and work, or to retrain for a new career.

To support an entire family on just 40 hours of employment per week may seem like a big stretch from where we are now: an unaffordable luxury. However, I remind the reader that 40 years ago, most families were supported by 40 hours of paid employment per week. Families were bigger back then, and a worker's hourly output was about half of what it is now. A 20-hour workweek, with two breadwinners per family, merely reduces the average work load to what it was 40 years ago. We can certainly afford that!

THE HEAVEN-OR-HELL CHOICE

We face a very clear choice. A generation from now we can have a prosperous economy and a sustainable relationship with the environment, if workers work 20 hours per week, nine months of the year—or any equivalent configuration.

If the reduction in working hours is significantly less than that, we will face massive unemployment, an inefficient economy, and environmental disaster.

The choice is ours.

25

Take Back The Nation!

*What we need now is a new shared vision of Canada, of
the kind that has been pathetically absent in recent years
in far too many of our political and corporate leaders.
We need a new vision of a free, democratic, and
independent Canada, a Canada where we are able to
maximize our abilities to determine our own future.*

MEL HURTIG

We do not have to set firm national boundaries to reap benefits from
shorter working hours. Shorter work hours will reduce unemployment and overcapacity in Canada. This, in turn, will increase
the efficiency of Canadian businesses and ease our tax burden, both
of which will help our competitiveness in the global economy.

However, insofar as the global economy is suffering from worsening
overproduction problems, it will continue to influence the Canadian
economy adversely. The counterbalancing effect of exchange rate
fluctuations will protect Canada from global overproduction per se,
but it will not protect us from the distortions and instabilities that global
overproduction creates. If world trade goes into a 1930s-style collapse,
and Canada is as dependent on international trade as we are today, it
will be a sledgehammer blow to our economy.

The most hopeful scenario is that the other major industrial
nations will recognize how positive the four-day workweek has been
for Canada's economy, and will agree to implement shorter workweeks. (Perhaps there would even be an agreement to impose tariff
penalties on any nation which didn't cut work hours.) With that kind

of international cooperation, the decline of the global economy could quickly be reversed.

In the absence of such cooperation, we are faced with a difficult and painful choice. The global economy is sick and getter sicker. Remaining part of the open system of world trade leaves us vulnerable to impending global economic collapse.

Insulating ourselves from the global economy will also hurt, and hurt more immediately. Canada is heavily involved in global trade. To restrict our international trade will cause dislocations and job losses in the hundreds of thousands.

However, voluntary changes now will hurt less and be more orderly than those which will occur if we wait until the global economy goes into free-fall. Most of the economic disruptions will be short term, with job losses resulting from lost exports being offset by new jobs arising from import replacement.

Five steps are needed to insulate Canada's economy from the global chaos which will ensue if the world's nations fail to agree on shorter workweeks: withdrawal from the GATT; abrogation of the Free Trade Agreement; the imposition of currency exchange restrictions; renewed federalism; and financial support for retooling.

Withdrawal From the GATT

The General Agreement on Tariffs and Trade is a fatally flawed agreement in that it does not set community standards by which signatory nations must abide. It gives countries like Burma and Malaysia free access to the Canadian market. Such countries have wage rates less than one dollar per hour, lack environmental and safety protection, and provide no social safety net — yet we expect Canadian companies to compete head-to-head with them!

In its current form, the GATT no longer serves Canadian interests. In the short term our best option is to insulate ourselves from global trade with high tariffs, and to work to restore Canadian self-sufficiency. Strong and swift anti-dumping provisions are also required.

If we wish to maintain international trade, new relationships with trading partners should be set via a multitiered tariff arrangement.

Trade partners would be assigned a tariff class based on the following criteria:

✔ The degree to which wage, environmental, and safety standards are enforced;

✔ The degree to which union activity is protected;

✔ The degree to which that trading partner has a balanced economy;

✔ The degree to which that trading partner has insulated itself from exploitive global trade.

Tariffs set by these guidelines would insure that Canadian companies and workers would not have to compete with exploitive firms in other parts of the world. Canada would not necessarily need to establish these trading rules unilaterally. A new General Agreement on Tariffs and Trade drawn up along these lines would be a powerful instrument against worldwide worker exploitation. When the GATT was first drawn up, an International Trading Organization was envisioned as a body to set community standards and to police trade practices. The ITO was never created — but it could be now. Such an agency would go a long way towards creating a fair basis for global trade.

Abrogation of the Free Trade Agreement

We face similar problems vis-à-vis free trade with the United States. The U.S. may close its borders to imports from outside of North America, which would create firm trade boundaries around the North American free trade zone. However, unless the U.S. makes reductions in its workweek similar to our own, U.S. overcapacity will continually flood out Canadian attempts to restore balance. Until the U.S. addresses the issue of overcapacity, free trade will only tie us to a drowning giant.

One of the terms of the Free Trade Agreement is that Canada can leave it at any time, with six months' notice. We need to give such notice and then set tariffs to protect ourselves from deterioration in the U.S. economy.

Currency Exchange Restrictions

Part of the thrust of expanding global trade has been to make it easier to change money from one currency to another and to move it from one country to another. As the global economy declines, we can expect that it will also become more volatile. The wild fluctuations in currency and interest rates seen in the fall of 1992 are only the beginnings of global monetary instability. We must make it harder to change funds to and from Canadian dollars, and harder to move money to and from Canada, if we are to insulate ourselves from the death throes of the global money market.

How can this be done? Numerous methods exist to restrict and slow down currency exchange and movement. Currency exchange can be limited to specific (and supervised) financial institutions. Exchanges of currency can be taxed — in both directions — which limits the ability of speculators to make windfall profits by creating short-term currency fluctuations. For many years after World War II, Britain restricted capital outflow with legal impediments; we could do the same. We even have the power to tax the foreign income of Canadians, should that be required to insure a stable supply of domestic capital.

Renewed Federalism

The constitutional wrangling of the past decade has had a disturbing theme. The provinces' willingness to agree to a new constitution has been directly proportional to the federal government's willingness to devolve powers to the provinces. If we are to maintain uniform community standards for employment and environmental concerns, these standards must be set at a national level. Similarly, potent economic policies will require the closed system of a strongly federalist Canada, rather than the open system of a loose federation of provinces.

I believe that much of the recent resurgence of Québec nationalism has its roots in the failed economic policies of the federal government. A strong vision for the future of Canada would win back the affections of many Québecois. It would also increase the likelihood that Québec would agree to stronger powers for the federal government — particularly if Québec gained stronger control over language and cultural issues at the same time.

Financial Support for Retooling

As we set firmer trade boundaries, the resulting shifts will help some Canadian industries while hurting others. Many firms will find that, although their export sales are dwindling, new domestic markets for other products have opened up. Retooling equipment and production processes will enable such companies to shift from export to domestic sales. This retooling could be made faster and less painful by providing low-interest government loans.

Standing up to the Transnationals

The fear exists that if Canada refuses to play the hardball of international trade, transnational corporations will suck the wealth out of Canada, leaving us destitute. To challenge this fear, let's review what they can not take:

THE CANADIAN MARKET: We have the power to insure that companies which want to sell products in Canada must produce those products here.

THE CANADIAN LABOUR FORCE: If companies want our highly skilled workforce, they need to operate here.

CANADIAN REAL ESTATE: Even if particular transnationals decide to leave Canada, they are limited in what they can take with them. The land cannot be moved and it would be prohibitively expensive to move most factories and offices. It would be possible to move some production equipment but, insofar as that equipment was producing for the Canadian market, it will have less value elsewhere.

CANADIAN POLITICAL STABILITY: Part of the reason that corporations continue to locate in Canada, rather than in the Philippines or Nicaragua, is that civil war and violent insurrections are less likely to destroy their factories here. Similarly, many individuals of great wealth stay in Canada, despite our higher levels of taxation, because they feel that they and their wealth are safer here.

CANADIAN FINANCIAL WEALTH: Currency exchange and capital flow restrictions give us the power to insure that the lion's share of Canadian financial wealth remains here.

Transnationals will undoubtedly dislike it when Canada sets firm trade borders. Nonetheless, most will find they stand to lose more by leaving Canada than by staying — particularly as our economy becomes healthier. Should they decide to leave, Canada has plenty of domestic capital available, so long as we design the tax system to reward productive investment and to punish speculation.

WE HAVE EVERYTHING WE NEED!

We have everything we need to be masters of our own house: abundant land and raw materials, an educated workforce, adequate investment capital, and a strong industrial base. Reclaiming economic self-sufficiency will require that we voluntarily undergo a painful retooling of our economy. The alternative is to remain as reluctant passengers while the global economy sinks slowly — or quickly — into oblivion.

26

Undoing the Damage

We have been living in a distorted economy for a long time. A shorter workweek can restore the balance between production and consumption. Further steps will be required to undo the damage of the past 30 years.

Equality and Democracy

A subtle but profound effect of living in a sick economy has been the gradual erosion of social equality. By reducing unemployment, a shorter workweek will shore up the power of unions and individual workers. Employees who see that they have other choices will be less easily threatened by employers.

Setting firm trading boundaries will curb the power of transnational corporations, making them more responsible to local community interests.

While these changes are important, other changes are required to restore Canadian democracy to health.

■ AFFIRMATIVE ACTION IN GENDER POLITICS

Part of the reason women lack power and influence in Canada is because they lack a voice in government. Despite being half of the population, women still hold only one seventh of the seats in parliament.

I agree wholeheartedly with the argument that people should be elected as persons, rather than on the basis of gender. To assign political seats by gender is undesirable.

Unfortunately, gender-based elections are what we have in Canada today. If Canadians elected their federal politicians on character and policies alone, we would expect to see a parliament roughly 50% female in make-up. A parliament which is 87% male is evidence that political seats *are* assigned on the basis of gender. This gender assignment is no less real for being covert and random.

Affirmative action is needed to overcome age-old prejudices against female leaders. Affirmative action will create models and mentors for future female leaders.

■ ELECTION EXPENSES REFORM

It could be argued that Canadian big business bought the last election for the federal Conservative party, with donations to the party itself and with a massive "non-partisan" campaign on behalf of the Conservatives' major election platform: free trade. This subversion of democracy must not be repeated.

The most straightforward way to limit the power of big business and the wealthy is to restrict political contributions to individuals, and to restrict individual contributions to $500 per year. Party nomination races could be subject to the same limitations. Special interest lobby campaigns (like that for free trade) would face similar restrictions. (Given that the wealthy in Canada are predominantly male, and the poor disproportionately female, such reforms would also support affirmative action goals.)

■ A HUMAN SCALE FOR BUSINESS

Setting firm trade boundaries will make Canada less vulnerable to transnational blackmail. Solving the problem of overcapacity will remove much of the incentive for further corporate concentration. Nonetheless, years of corporate concentration have made much of the corporate world so large it no longer operates at a human scale.

Canadian-owned businesses are more likely to function in Canada's interests. Foreign-owned companies could be taxed on their gross sales in Canada. (A tax on sales is advised because businesses would not be able to escape it through transfer price manipulations.) Such a tax would not prevent foreign investment within Canada — but it would provide strong incentive for new and existing foreign investors to be minor partners rather than outright owners.

Businesses are more likely to function in the interests of their employees when employee-owned. Companies which are more than 50% owned by employees could be assessed a lower rate of corporate tax.

There is also a need for stronger anti-trust legislation to break up corporate concentration. As Herman Daly maintains: "To the extent that competition is self-eliminating we must constantly re-establish it by trustbusting."

■ A HUMAN SCALE FOR COMMUNITIES

It is attractive to many to live in a small town rather than a large city. It's safer, cleaner, quieter, and more personal. Smaller centres are friendly to the democratic process. It's harder to buy votes in a small town; too many people know the candidates.

The Conservatives have abandoned regional economic development in Canada, claiming past development programs have failed at vast public expense.

What needs to be abandoned is not the goal of regional development but the methods by which it has been sought. Past efforts at regional development focused on giving large, one-time grants to megaprojects coming in from outside the community. Major corporations often took unwise gambles in building new factories, because government was paying the bills and taking all the risks. Other strategies offer greater promise as vehicles of regional development:

SMALL IS BEAUTIFUL: Much publicity has been given to the failures of regional development megaprojects. What hasn't been reported is that small, locally based initiatives have had much higher success rates.

TAX INCENTIVES: Lower property taxes on corporations in small towns and economically depressed regions can provide a solid incentive to locate in these regions — without bankrupting local governments. These incentives can be funded by a tax surcharge on corporations in big cities.

ELECTRONIC INFRASTRUCTURE: A stronger electronic infrastructure would increase the attractiveness of small towns for businesses.

LETS: Local Exchange Trading Systems are community-based currencies which represent a huge improvement on barter networks. Participants in a LETS program buy and sell products using "green dollars," a scrip currency which must be spent within the local community.

Regional economic development will move jobs to the people. Aside from its value in promoting a human political scale, decentralisation will ease inflationary pressure on land prices in our metropolitan areas and the environmental stress caused by big cities.

■ **PUBLIC INPUT INTO MARKETING AND PROFESSIONAL BOARDS**

Marketing boards set prices which we, as consumers, must pay. Professional associations also set prices, either directly or indirectly, and establish educational standards involving large public expenditures. Both types of boards have self-interests not necessarily in alignment with the needs of the public.

Marketing boards for agricultural commodities have been structured to acknowledge the public interest. Such boards include representatives from both government and consumer groups, and their actions are subject to close scrutiny. Other marketing boards and professional associations should have a similar level of public representation to insure that the interests of the larger community are protected.

Housing

Declining unemployment will push wage rates up, creating some inflationary pressures within the economy. If we are to forestall renewed inflation, we need to keep real estate prices rock steady. A government commitment to keep average real estate price increases below the rate of inflation will discourage real estate speculation. Policies to implement such a commitment could include:

✔ No capital gains exemptions on speculative profits;

✔ Taxes for non-resident owners higher than those for resident owners;

✔ Conversion of crown land to building lots;

✔ Active support for cooperative housing and co-housing;

✔ More active regional development programs, perhaps including tax surcharges on businesses in overheated real estate markets;

✔ Lower immigration levels, restricted to family reunion and compassionate grounds, will reduce the pressure on the real estate market.

Between these various strategies, government has the tools it needs to keep real estate prices stable. Stable real estate prices will put the brakes on inflation.

Education

The change to a two-shift system will automatically reduce the capital costs associated with school buildings. Reduced numbers of involuntary students will mean lower education costs. Beyond that, two themes are important:

A SHIFT TO COMPETENCY-BASED QUALIFICATIONS: Currently, university degrees are used as much to keep people *out* of certain professions as to help them be competent in their jobs. It could be made easier to challenge university and college courses — that is, to gain credit for any course by passing an exam. Expanded on-the-job training and supervised apprenticeships could increase opportunities to learn and earn. If nursing training, for instance, were done through a series of skill grades, we could make the path to such professions easier and recognize more fully the role of paraprofessionals.

A LEARN-TO-PLAY FOCUS: Schools and colleges have an important role to play in assisting people to make rich and full use of their leisure. A life-long learning approach will counterbalance our cultural tendency to workaholism and help insure that retirement years are rich, not empty. Learning for the sheer joy of it can be encouraged and supported.

Taken together, these changes can result in a stronger integration between school and community.

Health Care

By eliminating unemployment and creating more leisure, a shorter workweek will act to cut health care costs related to stress. A good beginning, but not enough; active promotion of healthy lifestyles is also required.

The medical profession makes no bones about the fact that the lifestyles of their patients have far more influence on their health and longevity than anything a doctor can do. We need to structure our medical profession around this obvious truth and shift monies away from heroic interventions, towards community health programs. The promotion of healthier diets, more regular exercise, stress management skills, anti-smoking programs, drug and alcohol treatment programs, individual and family counselling, and regular medical check-ups will keep more of our population alive and healthy, at less cost.

Debt and Taxes

A legacy of a labour-surplus economy is that the rich have become richer and the poor, poorer. To cope with the problem that the working class can not afford to buy all it is producing, we have run up massive amounts of both public and private debt. What is required to restore our economy to fiscal balance?

By eliminating the oversupply of labour, a shorter workweek will restore part of the balance. Low unemployment will lead to higher wages for the working population and lower profits for the rich.

Active intervention by government to insure stable real estate prices will help keep inflation to a minimum. Low inflation, in turn, means that interest rates can be kept low, which will keep down the costs associated with both public and private debt. Lower ceilings on the interest rates that can be legally charged for credit card and mortgage loans could help insure that private interest charges come down in sync with the Bank of Canada rate. The lower taxes that will result from a healthy economy will also give working people some room to pay down personal debts.

Nonetheless, our economy is unlikely to show anything like dynamic health so long as much of its private and public income is bled off in debt servicing. As well, the presence of undue amounts of investment capital will continue to be a loose cannon in our economic system.

These two problems present us with an obvious strategy: pay down the public debt with taxes on the rich. Two steps would be required: the elimination of current deficits, followed by debt repayment.

Reforming Canada's tax system could achieve the first goal. In 1968, Kenneth Carter produced a very careful Royal Commission report on how Canada's tax system could be made more equitable by reducing tax breaks and by treating all forms of income equally. Canada's former auditor general, Kenneth Dye, has a wonderful metaphor to describe how tax breaks for the rich leak away huge amounts of government revenue: "A cost-conscious parliament is in the position of a team of engineers trying to design a more fuel-efficient automobile. They think they have succeeded, but the engine seems to go on consuming as much gas as it did before. They cannot understand the problem until they notice that, hidden from view, myriad small holes have been punched through the bottom of the gas tank. This is too often the way of tax expenditures. Revenue leaks away, and MPs do not know about it until it is too late." In *Behind Closed Doors*, Linda McQuaig presents evidence that such tax breaks go overwhelmingly to the rich, and that if these breaks were eliminated, the revenues saved would be enough to wipe out current federal government deficits.

Taxes on the rich could then be used to pay down the national debt. Possible revenue sources could include:

✔ Scrapping the $100,000 capital gains tax exemption;

✔ A higher rate of tax on high-income Canadians (one option would be to restore the top tax rate for wealthy Canadians from the current 44% to its former 65% rate);

✔ High inheritance taxes on large estates;

✔ Taxing the foreign income of Canadian residents;

✔ A separate wealth tax on rich Canadians (Canada is one of the few countries in the developed world without such a wealth tax);

✔ Making corporations pay their fair share of tax. As Mel Hurtig notes: "In 1950, corporations and individuals each paid about half of the income tax collected in Canada. In 1989, individuals paid 88.1% of all income tax and corporations only 11.9%."

Guaranteed Employment

A shorter workweek will end the need for a large-scale UIC program and cut back sharply the numbers on welfare. Most of the unemployed will be individuals temporarily between jobs, with the remainder being single parents of young children, workers with few skills, and individuals with alcohol or personality problems. With a small population needing income supports, we could afford higher levels of support.

That being the case, why have unemployment at all? Why not have the government provide guaranteed employment instead? With only a small portion of the workforce to support, providing guaranteed employment at the minimum wage would cost Canada far less than we're now paying out in UIC and welfare.

In a labour-surplus economy, we have been afraid to put the unemployed to work, for fear they will take jobs away from those who are employed. That policy has wasted the energies and talents of those without jobs. There is a wide range of useful tasks that aren't "economic" in a market economy and still have social utility. In my own province of B.C., for example, we could be doing more of the following:

✔ Spacing second-growth forests to improve yields;

✔ Culling logged areas for firewood;

✔ Creating and maintaining hiking trails;

✔ Salmon-enhancement activities;

✔ Cleaning up litter, and pollution watchdog patrols;

✔ Big brothers/big sisters for teenagers at risk;

✔ Supplemental staffing for non-profit societies.

People unable to find jobs because of limited skills, personal problems, or family responsibilities should not be thrown on the scrap heap. Rather, a guaranteed employment program could be authorized to include any of the following as part of the participants' responsibilities:

✔ Skills training;

✔ Communication and human relations training;

✔ Drug and alcohol counselling;

✔ The care of infants by single parents;

✔ A job-search program on the Job Club model.

Those with serious health or emotional problems could be offered limited tasks, in recognition of their needs and limitations.

A guaranteed employment program would quickly get very expensive if the number of participants was more than a few percent of the workforce — but that perhaps is a good thing in that it would provide government with strong incentive to adjust work hours frequently to keep the economy in healthy balance.

International Relations

The Cold War is over. With the advent of shorter work hours, we will no longer need huge military expenditures as giant job-creation programs. These two changes offer an opportunity to rethink Canadian defence policies. A starting point might be a change of name, and change of heart, to the Department of International Relations.

What would this new department do? For starters, we can withdraw from NORAD and NATO, alliances based on the Cold War. We can bolster our support for the United Nations as the legitimate body to avert or contain international disputes. We can shift our focus to activities which increase the security of Canadians or earn international goodwill — our best guarantee of peace and justice in international relations. We can expand the most constructive functions of the Canadian military:

✔ Expanded search and rescue services;

✔ More United Nations peace-keeping units;

✔ Mobile disaster relief units, to respond to domestic or foreign disasters of flood, fire, or earthquake;

✔ Surveillance patrols against smugglers and polluters;

✔ Expanded weather reporting and monitoring.

Such a shift would require similar numbers of personnel, but less hardware — and a smaller budget.

Prison Reform

As unemployment falls, crime and its attendant policing expenses can be expected to fall. Prison reforms can add further improvements.

In a labour-surplus economy, we have been afraid to demand useful work of the prison population, which only encourages that population to feel useless and incapable. If prisoners worked similar hours to the general population, it would help build their self-worth and allow them to maintain the habits of gainful employment. Time off from work could be given for counselling, drug and alcohol therapy, or vocational training. The labours of the prison population would defray part of the cost of the prison system, plus provide restitution for crime victims. Inmates could also build nest-eggs to help reestablish themselves on their release.

In the next chapter we will focus attention on rehabilitating that other casualty of a labour-surplus economy: the environment.

HEALTHY AGAIN!

The initiatives listed in this chapter will rebuild our country in important ways:

- ✔ Restore a community-based democracy;

- ✔ Fight inflation — while stabilizing housing prices;

- ✔ Improve the quality of education — while containing education costs;

- ✔ Improve our health — while trimming health-care costs;

- ✔ Cut government debt — while distributing wealth more fairly;

- ✔ Eliminate unemployment — while performing socially useful tasks;

- ✔ Increase national security — while reducing defence costs;

- ✔ Reduce crime — while cutting prison costs.

27

Protecting
the Environment

The great obstacle is simply this: the conviction that we cannot change because we are dependent upon what is wrong. But that is the addict's excuse, and we know that it will not do.

WENDELL BERRY

Our attempts to expand consumption endlessly have gravely damaged the environment. Even after it has become clear that our actions threaten all life on Earth, we persist with unsustainable levels of resource use, waste, and pollution. In either/or choices between jobs and the environment, the environment has usually lost.

A shorter workweek itself is an environmentally friendly act of the first magnitude. It will mean less commuting and less consumption generally. The move to a two-shift economy will even out traffic flows, meaning that less of Canada will disappear under asphalt. A slowdown in construction will ease the pressure on our forests.

Once we realize that we can have full employment *and* reduce consumption, the stage will be set for solid environmental action. The following are among the kinds of steps that could be taken.

Green Taxes

The Goods and Services Tax has been an incredibly unpopular tax. The cost and complexity of collecting it separately from provincial sales taxes have been very high, both for governments and for business.

Both taxes could be replaced by a single Green Tax Program. Every product sold could be assessed a Green Tax Code from zero to ten, based on three factors:

❶ **The amount of waste or pollution involved in the product's manufacture and packaging;**

❷ **The resources used in the item's production;**

❸ **The amount of environmental or social damage that use and disposal of the product will entail.**

Green taxes would be set on a sliding scale based on their Green Code. If a product were environmentally benign, it would be Green Code 0 — tax-free. A product which had a mild impact on the environment might have a Green Code of 2 and its retail price would include a 10% tax. A product which was an environmental no-no (a pesticide or a gas-guzzling car) might have a Green Code of 10 and be hit with a whopping 50% tax.

Store prices would all be posted with the tax included. Each item would have its Green Code on the price tag so consumers would know at a glance whether a product was environmentally friendly or harmful. Consumers could escape paying green taxes by buying environmentally friendly products.

A green tax system would require a lot of work to set up. Once in place, it would function as an ongoing environmental audit, sensitizing producers and consumers alike to the environmental impacts of any product.

Organic food production would be given a boost when non-organic farmers paid heavy taxes on their pesticides and chemical fertilizers. Heavy polluters would find their products more expensive than those of environmentally responsible companies. Excessively packaged products would still attract attention — but they'd cost more at the checkout counter. Imports would be subject to the same tax structure, so environmentally harmful imports would cost more than products made by responsible domestic firms. Reusable containers for food products would earn a lower Green Code, as would extended warranty provisions for appliances and tools; both would reduce the waste stream. The use of recycled materials would win products a low Green Code and thereby create better markets for recycled paper, glass, metal, and plastic.

Because green taxes are incentives, they wouldn't restrict people's freedom to choose. Nonetheless, as a gentle but insistent pressure towards environmental responsibility, they would nudge us to a sustainable relationship with the environment.

Adbusting

Advertising is environmentally unfriendly. It wastes vast amounts of time, energy, and resources in an activity which does not produce a socially useful product. It manipulates people to buy products they neither need nor want. Stiff green taxes assessed on advertising could discourage excessive advertising. Monies raised in this way could fund *Consumer Reports*-type tests on the quality, price, and user satisfaction of various products, or could go into an "adbusting fund" to create anti-commercials. Anti-commercials would:

- ✔ Provide consumer education to make consumers aware of how advertising manipulates and distorts;

- ✔ Provide rebuttals to questionable claims or promises made by specific advertisers;

- ✔ Publicly acknowledge businesses and individuals who have shown environmental responsibility;

- ✔ Promote non-materialistic values.

Building an Electronic Infrastructure

We spend vast amounts of public money supporting environmentally damaging public works. We could achieve the same results far more cheaply, and in an environmentally benign fashion, by building an electronic infrastructure instead, with high-tech phone links, electronic libraries, and telecommuting. (Telecommuting means working from one's home or a neighbourhood office, linked to the main office by a computer, fax, and phone.)

If we were to lay fibre-optic telephone lines between most towns, we could quickly and relatively inexpensively create a powerful phone network. No long-distance charges would be necessary for calls anywhere within Canada. This, in turn, would reduce highway traffic and overcrowding in cities, lessening air pollution and the need to construct super-highways.

We now have the technology to create electronic libraries. One library can serve an entire province or region. Every book in the library is always "in," as borrowers take only an electronic copy. Even if you live in a small, isolated town, you can access all the resources of big city libraries via your home computer. Electronic books and newspapers require no paper, so no trees need be cut down for their production; there is no waste to recycle.

Active promotion and support of telecommuting offers both financial and environmental benefits.

Vancouver is a growing city; as the city gets larger, so does the amount of time commuters spend on the road. Average daily commuting time increased from 30 minutes in 1980 to 55 minutes in 1990. About 85% of the air pollution in Vancouver comes from automobiles. To cope with rising peak traffic volumes in the Vancouver area, new road, highway, and bridge construction worth $1.2 billion has been recommended for the next 10 years.

Steve Finlay, in a research paper for Simon Fraser University, has estimated that these costs could be avoided through the promotion and support of telecommuting. Government could buy all the computers and electronic equipment needed to enable part of the workforce to telecommute, for a fraction of the cost of getting those same people to work by car.

Some telecommuters could work at home, but most would probably prefer the social environment of a neighbourhood satellite office. BC Tel, B.C.'s provincial phone company, has an experimental satellite office in Langley; it reports that productivity rose by up to 25% and absenteeism dropped by 50% since employees at the centre traded the long commute to Vancouver for a quick walk or bike ride to work.

Telecommuting need not be restricted to a city's suburbs; neighbourhood telecommuting centres could be set up in small towns anywhere, reducing joblessness in these communities and slowing the cancerous growth of cities.

The creation of an electronic infrastructure will reduce the use of fossil fuels, save money, and improve our quality of life.

Full-Scale Recycling

Green taxes will provide strong incentives to reduce and re-use. We must also pay more attention to recycling. Most household garbage can be recycled. I recycle the items below; it takes about an hour a week.

MATERIALS IN HOUSEHOLD GARBAGE

Compostables, including lawn waste	35%
Newspapers	15%
Other paper and cardboard	21%
Glass	9%
Tin cans	5%
Plastic	5%
Total fraction of average household waste	90%

If each of us made the commitment to invest one hour of our new-found free time in sorting our household waste, we could slash waste dramatically. Community blue box programs could be expanded to include all recyclable items. Centralized composting facilities would create large amounts of organic fertilizer for municipalities and home gardeners alike. A full-scale recycling approach would create new employment, at least partly offsetting the job losses caused by consuming and wasting less.

Hornby Island, a small community off the east coast of Vancouver Island, has had a full-scale recycling program for a number of years, including a "free store" for used goods and clothing. The program has proven extremely effective both at reducing waste and at creating local employment.

Let's Park!

To remain healthy over many generations, wild species need to breed among large populations of their kind. If we are to maintain diversity of wild plant and animal species for future generations, we need more parks and wilderness areas. If we have less fear of loggers and miners being unemployed, perhaps we will be willing to preserve more of our crown land as parks and wilderness reserves.

Preserving open space and green space also requires a repudiation of the compulsive growth mentality of the past. We need neither a growing population nor rapid economic growth to maintain prosperity, just a commitment to share the work.

RESTORED IN BEAUTY

The ideas we have explored in this chapter are not new and represent only some of the steps we could take to establish a sustainable relationship with the environment.

> When we're no longer blackmailed by the either/or choice of jobs or the environment, we can take the needed steps to establish a friendly and sustainable relationship with the natural beauty of Canada's environment.

28

A New Worth Ethic

Learning is work, caring for children is work.
Once we accept the concept of work as something
meaningful — not just as the source of a buck — we
don't have to find enough jobs.
STUDS TERKEL

Political and economic changes alone will not create a happier future. We must also replace the toxic values of the past with life-affirming beliefs.

In this process it is not necessary to invent new virtues but rather to promote existing, healthy values. Healthy values must be promoted at all levels: in schools and churches, in the media, at work, and at play. Government will need to clean its own house, to root out policies which promote work addiction. Government can highlight healthy values in adbuster ads.

Individuals will play an important role in the process, insofar as they stand as *models for change*.

Intrinsic Self-Worth

It is important that we create social support for individuals to base their sense of worth on who they are, rather than on what they do or what they own.

Intrinsic self-worth is supported when we recognize there is something sacred in every human being. Each human being has the potential to be a force for love and creativity in the world. Each of us enters the world with a unique perspective and our own unique gifts.

Acts of ego are the practical decisions of a bargain- or trade-based economy, decisions based on fear or self-interest. Acts of self are the free choices we make from love and creative exuberance: acts of service, acts of love, acts of friendship, acts of passionate curiosity.

Healthy self-worth is based not on career or possessions, but on character and on acts of self.

Recovery from Addiction

As any recovering alcoholic can tell you, the first and most important step in overcoming addiction is to acknowledge the addiction. We have a culture that is addicted to work, and which has an overarching pattern of addiction. We cannot address our addictions without first acknowledging their extent, severity, and cost.

A starting place would be widespread public education on the nature of the addictive process. Workaholics Anonymous has a set of 12-step teaching manuals modeled on those of Alcoholics Anonymous.

If we can afford to spend thousands of dollars on heart and liver surgery, we can afford to spend similar amounts through Medicare on addictions therapy which will obviate the need for much surgery.

In the workplace we can acknowledge addictive behaviours within organizations, and treat them through workshops and in-service training. Organizations can help their staff deal with addiction and co-dependency issues through Employee Assistance Counselling programs.

Right Livelihood

Right livelihood is a commitment to earn one's daily bread in a fashion which benefits rather than harms the community and the environment. Right livelihood is a co-requisite to healthy self-worth; it's difficult to feel good about yourself if your work is useless or destructive.

Low unemployment will allow individuals to push for work

which is positive in its effect on the world. A right livelihood ethic will put pressure on businesses which engage in useless or environmentally toxic activities. An ethic of fair value for fair measure is the business counterpart to right livelihood.

Simple Living

The doctrine of simple living offers a healthy antidote to consumerism. In North America, a high standard of living has gone hand in hand with a low quality of life.

Time spent on possessions is time we are unavailable to our loved ones. A surfeit of material possessions distracts us from our emotional needs.

Possessions possess us as much as we possess them. Consider for the moment all the time you've spent buying, cleaning, fixing, and paying for all you own. How many of the things in your world do you really need? How could you live better with less?

Every item I buy has some degree of resource depletion, waste, or pollution involved in its manufacture and use. A conscious decision to eliminate unnecessary consumption nurtures the Earth.

When we no longer need to endlessly expand consumption to create jobs, we can conserve, repair, and re-use. When my self-worth is no longer contingent on the number or value of my possessions, I am free to wear comfortable clothes, even if they are old or out of style.

Many of us are so dominated by fears of scarcity that we fail to recognize that our lives are stressful because they are too full. It clears the mind to remove the clutter.

A companion value of simple living is valuing substance over image — to look past the designer clothes and the designer bodies to ask, "Who's inside?" We must dispel the confusion between who people are and their external trappings of clothes, possessions, and status.

An Ethic of Service

In *The Gift*, artist Lewis Hyde suggests that capitalism has altered our basic way of being in the world. Hyde suggests that the idea of the trade or bargain has become the model for all relationships in our society and that other cultures see life very differently.

For many cultures, trades are seen as a secondary or lesser form of relationship. Because trades are acts involving means and ends, they are not free acts in the same sense that gifts are.

Gifts require a mind-set of abundance, a belief that I have so much that I can give it away. Gifts are acts of free choice, unencumbered by any expectation of the other. Service is a potent antidote to isolation; my aloneness disappears when I surrender to something larger than myself.

We must recognize and value all gifts of service. It is dismissive to say a person is "just a volunteer." We must let go of the strange attitude that an activity is only worth what someone will pay for it. When we do that, we fail to recognize that much of what is important in our relationships with each other, indeed much of what will be required to insure our continued survival on the planet, is not necessarily "economic."

Is the service a Big Sister or a Big Brother provides less valuable because no money changes hands? Is it useless to recycle my newspapers because I don't get paid to do so? There is much essential work to be done in our society that the economic system does not, and sometimes cannot, reward.

What volunteers do is more, not less, important than paid employment. When I started the Work Well Society, I was a full-time volunteer. It was only after I became the paid manager of a paid staff that people started to thank me for the wonderful work I was doing. Yet by that point, truthfully, my vital contribution had been made. Once the funding and structures were in place, the job would have got done anyway. If I had been hit by a bus, there would have been people lining up to do my job. It was the work I did as a volunteer that would not have happened if I hadn't done it.

We are at a time of immense social change. The existing economic system does not foster change, but rather blunts and quashes the best efforts for change of those in paid employment. Most of the essential work of transformation in the next 10 years will be done by volunteers. Our survival as a species will depend not on what people do for money, but what they do for love.

Women Hold Up Half the Sky

It is not enough that women are able to work in jobs previously restricted to men, and that women reclaim personality traits like assertiveness which have been falsely identified as male. Two further changes are needed to create a healthy relationship between the genders.

The first is that we need more inclusive and flexible ideas about gender. Our culture has exaggerated and rigidified differences between the sexes. Even when we can say that *most* women or most men fit a particular pattern, human diversity is such that any putative gender pattern is burdened with a multitude of exceptions. To assign jobs on the basis of gender is to ignore this vibrant variability. Feminist writers have provided us with good resources for thinking about gender less rigidly.

The second issue is that gender traits identified as feminine must be recognized as being of equal value to traits labelled masculine. Traditionally female tasks must be seen as equal in value to traditionally male ones.

In our culture, traits labelled feminine have been undervalued. When women had no opportunity to engage in activities which had higher social status, this failure to value women's contribution did not prevent "women's work" from getting done. Now that women have the option to engage in higher status work, they have less incentive to put their energies into domestic and parenting tasks. Men have little incentive to take up the slack, with the result that family life has been getting short shrift.

If tasks traditionally identified as female have social status and financial remuneration equal to male-identified tasks, there will be no shortage of workers, both male and female, to complete those tasks. It doesn't really matter whether traditional women's tasks are done by men or by women; what matters is that the tasks are valued and rewarded.

The men's movement has an important role to play in this revaluing process. When men no longer fear the so-called feminine in themselves, they will feel less need to suppress and put down women.

Just Rewards

A commitment to a fairer distribution of income assists in the creation of a more harmonious society.

The first step is pay equity between the genders. The union movement has an important role to play in bringing about pay equity. The stance of the union movement is that women are underpaid and that their wages must be raised to equal men's. However, there has been little progress towards equity. After years of this policy, women's wages in Canada are still only two thirds those of men.

A pay equity policy with teeth would involve lowering men's wages to provide the funds to raise women's wages. Employers would have far less opposition to a policy which did not increase their costs.

A second step would be a commitment to reduce differentials between the highest- and lowest-paid workers, to bring Canada in line with Europe and Japan.

We need to develop a new model of social value. We must throw out the idea of a stratified society made up of winners and losers, and shift to a model of teamwork, a model that recognizes that the smooth functioning of society requires that all jobs get done.

We need street cleaners, waiters, garbage collectors, and cashiers every bit as much as we need town planners, managers, academics, and financiers. Indeed, the argument could be made that society would fall apart much more quickly if we took away the former group. Social status and financial compensation must be evened out, in recognition that everyone's contribution is needed to make society work.

A final step would be higher — and universal — family allowance payments, combined with larger tax deductions for dependent children. We must act to ensure the adequate parenting of future generations. It should be a top national priority to see that parents in Canada have the time, money and energy available for this crucial task.

THE TASK OF RECOVERY

> To have a healthy society, one which fills its leisure with healthy and life-affirming activities, we must replace the values of addiction with ideals based on sharing, caring, simplicity, integrity, and mutual respect.

29

The Rehabilitation of Pleasure

Love lifts us up where we belong.
BUFFY ST. MARIE

There are those who will ask, "If we work less, what will we do with all that free time?" They will express the fear that more free time will result in more time in front of the TV and heavier use of alcohol. My personal experience is very different. When I worked a three-day week I sold my TV, drank less alcohol, and was bored less often.

When I worked three days a week I had the time and energy for active and involved leisure. I socialized more with friends and had more intimate time with my partner. I went hiking, kayaking, and rock climbing more often, and spent more time in the garden. I was a more creative and imaginative cook. I read more. I was more involved in volunteer activities. My life was full and rich.

This is not to suggest that a shift to shorter working hours won't be difficult for some people. Bioenergetic therapist Alexander Lowen has suggested that many North Americans suffer from *anhedonia* — the inability to feel pleasure. Lowen suggests that when people's lives are dominated by fear and duty, their bodies armour themselves. Muscles go hard and tense. This is the body's natural way of protecting itself when threatened. Hardened muscles are less vulnerable to damage. A body which is heavily armoured also does not feel pleasure or strong desires — a small price to pay when under threat.

Lowen suggests that such body armouring can become chronic, a permanent stance in the world. The only way that many of us can cope with the demands of a 40-hour workweek is to place our bodies on permanent red alert. In a constant battle-ready state, the pleasures of love-making, human contact, good food, and body movement are muted, if they can be felt at all.

The rehabilitation of pleasure must be an active and conscious process. Change will not be immediate. People whose bodies are frozen in emergency readiness may go through a period of numbness and feeling lost. Massage, bioenergetic exercise, and relaxation therapy will help such people reclaim their natural capacity for pleasure.

Schools and community colleges must develop a strong leisure studies focus, introducing the public to meaningful leisure activities and helping individuals decide what kind of leisure would most satisfy them.

As a society, we must make friends with our bodies and with pleasure. Pleasure must be reframed, not as something to be feared or avoided, but as the body's cue that we are headed in a life-affirming direction.

The Play's the Thing

To rehabilitate pleasure, we must affirm and celebrate play. Children can be our best teachers in this joyful process. As adults, many of us sleepwalk through the wonders of everyday life. Children remind us that we are surrounded by miracles: fingers, kittens, sunsets, the hovering hummingbird, and the soaring hawk.

We must reclaim sport, not as serious work for the professional few but as exuberant play for the many. We need a democracy of creativity: music, drama, and art, for the people, by the people. The play's the thing; not who wins or loses.

We must reclaim sexuality from the pressure of performance and technique; our birthright is joyous love-play and love-making. Perhaps we need a new bumper sticker: "Make Love — Not Work."

We must honour the intimacy of partnership, encouraging couples not to get so caught up in being Mom and Dad that they forget to be lovers and friends.

We must honour passion. For the Greeks, the term "amateur" was a designation of great respect. What was done for love was considered a higher calling than what was done for money. The excellence of the amateur must be honoured and supported, whether the passion is for gardening, golf, bird watching, or medieval history.

We must honour family and friendship. European immigrants and First Nations peoples can teach us much about dinners that go on for hours, where the conversation is as rich and nourishing as the food. In our places of worship we must rediscover the fellowship of faith. The light within us shines more brightly when others reflect it back to us.

Finally, we also must honour silence and contemplation. The spirit speaks not in thunderbolts but in that still, small voice within. If we wish the spirit to fill our lives, we must give it the time and space to do so.

Community Rootedness

We need to re-establish rootedness. Ecologist Wendell Berry has suggested that "saving the planet" is an impossibly large goal. Rather, we need to concentrate on saving our own neighbourhoods. This is not to say that I shouldn't boycott grapes from Chile or send aid money to Guatemala. What it is saying is that the correct focus for my activities is my own community.

My home community is what I know, where I have most influence, what I am most able to monitor. The consumption of goods by me and by my neighbours is more under my control than is the far-off production of those goods. Though my power may be limited within my home community, I have more power to stop the cutting of trees, the paving of fields, and the fouling of streams in my own neighbourhood than I do anywhere else.

To become a true advocate for a tiny chunk of the planet requires a willingness to set down roots. Not "I'm here until I get a better offer," but "This is my home — and I will make it the best." If the earth is to survive, it will not be saved all in a piece. Rather, each river valley and hill must be defended by its own fierce circle of advocates.

True community requires time. If I'm not committed to staying in a neighbourhood, I will have only a half-hearted interest in its people. An extended family of friendship takes time to grow deep and rich.

Cooperation and Sharing

We must counteract our cultural manias for competition and individual ownership by active promotion of the values of cooperation and sharing.

We must acknowledge and reward teamwork, negotiation, and compromise. We must support new living arrangements of intentional community and cooperative housing. There is no need for every household to have its own washer, dryer, and lawn mower; it is more efficient, and gentler on the Earth, when such appliances are shared. We must reject the American model of private opulence and public squalor.

Loving the Earth

We need to change more than our behaviour towards the environment. We need to develop a deeper, more active connection with the Earth. We must think of ourselves as part of the ecology, subject to the laws of nature rather than in charge of the natural world. We must view the natural world as Gaia, a sacred unity, and not as a commodity for sale.

Original Blessing

We must embrace theologies which support the best rather than the worst in human nature. In *States of Grace*, Charlene Spretnak explores Buddhist, Native American, and mystic traditions — all of which can offer us gentler models for our relationships with each other and with the planet. Humanists and Unitarians also offer life-affirming spiritual paths.

Matthew Fox is a Dominican priest who teaches the Christian tradition of creation spirituality. Fox views creation not as a finite event but as an ongoing process, of which humanity is a part. Our connection with the divine means we begin not in original sin, but in original blessing.

Supporting the good in ourselves does not ignore or deny human shortcomings but simply applies what any wise parent or teacher knows — that what you look for in another human being is usually what you'll find.

TIME ENOUGH FOR LOVE

A shorter workweek is about having time enough for love:

✔ Time for a rich and abundant family life;

✔ Time to make whatever personal contribution we can to the creation of a better world;

✔ Time to appreciate our own unique selves;

✔ Time to follow our own passions;

✔ Time for a community of pleasure and laughter.

30

The Politics of Abundance

*The reason why our lives are not all that they can be is
that we have come to believe that nothing can be
changed. But things can be changed, in the most
fundamental ways. The greatest obstacle is our own
internalized sense that everything has to remain the
same, that the way people treat each other and live
together and work together is part of some fundamental
and unchangeable reality.*

MICHAEL LERNER

The change to a four-day workweek will be implemented by
government, but this does not mean it will be initiated by politicians.
In Canada, the term "political leadership" is an oxymoron. Politicians follow, not lead, public opinion.

Therefore, a change in the standard workweek requires the creation of a large grassroots movement of support — a bandwagon our
political leaders can climb upon. All of our major institutions must
become involved.

Creating a Movement for Change

When I began promoting the idea of a standard four-day workweek,
I was surprised by the universality of people's response: almost

without exception people would visibly lighten up, saying things like, "I'm ready" and "It's about time" and "Where do I sign up?" It isn't a matter of any great altruistic concern for the unemployed; people are just tired of the extent to which work dominates their lives, tired of being tired, tired of the insecurity of living in a high-unemployment society, and tired of feeling guilty about having a job when so many do not.

Met with such a positive response, I initially thought that my job would be an easy one, like starting a grass fire on a dry prairie field. But what I next discovered is that, while people wanted a four-day workweek and believed intuitively in its effectiveness, when it can time to volunteer, they disappeared.

I've recruited volunteers before, so I'm familiar with that gap between what people believe in and what they will actively work to support — but in this case the gap was enormous, which confused me at first. As I talked with people in greater depth, the problem became clearer.

Most Canadians think of the economy as being like the weather: a huge, mysterious force totally outside their control. Our governments have been using unworkable economic strategies for so long that many people have come to the conclusion that our economic problems are insoluble. The so-called experts have thrown up such a wall of economic bafflegab that most people are confused about the economy, afraid to trust their own intuitive understanding that work hours must go down.

The belief that our economic problems are insoluble makes them so — for now, but not for long. There are four factors which make change inevitable.

■ THE FRAMEWORK OF 'SHARING THE WORK'

The first factor I have observed is that simply talking about our economic problems within a framework of sharing the work — as opposed to "creating jobs" — seems to shift individuals' willingness to act.

We are quickly approaching a *paradigm shift*, a basic shift in how we see the economy. As a counsellor, I know that half the job of solving any problem is coming up with a productive way of seeing one's situation. The counselling term for this process is *reframing*.

Our economic problems are transformed by reframing them. Instead of seeing the problem as a scarcity of work, we can view it as the opportunity for an abundance of leisure. Instead of a lifeboat society dominated by fear, we can have an abundant society with time for love, play, and joy.

Our current economic framework is so outmoded it is like those old, derelict barns one sometimes sees in the countryside—one push in the right spot and the whole structure will come tumbling down. More than anything else, the shift to a new paradigm requires advocates who will keep nudging at the old framework till it crashes under its own weight.

■ THE CREATION OF A POSITIVE VISION

The second dynamic I have seen is that knowledge and vision contain power. The more people understand the nature of our economic fix, the more they are moved to do something. And when people become involved in creating a positive and concrete vision of the future, they get excited. Out of that excitement comes action.

The changes proposed in this book will create large and initially unsettling changes in our lives. The guidepost of a clear and positive vision of the future will be essential if we are not to sell ourselves out to fear and doubt.

This book has drawn a rough outline for a new vision of the future. In our churches, unions, and political parties we can join together to flesh that outline into a solid, comprehensive plan. The hopes, ideas and insights of many people will be needed if we are to build a powerful and energizing vision.

■ A NETWORK OF CATALYSTS

The third factor is that there are a few individuals bold enough—or crazy enough—to believe that they, personally, have a role to play in bringing about a future where there's a job for every Canadian who wants one, and where we take better care of the environment and ourselves.

It is these individuals who will be the catalysts for a much larger network. They, in turn, will prod others to join what, by then, will be a movement.

One final factor is making the job easier with each passing year. As our economy deteriorates, its problems are becoming glaringly obvious, and individuals become more willing to trust their own instincts over the nonsense of the experts.

■ THE WORK WELL NETWORK

The creation of a new paradigm for employment involves the willingness of hundreds of ordinary Canadians to speak up, insistently and persistently. We will be the catalysts for the shift to a new economic order.

The Work Well Society is coordinating the efforts of individuals and organizations to lobby for a shorter workweek. This new network, modelled on the Pro-Canada Network, provides a mechanism for individuals and organizations to work together for change.

Financial contributions to the network underwrite the cost of short publications, advertising, and a paid coordinator.

Network members work to change how employment issues are framed in the public forum. They lobby for a change in thinking at any institution they're involved with, be it a church, social club, workplace, union, or political party.

Debate is fostered by letters to the editor, calls to open-line shows, questions from the floor at political forums — even through conversations among friends.

■ STUDY CIRCLES

Work Well is currently preparing a resource guide for setting up study circles to examine employment issues. Early in this century, the Swedish government facilitated the establishment of study circles which involved more than a million Swedes, to examine social and economic issues. Many credit the study circle process for Sweden's impressive economic performance over the past 70 years.

Study circles provide an easy and social way for individuals to educate themselves about work issues. They also create a solid commitment among those who are attracted to the idea of a shorter workweek. Study circles are also circles of mutual support for political action. (For those wishing to use *Working Harder Isn't Working* as a basis for study circles, bulk purchases can be made from New Star Books at a reduced rate.)

■ CHURCH INVOLVEMENT

Sharing is a fundamental tenet of most faiths. It is appropriate that there be religious services on the theme of sharing the work. It is also a proper focus for church-based study circles and social-action groups.

Union Rebirth

The Canadian Autoworkers Union, one of Canada's largest and more progressive unions, has taken an important step with their 1993 pamphlet *More Time for Ourselves, Our Children, Our Community*, in which they proclaim, "It's time to have a national debate on reducing work time." The Canadian labour movement needs to join with the CAW in making a heartfelt return to the ideal of solidarity. Every union must recognize that only by creating justice for all workers will unions have the power to protect their own memberships.

As an initial step, the union movement must replace its current policy—a shorter workweek with no loss in pay—with more practical policies of the type described in this book. It should also replace a focus on individual union action with a move to collective action. An across-the-board change to a shorter workweek creates systemic benefits which are absent when individual unions bargain separately.

Unions can express this renewed commitment to solidarity by allocating a portion of all union dues to organizing a broad-based coalition for change, like the Eight Hour Movement of the 1870s and the 30-Hour Workweek Campaign of the 1930s.

From this campaign fund, the union movement could fund national initiatives, such as:

✔ A national advertising and media campaign;

✔ Study circles on the economy;

✔ Pamphlets on the need for a shorter workweek;

✔ Public forums and workshops on employment issues;

✔ Debates on the economy during federal and provincial election campaigns.

Unions must also more actively stand in solidarity with the unemployed. The Canadian union movement could help fund a national Want To Work Union for the unemployed of Canada. This union would provide job-search training and support, advocacy services for UIC and welfare difficulties, and crisis counselling. A Want To Work Union would also serve as the voice of Canada's unemployed, and organize for political action on their behalf.

Unions must abandon their traditional opposition to part-time work. Instead, they should fight for expanded opportunities for qual ity part-time work with equal hourly rates of pay, fixed schedules, prorated benefits, seniority protection, and union membership. As an interim step, the union movement can express solidarity with the unemployed by demanding that all extra work hours be covered by relief staff rather than by overtime.

It was the union movement that provided the prototypes for structures which reduced unemployment and kept the economy in balance in years past. By creating large-scale models for the four-day workweek, unions can resume their proper role as social innovators. Unions should target industries where layoffs are threatened for early introduction of a shortened workweek. Even if members of those unions need to take a cut in take-home pay, the attitude of solidarity implicit in such job-saving action will bring renewed support for unions and provide clear models for change. The Canadian Autoworkers Union has shown leadership in this regard, bargaining fiercely in its most recent contracts for overtime restrictions, phased retirement provisions, and a shorter workweek.

Reinventing the Corporation

The corporate world as a whole will probably continue to be myopic for years to come, opposing a shorter workweek as "too expensive" and firm trade boundaries as "bad for business."

However, we must remember that even transnational corporations are staffed by human beings who have friends, children, and neighbours suffering from unemployment. Even the most hard-nosed of executives realizes that a depression will hurt corporate profits.

Except for those who have been blinded by ambition, most corporate executives realize that they are expendable. And the sicker the economy becomes, the more likely their jobs will be threatened.

I expect that at least some of the upper echelon of Canadian business will recognize the unworkability of the 40-hour workweek, and will support lower-level managers in activities which indirectly promote a shorter workweek:

✔ Policies on job sharing, permanent part-time, and relief staffing pools;

✔ Workplace programs to combat workaholism;

✔ Workshops/seminars on the addictive organization;

✔ Personnel department reports exploring the feasibility of short workweeks built around double-shifting.

Whether you work for a large company or a small one, lobbying for such activities offers avenues for your organization to support the principle of sharing the work.

A New Political Agenda

Once grassroots support for a four-day workweek is in place, the first political party to promote it as party policy will soar in popularity.

For those who are active members of political parties, this opportunity must be highlighted in platform planning. For the rest of us, we can ask questions and express opinions at political rallies. During election campaigns we can write letters to the editor and phone in to talk shows. Once a political party makes a shorter workweek official party policy, we can make donations to that party — and vote for it. Individual Canadians can run for federal office on the platform of a shorter workweek.

THE AUSPICIOUS MOMENT

Changes to government policy will be the prime mechanism for implementing shorter working hours, but the push to create that change must involve all of our major institutions: unions, churches, corporations, community organizations, political parties, and the media.

In the six months since this book first appeared in print, Bell Canada and Volkswagen in Germany have both gone to a four-day workweek. France has been exploring a plan to move the whole country to a four-day workweek by 1995.

Canada's new Liberal government has established an Advisory Committee on the Distribution of Work to study the role of shorter work times in reducing unemployment. The Canadian Labour Congress chose shorter work hours as the theme of its annual convention in 1994. Both the Green and National parties are considering the adoption of the four-day workweek as official party policy.

The time for change has come.

> **Strong public support for shorter working hours is essential. Where the people lead, our political leaders must eventually follow.**

31

What to Do Until the Revolution

If I can't dance, I don't want to be
At your revolution, that's no solution
If I can't sing and shout, you can count me out.
I'll dance my way to freedom.

AL GIORDANO

What can you and I do until the revolution of a shorter workweek is upon us?

Be an Optimist

Norman Cousins, in his book *Head First*, describes being admitted to a tuberculosis sanatorium at age 10. In those days, tuberculosis was a very serious disease; statistically, you were likely to die.

Cousins found two types of people in the sanatorium: realists and optimists. The realists knew that they had a disease that was probably fatal. They were sombre, depressed, and resigned. They lived in the shadow of death and waited to die.

The optimists, on the other hand, knew that some people recovered from tuberculosis. They lived with gusto, developed

266

strong bonds, made plans for the future. They fought the disease with passion and determination.

Most of the realists withered away and died. The optimists lived rich and passionate lives. Some of those lives were short, bright candles. Most — like Cousins' — were long and full.

Optimism is very different from denial or wishful thinking. Cousins and his optimist colleagues did not deny the seriousness of the threat to their lives. Indeed, *healing* was the prime focus of their lives. The optimists' commitment to life was so strong that it mobilized the healing energy of every cell of their bodies.

We are in a time of crisis. It is not enough to wish for a better future. If we are to have a positive future together, we must live like people who have a positive future. Only by laying claim to the future, by staking our creative energies and our best efforts upon it, can we bring that future into being.

Part of creating a future of leisure and prosperity is to *work* for change doing all of the normal things one does to create a social and political movement.

Part of the revolution is to sing and dance — and *play*. By doing what you can to establish a simple, balanced, and happy life for yourself *now*, you will act as a beacon for others to follow. By expressing and supporting healthy values, you can encourage others along the same path.

If you think that you can't work less because you're already spending more than you're making, I recommend starting your own leisure revolution by reading *Your Money or Your Life* by Joe Dominguez and Vicki Robin. You don't have to wait for the system to change to begin moving your own life in the direction of joy and play.

The challenge I and the Work Well Network offer you is to change the world — and have fun doing it.

The following two checklists summarize individual opportunities for action. Check through the "Notes and Sources" section for suggested readings (marked by a ☞), addresses, and phone numbers.

■ **ACTION STEPS: WORK FOR CHANGE**

✔ Speak up: In talk shows, letters to the editor, conversations with friends, let your voice be heard.

✔ Lobby any group with which you are affiliated: Nudge your church, union, employer, or political party towards active support of a shorter workweek.

✔ Educate yourself: Recruit friends and form a study circle. (Kits are available from the Work Well Network.)

✔ Join the Work Well Network: Participate with others in a coordinated program for change. If there isn't a local chapter yet — form one.

✔ Be politically active: See that the idea of a shorter workweek is raised at every political forum. Press candidates to take a stand, and vote accordingly.

✔ Make the paradigm shift: Whenever you hear our problems described as a shortage of jobs, reframe it as a surplus of labour. Reframe the problem of a scarcity of jobs as an opportunity for abundant leisure.

✔ Spread the word: Share this book with your friends — or circulate several copies.

✔ Contribute to the cause: Financial contributions to Work Well help it in its work.

✔ Make the Work Well commitment: Commit yourself to working for change — and to living it.

■ **ACTION STEPS: LIVE THE REVOLUTION!**

✔ Live simply: Begin rigorously asking yourself before each purchase: "Do I really need this?" Find your pleasures in human contact rather than things.

✔ Work less: Do whatever you can to start your own leisure revolution — job share, work a four-day week, turn down overtime, or take extra weeks of vacation.

✔ Confront your addictions: Addictions to work and alcohol can make us numb — and ineffective as agents of social change.

✔ Confront addiction where you work: Workshop kits are available from the Work Well Network.

✔ Choose a life-affirming spiritual path: Seek a spiritual path which supports what is good in you.

✔ Embrace pleasure: Do massage, exercises, or sense relaxation to soften any armouring your body may have. Make room for fun, play, and intimacy.

✔ Deepen your roots: If you haven't already done so, set down roots. Declare yourself a steward of that little piece of Earth that is your home.

✔ Develop an ethic of service: The experience that we have enough is strengthened by giving to others.

✔ Seek balance: Healthy self-esteem is grounded on a balanced life: family, spirituality, solitary time, community service, and friendship — as well as work.

✔ Respect the earth: Develop an active appreciation for nature. Reduce, re-use, recycle, and telecommute.

✔ Experience abundance: Abundance is an attitude. When we slow down, we find ourselves surrounded by riches which are invisible in the hurly-burly of life.

AWAKENING TO ABUNDANT LIFE

The River is moving in our direction. Machines and computers are doing more and more of the work that used to fall to human hands and minds.

Fighting this wonderful opportunity has made our lives harder and harsher, and hurt our home, the Earth — but we can choose differently whenever we tire of the pain. Embracing the vision of leisure will create lives of richness and abundance — even if there are those among us who must be dragged, kicking and screaming, into paradise. The time has come to claim the future of our dreams.

I would like to leave the last word to Eric Hoffer. Hoffer was a longshoreman who wrote books of philosophy. He wrote the following passage in 1967, but its simple eloquence rings equally true today.

> "The fact is that the mad rush of the last hundred years has left us out of breath. We have had no time to swallow our spittle. We know that [technology] is here to liberate us and show us the way back to Eden; that it will do for us what no revolution, no doctrine, no prayer, and no promise could do. But we do not know that we have arrived. We stand there panting, caked with sweat and dust, afraid to realize that the seventh day of the second creation is here, and the ultimate sabbath is spread out before us. "

Notes and Sources

Part of the price of keeping the main text free of footnotes and citation numbers is that it requires a little more effort on the reader's part to root out the source of a particular idea or statistic. This section is arranged by chapter, with key words in boldface type introducing each notation.

Publishing information for book citations is given in brackets in the form: (City of Publication: Publisher, Year). Suggested readings are noted with the symbol (☞).

Abbreviations in boldface are commonly cited sources, which are listed below. KEY stands for key statistics, listed on the next page.

I have included numerous citations from the *Canadian Global Almanac* and the *Canada Yearbook*, even when original Statistics Canada sources are cited, as these references are more easily and widely available.

Where there are numerical discrepancies between the main text and the notes, the notes are accurate to sources. Figures in the main text have often been rounded to keep their level of precision to that which can be justified.

Readers are warned that the notes contain a lot of the kind of economic jargon I have railed against in the main text. Unfortunately, if I am to defend myself against the multitude of tunnel-visioned economists who will wish to dismiss this book, I must speak their language.

Frequently Cited References

BCD: ☛ *Behind Closed Doors: How the Rich Won Control of Canada's Tax System* by Linda McQuaig (Toronto: Viking, 1987). An excellent summary of tax issues in Canada.

BOC: ☛ *Betrayal of Canada* by Mel Hurtig (Toronto: Stoddart, 1992). A scathing, well-documented indictment of current government policies.

CGA: *Canadian Global Almanac: A Book of Facts* by John Robert Columbo (Toronto: Macmillan, 1992).

CYB: *Canada Yearbook 1992* from Statistics Canada (Ottawa: Statistics Canada, 1992).

FCG: ☛ *For the Common Good: Redirecting the Economy Toward Community, the Environment, and a Sustainable Future* by Herman E. Daly and John B. Cobb (Boston: Beacon Press, 1989). A community economics primer which ably demolishes some old economic truths — albeit in an academic style.

HTH: ☛ *Head to Head* by Lester Thurow (New York: William Morrow, 1992). Thurow offers intelligent and articulate economics with tunnel-vision — looking at the global economy without any real analysis of what's wrong.

KEY: Stands for the Key Statistics that follow.

PEA: *Planning Environment Assessment Document* from Canada Employment and Immigration (Ottawa: Supply & Services, 1988).

TOA: ☛ *The Overworked American: The Unexpected Decline of Leisure* by Juliet B. Shor (New York: Basic Books, 1991). Shor is strong in itemizing what has gone wrong, but skimpy in prescription.

Key Statistics

Canadian population: 27,297,000 in 1991, from **CGA**, p. 40.

Numbers of households: 10 million Canadian households, from p. 16, StatsCan's *Household Facilities and Equipment 1992* (Ottawa: Statistics Canada, 1992).

Average family income: $53,535 in 1992, from **CGA**, p. 234.

Tax costs per family: Are based on the average family paying out 44% of their income in direct and indirect taxes, from **CGA**, p. 234.

Dollar conversions: Estimates which convert dollars to 1992 Dollars are based on the chart in **CGA**, p. 230.

Total government tax revenues: Are based on Statistics Canada's *National Income and Expenditure Accounts, 1980-91* (Ottawa: Statistics Canada, 1992), p. 49, which show direct taxes on individuals for 1991 of $136 billion, indirect taxes of $95 billion, and corporate taxes of $14 billion for a total of $245 billion. Of that total, all federal taxes made up $108 billion, and federal and provincial income taxes totalled $126 billion.

Official labour force: Statistic Canada's *The Labour Force for November 1992* (Ottawa: Statistics Canada, 1992) listed 10,194,000 Canadians as full-time employed, 2,059,000 as part timers (for a total of 12,253,000 employed) and 1,645,000 unemployed, for a total official labour force of 13,898,000. The given participation rate of 65.6% gives a total of 7,288,000 not in the labour force and a working age population of 21,186,000.

1. The Dream That Disappeared

Arthur Clarke quote: From p. v, *Yesterday's Future* (cited below).

The future as seen from the past: Reading predictions on "The Future" from the 1960s, it is clear that we were entranced by technology. Our faith in technology now seems naive. Much was written about how technology would make our lives easier, and almost nothing about the practical mechanisms of change. A good resource is ☛ *Yesterday's Future: Past Visions of the American Future* by Joseph Corn and B. Horrigan (New York: Summit Books, 1984).

3-day workweek: Early visions of the future were starry-eyed, as described by Robert Kahn in *Work and Health* (New York: Wiley, 1981): "In the years immediately following World War II, the introduction of automated machines and the increasing use of the computer generated a vision of a world without work." Optimistic scenarios for the future continued until the early 1970s. From p. 136 of *The Future of Work and Leisure* by Stanley Parker (London: MacGibbon and Kee, 1971), we have the following: "A second development making for a revaluation of work and leisure is the reduction of working hours which the mass of people may expect. Estimates of the probable rate of reduction vary but few question the general direction of the trend." From p. 152 of the same volume: "One optimistic estimate for Germany is that, assuming no increase in the 1968 level of the gross domestic product, a 4.5% average annual growth rate of productivity could make possible by 1985 a halving of the weekly hours and half the year as paid leave." In *Work and Leisure in Canada*, edited by S.M.A. Hameed and D. Cullen (Edmonton: University of Alberta, 1971) reference is made on p. 33 to the "leisure problem" that shorter hours may create. On p. 129, we have: "the workweek could fall to 22 hours by 1985."

Number of breadwinners per family: From **CGA**, p. 85, "In 1989, less than one third of Canadian households relied on a single income." From **TOA**, p. 29, two thirds of married women are now in the labour force, up from 20% in 1948.

Productivity doubled: From **TOA**, p. 2 — quoted for U.S. in 1948, but the economies are similar enough it makes a good ball park figure. See also the section on Increasing Productivity in the notes for Chapter 5. Output/hour for industrial and manufacturing sectors has risen much faster than the workforce as a whole, at something close to 3% per year, and many economists feel this is a more accurate indicator of the real potential for shorter hours. Compounded growth of 3% per year means that a 1992 industrial worker produces 2.5 as much output/hour as their 1960s counterpart. At this rate, a 1992 worker working 3 days per week could produce 1.5 times as much as their 1960s counterpart on a 5-day workweek.

2-day workweek: The output/hour of all Canadian workers grew at an annual rate of 1.2 between 1960 and 1990, according to the Organization for Economic Cooperation and Development figures given in **BOC**, p. 112. If we compound 1.2% through the 23 years from 1970 to 1993, the cumulative growth in productivity is 30%. Working 40% as many hours by twice as many workers working at 1.3 times the hourly output would give 1.04 times the average weekly output today as in 1970.

CMHA books: *Work and Well-being: The Changing Realities of Employment* authored by the Canadian Mental Health Association (Toronto: CMHA, 1984), and *Unemployment: Its Impact on Body and Soul* by Sharon Kirsh (Toronto: CMHA, 1983).

Work Well: Mailing address is Box 3483, Courtenay, B.C. V9N 6Z8. Phone (604) 334-0998. Work Well published the first edition of *Put Work In Its Place* (Victoria: Work Well Publications, 1988).

Life is harsher because we didn't let it get easier: In *The Next Left* (New York: Henry Holt, 1986), Michael Harrington skirts this idea.

Economists: It is unfair to tar all economists with the same brush. Herman Daly, on p. 138 of **FCG**, makes the following observation: "Aristotle made a very important distinction between 'oikonomia' and 'chrematistics.' Chrematistics . . . can be defined as the branch of political economy relating to the manipulation of property and wealth so as to maximize short-term monetary exchange value to the owner. Oikonomia, by contrast, is the management of the household so as to increase its use value to all members of the household over the long run. It appears in modern usage the academic discipline of economics is much closer to chrematistics than to oikonomia." Most modern economists should properly be referred to as chrematists. Within the socially responsible definition of economics associated with oikonomia, we might include such practitioners as Hazel Henderson, E.F. Shumacher, Kenneth Boulding and Robert Heilbroner, Michael Mascall, Johan Schuyff and David Weston.

Pogo quote: The famous Walt Kelly cartoon quote is in fact a tongue-in-cheek corruption of a quote by Oliver Perry at the battle of Lake Erie in 1813: "We have met the enemy, and they are ours."

End of slavery: The argument has been made (by Eric Williams, among others) that slavery ended for economic reasons rather than social justice reasons. My belief is that social pressure caused slave owners to rethink the economics of slavery and seek out other arrangements. Our current economic structuring benefits no-one in the long run — and, undoubtedly, after social pressure has caused it to change, historians in the distant future will claim that the changes were made in the economic self-interest of participants.

2. The Stress and Pain Triangle

David Vice quote: From p. 8 of Linda McQuaig's ☛ *The Quick and the Dead* (Toronto: Viking, 1991).

Numbers of employed mothers: From **CYB**, p. 146: 73% of mothers of school-age children are working.

Time-poor families: The imbalance of the modern lifestyle is nicely summed up by a Canadian Press article entitled "More Time for Job, Less for Children," from the Victoria *Times-Colonist* of March 10, 1989 (p. C3). "Most business people are working longer hours and spending less time with their children, a survey by a Vancouver company indicates. A study by Priority Management Systems Ltd. found 75% of 1000 business people surveyed worked more than 45 hours per week and 44% spent fewer than two hours a week with their children." From **TOA**, p. 1, Americans now have only 16.5 hours of leisure per week. See also ☛ *When the Bough Breaks: The Cost of Neglecting Our Children* by Sylvia Ann Hewlett (Cambridge, Mass.: Harvard University Press, 1991) and *Second Shift* by Arlie Hochschild (New York: Viking, 1989).

Typical adult workload: According to **TOA**, the typical (single breadwinner) family of the 1950s spent 39.9 hours on employment (p. 79) and 52 hours on housework (p. 87) for an average of 46 hours. In the late 1980s the typical two-job family spent 80.8 hours on employment (p. 30) and 49 hours on housework (p. 87) for an average of 65 hours. In *Second Shift*, Arlie Hochschild presents evidence that women usually carry a greater share of the domestic load even when the job hours of both spouses are comparable. In **TOA** Shor estimates that, including housework, employed mothers now work an average of 70 hours per week.

High-stress lifestyle: See the section on family mental health in the author's *Work and Family Employment Policy: A Selected Bibliography* (Victoria: Work Well Publications, 1990). See Ellen Galinsky's ☞ *Family Life and Corporate Policies* (New York: Families and Work Institute, 1986), "How America has run out of time" in *Time* magazine, April 24, 1989, pp. 48-55, and *The Politics and Reality of Family Care in America* by John Fernandez (Lexington, Mass.: Lexington, 1990).

Working harder: TOA, p. 29, reports that the work year for the average worker in America has increased by 168 hours since 1969 (approximately 3 hours per week). **TOA**, p. 2, reports: "U.S. manufacturing employees currently work 320 more hours [per year] . . . than their counterparts in West Germany or France."

Working: By Studs Terkel (New York: Avon Books, 1983).

One in six in poverty: From StatsCan's *Income Distributions by Size in Canada 1991*. 4,227,000 Canadians or 16% of Canada's population live in families with incomes below the poverty line.

Emotional cost: For a good overview of the human impact of unemployment in Canada, see ☞ *Unemployment: Its Impact on Body and Soul* by Sharon Kirsh (Toronto: CMHA, 1983).

Brenner statistic and calculation: In "The Influence of the Social Environment on Psychopathology: The Historical Perspective" in *Stress and Mental Disorder* edited by J.E. Barrett (New York: Raven, 1979), pp. 141-169, Brenner found that an increase in unemployment of 1 million persons over a 5-year period could be expected to result in an additional 63,000 admissions to psychiatric wards. If we are to consider the annual toll on Canada's 1.64 million unemployed, it works out as 63,000 x 1.64/5 = 20,000.

Disposable diapers statistic: In "Durable Not Disposable" from p. 60 of the Winter/Spring 1991 issue of *Women & Environments* magazine, we have the figure of 7,000 diapers per child. At 7 ounces per diaper that works out to over 3000 pounds.

Environmental crises: All of these crises are outlined in more detail in ☞ *The Canadian Green Consumer Guide* by Pollution Probe (Toronto: McClelland & Stewart, 1989). The cancer statistic is from p. 4 of that book. See also ☞ *A Matter of Survival* by Anita Gordon and David Suzuki (Toronto: Stoddart, 1990).

3. The Financial Costs We All Pay

John Ward Pearson quote: From *The Eight-Day Week* (New York: Harper & Row, 1973).

Decline in wages: Developing a meaningful statistic on wages is fraught with perils. If we measure changes in the average wage of all Canadian workers, it overstates the decline relative to particular occupations, as an increase in low-paying service jobs is responsible for much of the decline. If we measure wage settlements only in the industrial sector, it understates the impact of recent economic changes on the average Canadian worker. Settlements for specific occupational niches are most easily available from union contract agreements — but the unionized workforce is more able to protect itself from falling wages than non-unionized workers are. We can get some guideposts however. The Ministry of Finance's *Quarterly Economic Review* of June 1991 (Ottawa: Supply and Services, 1991) gives both inflation and unionized wage rates for the period 1978-90. By these estimates, wages have fallen only 0.7% behind inflation. StatsCan's *Canadian Economic Observer Historical Supplement 1991/1992* gave an average hourly wage of $9.85 for 1983 and $13.33 for 1991. Converted to 1992 dollars these are $14.18 and $13.46 respectively, for a 5% drop in the average wage over 8 years. From *Canadian Jobs and Firm Size: Do Smaller Firms Pay Less?* by René Morrisette (Ottawa: StatsCan, 1991) we have the information that large firms paid an average of $13.55 per hour and small firms only $8.85. *Time* magazine, September 28, 1992, p. 18, comparing private, hourly, U.S. non-farm wages from 1972 to 1992, reports: "Adjusted for inflation, wages are down 13%." From **HTH**, p. 53: "Between 1973 and 1990 America's real per capita GNP rose 28%, yet the real hourly wages for non-supervisory workers . . . fell 12%, and real weekly wages fell 18%. . . . In the late 1980s and the early 1990s real hourly wages were declining at one percent per year." Even if we assume wages are falling faster in the less-unionized U.S., estimating a 10% decline in wages in Canada likely underestimates the loss.

Increases in productivity: The output/hour of all Canadian workers grew at an annual rate of 1.2% between 1960 and 1990 according to OECD figures given in **BOC**, p. 112. Compounded over a 15-year period this works out as 20%. (This figure probably understates the true increase in productivity because it is pushed downwards both by chronic overcapacity — and the inefficiency which that causes — and by a workforce shift from manufacturing to the service sector.)

25% less work: On the surface, we would expect to need 30% less work if wages went up 20% instead of down 10%, but percentages change when we change the base figure. To earn 90% as much, working at wage rates 20% higher would require 90/120 times as much time, or 75% of the current workweek. Measured against current income, the percentage is more impressive: workers should be paid 120%/90%, or one third more.

10 hours per week for free: 25% x 40 hours = 10 hours/week.

Real, after-tax income: StatsCan's *Income After Tax, Distributions by Size in Canada 1992* gave 1980 average family after-tax income as $44,525. The corresponding figure in 1991 was $42,612 (Both figures in 1991 dollars) for a drop in real income of 4.2%.

Cost of UIC contributions: The term "unemployment insurance" is, to my mind, misleading in that employees have no option about whether or not to buy this insurance coverage. (Provincial health insurance plans, in contrast, allow individuals to choose whether to buy medical insurance.) UIC is a *de facto* tax on the working population. Government pays for the costs of short-term unemployment through a levy on wages of the working population. The employee contribution to UIC is now 3.0% of wages, and the employer contribution is 4.2% of income (both statistics from **CGA**, p. 163). If we consider that the employer's contribution would otherwise go towards a worker's salary, the two contributions together amount to 7.2% of 104.2% or 6.9% of employee's wages. Workers earning over $25,000 per year would pay a somewhat lower percentage due to the ceiling on UIC contributions.

Average cost of UIC: From **CGA**, p. 163, total UI benefits paid out were $17.7 billion. If we assume an overhead of 20% for administering the system (including employer's administration costs) this raises the figure to $21 billion. Dividing $21 billion by 10 million households gives $2100. On an average income of $53,535 (see **KEY**) this represents almost 4% of income.

Proportion of B.C. on welfare: The number of people in B.C. on welfare rose to more than 10% of the population in the spring of 1992. From "Joblessness a Fixture, Minister Fears" on p. A1 of the Vancouver *Sun* of June 6, 1992, we have "One in ten British Columbians now depend on social assistance." Furthermore "the number on welfare has nearly doubled since 1982" and the province spends "$2.3 billion" on welfare. In "The Wilson Depression" in *Canadian Forum*, December 1992, Duncan Cameron offers the statistic that 2.6 million Canadians are now on welfare — 9% of Canada's population. Expenditures on welfare have risen dramatically. Figures derived from **CGA** show:

	1970	1991
Federal welfare payments	$456 million	$6602 million
In constant 1992 dollars	$1,883 million	$6668 million
Including prov./munic. costs	$3766 million	$13,336 million
Per capita cost	$174	$488

Even correcting for inflation and population growth, welfare costs have more than doubled in the past 21 years.

Cost of welfare and UIC: Individual contributions towards UIC and welfare taxes will vary somewhat depending on income level, number of deductions, and province of residence. Welfare costs are spread between federal, provincial, and municipal taxes, so they are difficult to itemize exactly in the form of individual taxes. However, we can work backwards to an approximate figure by calculating welfare costs per household in Canada. From **CGA**, pp. 162-163, we have welfare payments for 1990 of $6.6 billion, or $13.2 billion if we include matching funds for the provinces/municipalities. Adding 20% for administration costs would bring this total to $15.8 billion. From **KEY**, we have 10 million Canadian households, or $1580 per household. Given an average family income of $53,535 (see **KEY**) this represents $1580/$53,535 = 3%. Added to the 4% of income that goes out for UIC, this sums to 7% of income. On a 40-hour week 7% translates to 2.8 hours.

Second breadwinner expenses: The North Island *News* did a survey to come up with comparable data for Canada, and released its results in their February 3, 1991, issue. For a second spouse to return to work in a family where the primary wage earner is making $30,000 per year, the first $14,260.57 of the second salary goes out in additional expenses. Child care, at $7958.40, was the largest single item.

Average cost of second breadwinner: Costs of $14,260.57, measured against an average family income of $53,535, works out as 26% of total family income. To remove taxes from that total, we must remove the 44% of income that goes towards taxes from that 26%, or 11%, leaving 15%. Actual non-tax family costs will vary depending on income levels, and whether the family has daycare costs, usually running in the range of 5%-15% of family income. There is no good way that I have found to come up with an average figure, but if we consider that roughly half of Canadian households are dual-breadwinner, and that this group spends an average of 10% of its income on the non-tax costs of having two breadwinners, that would reduce to 5% of income averaged against all households.

Educational inflation: See Lester Thurow's "Education and Economic Equality," in *The 'Inequality' Controversy: Schools and Distributive Justice* edited by Donald Levine and M. J. Bane (New York: Basic, 1975).

Cost of education: From **CGA**, p. 75, we see the following:

	1975	1992
Total education costs	$11.0 billion	$50.6 billion
In 1992 dollars	$32.2 billion	$50.6 billion
Per capita	$1405	$1825

Education costs rose 30% faster than inflation and population growth in the period from 1975 to 1992. Total educational expenditures of $50.6 billion amount to $5060 per Canadian household (based on 10 million households — see **KEY**). If roughly 20% of this figure went to added costs associated with high unemployment, this would be $1012 per family, or just under 2% of average family income of $53,535. Two percent of a 40-hour workweek is 48 minutes.

Brenner data: See "Estimating the social costs of national economic policy: Implications for mental and physical health and criminal aggression," by M. Harvey Brenner (Report to the Joint Economic Commission, Congress of the United States, 1976). From Brenner's book *Mental Illness and the Economy* (Cambridge, Mass.: Harvard University Press, 1973), p. ix, "Instabilities in the national economy are the most important source of fluctuation in mental hospital admissions." Also, from "The Death of Leisure" in the *Globe & Mail* of May 25, 1991, we have a health statistic from the overwork experts: "An estimated 10,000 Japanese a year die of karoshi — death by overwork — roughly the same number as die in traffic accidents."

Brenner quantitative data: In "The Impact of Social and Industrial Changes on Psychopathology" in *Society, Stress and Disease* edited by Lennart Levi (New York: Oxford University Press, 1981), p. 47, we have data suggesting that a 10% rise in the unemployment rate will lead to:

💧 a 19% increase in heart disease mortality,

💧 a 19% increase in cirrhosis of the liver,

💧 a 41% increase in the suicide rate,

💧 a 57% increase in the homicide rate,

💧 a 34% increase in mental hospital admissions, and

💧 a 40% increase in prison admissions.

Personal cost of health care estimate: On p. 2 of *The Health Care System in Canada and Its Funding: No Easy Solutions* (Ottawa: Supply and Services, 1991) Bob Porter reports 1990 health care costs of $60.2 billion dollars, or about $6000 for each of 10 million Canadian households. Thirty percent of that would be $1800 per household, or $1800/$53,535 = 3.4%. On a 40-hour workweek, this is just under 1.5 hours.

Brenner data: See the Brenner article cited above.

Second highest incarceration rate: See "U.S. Leads the World in Jail Population" in *The Futurist*, July 1991, p. 47.

Prisoner rate data: From **CGA**, p. 169, there were 2.8 million (non-traffic) crimes in Canada in 1991. In 1990 there were almost 30,000 prisoners in federal and provincial jails at any given time. Property crimes increased by 9% from 1990 to 1991. In 1975, there were 861 prisoners for every 100,000 Canadians. By 1990, the rate had risen to 1075, an increase of 25%.

Prison cost data: From **CYB**, pp. 256 and 261, we see that Canada spent $1.47 billion on corrections programs, of which 79% was spent on prison-related costs. For Canada's 29,154 prisoners, this divides out to $39,833 per prisoner per year.

Cost of crime: From StatsCan's *The Daily* of October 23, 1992, we have total policing costs of $5.3 billion dollars in Canada. From *The Daily* of December 3, 1992, we have total corrections expenditures of $1.8 billion, for a total of $7.1 billion.

Per capita crime costs: If we conservatively estimate the costs of crime itself as matching the $7.1 billion we spend fighting crime, and then take 40% of that amount as the portion which Brenner's research would attribute to a 10% unemployment rate, and divide by 10 million Canadian households, this works out as: ($7.1 billion x 2 x .40)/10 million = $568 per household. This is 1% of average family income, or 25 minutes/week.

World defence spending: From the *Universal Almanac 1990* edited by John Wright (New York: Andrews & McMeel, 1989), p. 534, total world military expenditures are quoted as exceeding $1 trillion per year since 1987.

Canadian defence spending: From **CGA**, p. 181, Canadian military expenses in 1991 were $12.3 billion, out of total federal tax revenues of $109 billion (see **KEY**). This works out as 12.3/109 or 11% of all federal taxes.

Per capita cost: If the end of the Cold War represents an opportunity to cut our military budget in half, this would represent a savings of 50% of $12.3 billion, or $6.15 billion. For 10 million households, this represents $615 each, or $615/$53,535 = 1.15% of average income. Expressed as a proportion of a 40-hour workweek, this is 28 minutes.

High prices: The inefficiencies brought about by overcapacity would have probably pushed prices higher still if debt-induced exports of raw materials from the Third World had not pushed down world commodity prices (see Chapter 9).

High prices calculation: In 1992, businesses worked at an average 78% of capacity (see "Symptoms of Overcapacity" in the notes for Chapter 6). This means companies carried 22% of their overhead as wasted capacity. If, as a ball park figure, 25% of the selling price of an item represents overhead costs, this wasted overhead could be expected to add 5.5% (22% x 25%) to the cost of most items. Purchases of goods and services make up only part of individual family expenses. However, higher taxes result when government must pay more for its purchases due to high prices. Being conservative, let's consider only the portion of the family income that does not go to taxes or housing. (Taxes make up 44% of average income, and non-tax housing costs about another 20% — leaving about 36%) Prices 5.5% higher on the 36% of family income that doesn't go to housing or taxes is 5.5% x 36% = 2% of family income. Multiplying 2% x 40 hours = 48 minutes.

The money illusion: See *The Penguin Dictionary of Economics* by Baxter and Rees (Harmondsworth: Penguin, 1978). (Thanks to David Weston, an environmental economist at Simon Fraser University, for this and many other ideas!)

Inflated housing costs: From CGA, p. 241, we have the following:

	1975	1989
Average resale price of Canadian homes	$47,201	$148,737
In constant 1992 dollars	$137,354	$166,585

Real estate prices ran 21% ahead of inflation over the period from 1975 to 1989. Robert C. Beckman in *The Downwave: Surviving the Second Great Depression* (London: Pan Books, 1983) on p. 189, using U.S. data, reports: "Between 1950 and 1980 the average [land] plot price rose from $1060 to over $30,000, an increase of around 30 times, whereas the debasement of the currency measured by consumer prices was only 3.4 times." In real dollars, U.S. land prices increased in value eightfold over the 30-year period.

Per capita cost of inflated housing costs: If we were to estimate that real estate costs have doubled in the past 30 years in real dollars, an average 1992 home costing $150,000, should cost $75,000. Amortized over 50 years of home ownership, this amounts to ($75,000/50) or $1500 per year. $1500 as a percentage of average family income is $1500/$53,535 or 2.8% of average family income.

Advertising costs as a portion of selling price: In *Canadian Advertising in Action* (Scarborough, Ont.: Prentice-Hall, 1988) Keith Tugwell reports that advertising revenues grew by 8.8% per year through the early 1980s, and were worth $6.7 billion in 1986. In 1992 dollars this translates to $8.6 billion, or $860 for each of Canada's 10 million households. If we make the supposition that only one third of this advertising would be necessary in a healthy economy, unnecessary advertising represents $570 per household, or $570/$53,535 = 1% of average family income. If we estimate that excessive advertising causes the average family to spend another 2% of its income on products that are unneeded or unnecessarily expensive (including excessive packaging), this would raise the total to 3%.

Rapid inflation: From CGA, p. 180, the inflation rate for the decade running from 1973-83 averaged 9.2%.

Mortgage calculation: My handy, dandy computer mortgage program shows that a $50,000 mortgage, amortized over 20 years, compounded monthly, at 14% interest will cost $99,222.34 in interest charges. The same mortgage at 8% interest only costs $50,372.99. Higher interest rates thus cost an additional $48,849.35 in interest charges over the life of the mortgage.

Cost per family of high interest rates: StatsCan's *The Daily* of November 23, 1992, gave personal debts of $431 billion for Canadians — or $43,100 for each of our 10 million households. If we consider that most of that debt is at 10% interest or better, and that a fair rate would be closer to 7%, we can estimate the average annual cost per family at 3% x $43,100 = $1293. This is $1293/$53,535 = 2.4% of average family income.

High interest charges on public debt: From **BOC**, p. 126, "In 1991, all governments in Canada spent more than $65 billion paying the interest charges on their debts." Dividing this figure by 10 million Canadian households works out to $6,500. The public debt is held at average interest rates of about 10%. If it were at a more reasonable 7%, the per household cost of the public debt would drop from $6500 to $4,550. High interest charges on the public debt thus cost $1950 per household, or $1,950/53,535 = 3.6% of the average family income. Given that our annual government deficits only cover about $5,000 of the $6,500 in annual interest charges, we can consider that most of this $1,950 is actually paid out in higher taxes rather than being rolled over into more debt.

2.5 hours per week: If we add the 2.4% of family income paid out in high interest rates on consumer loans, to the 3.6% paid out on the public debt, it totals 6% of average family income. Six percent of 40 hours = 2 hours and 24 minutes.

Interest charges per household: From **BOC**, p. 126, "In 1991, all governments in Canada spent more than $65 billion paying the interest charges on their debts." Dividing this figure by 10 million Canadian households works out as $6500.

Per household cost of debt charges: With the $4,550/household figure above, taken against average family income of $53,535, debt charges (even after assigning 30% of the cost to high interest rates) amounted to $4,550/53,535 = 8.5% of average family income.

Deficit levels: For 1992, the budgeted federal deficit was about $29 billion, and combined provincial deficits at about $21 billion, for a grand total of $50 billion. (Provincial deficit figure from StatsCan's *The Daily*, October 26, 1992.) On a per household basis, this works out as $50 billion/10 million = $5000. Since this figure is more than the per household share of the debt charges, we can consider that interest payments on the public debt have been deferred in the form of increases in the public debt (excluding that which we earlier assigned against high interest rates).

Deficit/tax rate: Measured against total income tax revenues of $126 billion (see **KEY**), a combined deficit of $50 billion represents 50/126 = 40% of current income taxes.

Type of cost chart: Percentages in this chart are all taken from the notes for relevant sections of this chapter, with some rounding.

The full cost to your wage dollar: This chart can be expected to give only a ballpark picture, given that spending patterns (and work patterns) would be considerably different if Canadian salaries had risen to reflect productivity increases, rather than declining.

4. The True Scope of Unemployment

Benjamin Disraeli quote: From p. 8 of *Write Right* by Jan Venolia (North Vancouver: Self-Counsel Press, 1992).

Official unemployment rate: The *Globe & Mail*, December 5, 1992, reported an unemployment rate of 11.8%, or 1.64 million.

Maritimes equivalent calculation: From **CGA**, p. 40, we can determine that 66%

of the Canadian population is between ages 16 and 65. The populations of the four maritime provinces (also in **CGA**) total 2,522,000; 66% of this is 1.66 million.

Canada Employment's means of determining unemployment: Information from Statistics Canada's *Methodology of the Canadian Labour Force Survey 1984-1990* (Ottawa: StatsCan, 1990) and updated from a 1992 Labour Force Survey participant's brochure.

Dispirited workers: From StatsCan's *Historical Labour Force Statistics* we have a participation rate for males of 79.8% in 1966. According to *The Labour Force*, by November 1992 men's participation rate had fallen to 73.8%. In "Unemployment and Opportunity Lost" from *Perspectives* of Autumn 1990, Barry George reports that OECD analysis shows the labour force participation rate drops 0.83% for each 1% rise in the unemployment rate — which is the equivalent of 10,000 to 15,000 people leaving the workforce for each 10,000 added to the unemployment rolls. In **TOA**, p. 28, Shor reports that in a survey of men between the ages 55 and 64 who are "not in the labour force," almost half would prefer to be working. From the OECD's *Labour Force Statistics 1968-1987* (Paris: OECD, 1989) we have participation rates for the population from ages 15-64 for 1988 of 76.9% for Canada, and 85.8% for Sweden. One might expect that a good part of the discrepancy is that Canada has more dispirited workers. Finally, a front-p. *Globe & Mail* article of December 5, 1992, stated that the proportion of the population over 16 in the official workforce fell from 69.2% to 65.6% (a drop of 3.6%) in the period from 1990 to 1992. (This translates to 750,000 people leaving the labour force during a period when an additional 500,000 were added to the unemployment rolls.) The article went on to suggest that much of this group represents an increase in the number of discouraged workers.

Dispirited worker considerations and calculations: From *A Shorter Workweek in the 1980s* by William McGaughey (White Bear Lake: Thistlerose Publications, 1981) we have information on a U.S. Bureau of Labor Statistics follow-up survey of people "not in the labour force." It found that 19.4% had at least tried to get into the labour force one year later. McGaughey gives 13% as a "conservative" estimate of the proportion of the "not in the labour force" category who would prefer to be working. Thirteen percent of the 7,288,000 Canadians "not in the labour force" (see **KEY**) factors out as 940,000 people.

As an alternative way of arriving at a similar estimate, there were 1.4 million Canadians receiving UIC in May 1992 (see StatsCan's *Canadian Economic Observer*, August 1992). In the same month, there were about 1.5 million Canadians of working age collecting welfare, for a total of 2.9 million. This is 1.3 million higher than the official unemployment rate. If we estimate that one third of those on welfare or UIC are unable to work because of infirmity, maternity or infant care responsibilities, this again leaves about 900,000 Canadians as discouraged workers. The rate could be higher still: if we extrapolate the OECD findings back to a zero unemployment rate — and subtract reluctant students and the scarcely employed — we're left with 1.4 million dispirited workers.

Involuntary student rate estimates: There is at least some external confirmation for my anecdotal impressions. In an article from the *Globe & Mail*, November 19, 1992, p. D2, entitled "Universities Set New Enrolment Records," we have the following: "Both men and women have been going to university part time in growing numbers and returning to school after years in the workforce. The current recession has intensified the trend."

Doug Higgins quote: From the article above.

Proportion of adult population in school: From **CGA**, p. 74, 1991 full-time enrolment in colleges and universities was 878,000 students, representing 4.9% of the 18 million Canadians between ages 16 and 65. Twenty percent of 878,000 is 176,000 people.

Working Harder Isn't Working

Percentage of marginal part-time work: In ☛ *Part-Time Employment: Labour Market Flexibility and Equity Issues* (Kingston, Ont.: Industrial Relations Centre, 1988), Mary Lou Coates reports that 42% of part timers work 14 hours per week or less. From **KEY** we have 2,059,000 part timers in an official workforce of 13,898,000 (14.8%); 42% of this is 865,000 workers, or 6.2% of the workforce.

Percentage of involuntary part-time work: From StatsCan's *The Labour Force* of November 1992, we have 613,000 involuntary part time out of 2,137,000 part timers, or 29%. Taking 29% of the 865,000 who work less than 14 hours per week gives 251,000 involuntary, marginal part timers — 1.8% of the official workforce.

Unemployed group chart: To an official workforce of 13,898,000 (see **KEY**) we must add 940,000 discouraged workers and 176,000 involuntary students, for a total true workforce of 15,014,000. Expressed as a proportion of the true workforce we have:

Officially unemployed	1,645,000	11.0%
Discouraged workers	940,000	6.3%
Involuntary students	176,000	1.2%
Involuntary part-time	251,000	1.7%
Total Unemployed	3,012,000	20.1%

(You'll notice that percentages change slightly when measured against a true workforce which is larger than the official one. I have left numbers unchanged in the main text for ease of understanding.)

Six provinces metaphor: From **CGA**, p. 40, the total population of P.E.I., Newfoundland, Nova Scotia, New Brunswick, Manitoba, and Saskatchewan is 4.6 million — multiplied by 66% (see **CGA** p. 41) for the working age population, is 3.0 million.

Depression unemployment: from StatsCan's *The Daily*, Sept 8, 1992.

Economic Policy Institute statistic: From *Time* magazine, September 28, 1992, p. 19.

Seasonal/cyclical employment estimate: From StatsCan's *The Labour Force* of November 1992 we have 972,000 Canadians in the construction industry, of which 713,000 were employed. If we add in fishing, logging, and seasonal hospitality work, it is probably a good estimate that 1 million Canadians are involved in seasonal or cyclical unemployment — roughly 6% of the workforce. From StatsCan's *The Daily* of November 23, 1992, we have the statistic of 2.9 million temporary layoffs of Canadian workers per year.

Minimum-wage employment: In "Sinful Wages: minimum wages haven't kept pace with average wages and they're falling further below the poverty line" in *Perception*, Summer 1991, Melanie Hess reports that provincial minimum wages fell between 10 and 26% behind inflation in the past 10 years. One in twelve workers earns the minimum wage at some point in the year. The reported average minimum wage of $5.14/hour was listed at 69.8% of the poverty line, from which we may assume an average poverty line wage of $7.36. From Ernest Akyampong's "Working for the Minimum Wage" in StatsCan's *Perspectives* for Autumn, 1989, we have statistics that 1,180,00 Canadians were working at the minimum wage or less, and a further 1,151,000 worked at wages within $1 of the minimum wage — below the poverty line in most of Canada. 46% of those on the minimum wage worked part time, so, assuming a similar rate of part-time employment for those working at near the minimum wage, we have (1,180,000 + 1,151,000) x 54% = 1,258,000 people — more than 8% of the workforce.

Rate of involuntary underemployment: In *Part-Time Employment: Labour Market*

Flexibility and Equity Issues (Kingston, Ont.: Industrial Relations Centre, 1988), Mary Lou Coates reports that 58% of part timers work between 14 and 29 hours per week, and that 30% are involuntarily underemployed. From **KEY** we have 2,059,000 part timers out of an official workforce of 13,898,000 (14.8%): 58% of this group works out as 1,194,000 workers, or 6.2% of the workforce. Thirty percent of the remainder is 358,000, or another 2.6% of the official workforce.

Self employment: From StatsCan's 1988 publication *Enterprising Canadians: The Self-Employed in Canada*, we have the following: 1,556,000 out of a labour force of 11,634,000 were self-employed in 1986 (13.4% of labour force), 19.8% of them made less than $5000 per year, 15.8% made between $5000 and $10,000 per year, and 40% of Canada's self-employed work 50 or more hours per week. A 1986 income of $10,000 equals $12,900 in 1992 dollars, well below the poverty line in Canada, so we have 19.8% + 15.8% = 35.6% of entrepreneurs with poverty level incomes. Taking 13.4 % of today's official workforce of 13,898,000 and then taking 35.6% of the remainder leaves us with 680,000 people, or 4.5% of the workforce — which is conservative, given the rapid growth in self-employment.

Distressed group chart: Expressed as a proportion of the true workforce of 15,014,000, we have:

Actual unemployed	3,012,000	20.1%
Seasonal work	1,000,000	6.6%
Low wages	1,225,000	8.1%
Underemployed	358,000	2.4%
Non-viably self-employed	680,000	4.5%
Aggregate total	6,275,000	41.7%
Less overlap	1,225,000	-8.1%
Net total	5,050,000	33.6%

Spin doctors: This is the slang term for public relations specialists — who try to put the right "spin" on every media report.

Government employment statistics: Canada's opposition parties have been remarkably slow to challenge the government on its fictional unemployment figures. However, in NDP MP Robert Skelly's November 1992 householder mailing we have: "Official Canadian unemployment rate in October 1992: 11.4 per cent. The number of Canadians who cannot find work, have given up looking, or want full-time work but can only find part-time jobs: 25 per cent."

PART TWO: WHAT IS THE PROBLEM HERE?

'Fine-tuning': A *Globe & Mail* article of April 21, 1991, p. B5, displays this attitude even in its title: "Wilson set to continue key role in economy: Former finance minister can now turn to fine-tuning."

Northern cod: See "The Northern Cod Crisis: Fighting Back" by Lana Payne, in *Perception*, March 1993.

5. Too Much: The Problem of Overproduction

Balancing production and consumption: Most economists will try to make this balance more complex, but their formulas amount to the same thing if we're looking at the big picture over the long term. A first-year university economics text will give a formula of "Production + Savings = Consumption + Investment + Government." For our purposes here, savings can be considered a stored form of production, and investment and government can be considered a form of consumption — which reduces our basic economic balance to Production = Consumption.

Market valuation: The market model presented here is an ideal — later in the book we'll see how other dynamics can affect prices.

War-time economic measures: See John Kenneth Galbraith's *Money: Whence It Came, Where It Went* (Boston: Houghton, Mifflin, 1975) for a good summary.

Productivity increases: From the *Report of the Business/Labour Task Force on Adjustment*, created by the Canadian Labour Market and Productivity Centre in January 1989, p. 3, we have the following: "Since 1981, output per hour in manufacturing has advanced at a 3% rate [per year]." For the Canadian mining industry: "since 1981, because of technology-driven productivity gains, output per worker has risen by 84%, and employment has fallen by 19%." From Canada's Department of *Finance Quarterly Economic Review* (1991), p. 70, we see a 20% increase in output per person hour from 1975 to 1990.

Doubling every 21 years: 3.3% per year is considered a moderate growth in industrial productivity, and it equates to a doubling every 21 years. See **HTH** p. 165.

Sectoral differences in productivity changes: In most industrial sectors, we see output increases in the range where between one half and one quarter fewer production personnel are required to produce the same number of goods. Sometimes these gains are partially offset by increases in personnel for sales, advertising, etc., but this should be seen as an indirect result of overcapacity, rather than as a function of need. Differences in the service sector are much more difficult to quantify and, again, the inefficiencies created by overcapacity confound attempts at measurement. For all these reasons, increases in overall output can only be measured roughly.

B.C. forest industry statistics: See Bob Nixon's article in the June, 1991 issue of *Forest Planning Canada* which presents forest employment data prepared by Ray Travers.

Desktop publishing: Even desktop publishing is getting more efficient. *Working Harder Isn't Working* was typeset in a few days on a personal computer and laser printer. My previous book, *Put Work In Its Place*, required $5000 worth of desktop publishing services to accomplish the same goal.

Average hourly output: From **TOA**, p. 2: "the level of productivity of U.S. workers has more than doubled since 1948."

New norms on number of breadwinners/family Size: From **PEA**, p. 10, we can see the magnitude of the shift in family patterns. In 1971, 68% of two-parent families had the husband as the sole breadwinner, while 38% had both husband and wife participating in the labour force. By 1986, the figures had practically reversed, with 59.6% of families headed by two breadwinners, and only 40.8% headed by a sole breadwinner.

Average workweek: TOA, p. 29, reports that the work year for the average worker in America has increased by 168 hours since 1969 (approximately 3 hours per week).

Productivity increase examples: The examples given for productivity increases are made for argument rather than being based on actual statistics, but are all in the range of possibility.

Midas World: By Frederik Pohl, (New York: St. Martin's Press, 1983).

Environmental limits: The concept was first introduced by the Club of Rome in *Limits to Growth* by D.H. Meadows, et al. (New York: Universe Books, 1972).

Lighter automobiles: From Hardin Tibbs' "Industrial Ecology: An Environmental Agenda for Industry," published in the Winter 1992 edition of the *Whole*

Earth Review on p. 13, we have the statistic that the average weight of U.S. automobiles dropped 20% from 1975 to 1985. Unfortunately, an assumed 3% annual increase in productivity for auto workers means that the annual tonnage of cars per auto worker is still increasing.

Beyond Oil: By John Gever, et al. (Cambridge, Mass.: Ballinger, 1987).

Techno-optimists: See ☞ *The Resourceful Earth: A Response to Global 2000*, edited by Herman Kahn and Julian Simon (Oxford, UK: Basil Blackwell, 1984) if you want to escape to fantasy land.

Limitations of the free market: For more information on debates within the economic profession, see **FCG** pp. 44-61.

6. Efficient Inefficiency

Low productivity: Lester Thurow notes the effect of excess capacity on efficiency on p. 86 of *Zero-Sum Society* (New York: Basic, 1980).

Overcapacity: The *Globe & Mail* of December 5, 1992, p. B3, "Canada in Brief," reported that the highest capacity utilization of the past decade was 87.1%, reached in 1988. While this figure is designed to measure only industrial output, it is probably not a bad measurement of overcapacity in the economy. If we consider the 8% unemployment of 1988 to be another form of overcapacity, the total level of overcapacity must be on the order of 20%. The two figures cannot directly be summed because many of Canada's factories would require more staff to operate at full capacity. On the other hand, an official unemployment rate of 8% in 1988 probably translated to a real rate of 15%. The *Globe & Mail* article went on to say: "Canadian industry operated at 78.2% of capacity in the third quarter [of 1992] . . . according to Statistics Canada." Stated as a reciprocal, the overcapacity of Canadian industry is 21.8/78.2, or 27.8%. Again, if we add in the wasted productive abilities of the 20% of the Canadian workforce which is unemployed, we may estimate that at least a third of Canada's productive capacity was wasted in 1992. When we change the base figure to current production, wasted capacity represents half of current production.

The Elimination of labour: From *How to Profit From the Next Great Depression*, by John L. King (New York: New American Library, 1988), p. 55: "By the early 1980s about 65% of total investment capital was going for greater technological efficiency (labour displacement) and only 35% for augmenting the capacity upon which living standards depend."

Animal spirits: J. M. Keynes's famous metaphor for confidence.

7. The Unemployment Blues

P. Corrigal quote: This is the title of a chapter in *Work and Leisure*, edited by A.J. Veal (London: Leisure Studies Association, 1982).

Declining wages: See the section on "Declining Hourly Wages" under Chapter 3 in these notes. Speaking to the issue that shifts in the workforce are driving wages lower, from **PEA**, p. 5: "It is worth noting that over 70% of the new jobs (both full-time and part time) created between 1983 and 1986 paid less than $20,000 annually, with over 30% paying less than $10,000."

A modest disclaimer: Declining wages do open up some new employment, at the very bottom of the service sector, in operations which would not be viable if employees were paid a living wage. While this eases the oversupply of labour, it can hardly be considered a cause for rejoicing.

Story of Henry Ford II/UAW leader: Several of my sources have assured me that this story is in one of John Kenneth Galbraith's books, but I have been unable to track it down — so I don't know whether it is real or apocryphal.

The wage/price imbalance: This idea is as old as Karl Marx, and given a good précis on pp. 14-15 of *Cities and the Wealth of Nations* by Jane Jacobs (New York: Random House, 1984). John Maynard Keynes refers to this problem as "the missing markets."

Wages/prices in the 1930s: It would be more accurate to say that wages fell behind productivity before the 1930s, contributing to the onset of the Great Depression, and then fell further behind until the 1940s. Robert C. Beckman in *The Downwave: Surviving the Second Great Depression* (London: Pan Books, 1983), on p. 205, reports: "Labour productivity during the depression rose faster than at any time this century." Wages for those who were working actually grew somewhat during the Depression when adjusted for deflation, but because productivity rose much faster, the gap between what workers were able to produce, and what they could afford to buy, grew larger. As an interesting sidelight, Jack London, better known for nature fiction like *Call of the Wild*, wrote an economics treatise in the form of a novel, *The Iron Heel* (Brooklyn, N.Y.: Lawrence Hill, 1980). In that volume he identifies the disparity between wages and productivity as the source of the Depression.

Economics as a science: In FCG, pp. 25-31, Daly and Cobb make the argument that economics modelled itself on physics — when evolutionary biology was probably a better choice.

Accumulations of wealth: Interestingly, in *The Great Reckoning* (New York: Summit Books, 1991), James Dale Davidson identifies massive accumulations of debt as a major cause of all economic depressions, without making the rather obvious jump that the logical correlate of massive debts is the accumulation of extreme concentrations of wealth. However, when one is writing for those with the money, discretion in such matters is advised.

8. The Inflation Balloon

Lester Thurow quote: From HTH, p. 285.

Theories of inflation: See Chapter 3 of Lester Thurow's ☛ *Zero-Sum Society* (New York: Basic, 1980).

Stagflation: During the recession of 1981-82, despite several months of economic contraction, interest rates remained high — 12.4% in 1981 and 10.9% in 1982 — according to CGA, p. 180.

Inflation in real estate prices: See the note on "Inflated Housing Costs" in the notes on Chapter 3.

Interest rates as a means to control inflation: See Andrew Jackson's *Against John Crow* (Ottawa: Canadian Centre for Policy Alternatives, 1990).

Use value: See FCG, p. 139, for a discussion of the difference between use value and exchange value.

The rich get richer: From BCD, p. 38: the top 10% of Canadians own more than half of the wealth in the country, while the bottom 20% had negative net worth, i.e. they were in the hole. In "Drawing the Line on Inequality" in *Perception*, Winter 1991, p. 40, Barry George reports that the richest 1% of Canadians own 19% of the wealth, and the bottom 34% own only 2%. On p. 2 of *Poverty in Canada* (Ottawa: Library of Parliament, 1992) Helen MacKenzie states: "The poorest 20% of households had the same 5.2% of income in 1981 and 1991. In comparison, the top 20% of households increased their share of the pie from 39.9% to 41.9%. The remaining 60% of households, with incomes between $18,000 and $64,000, suffered a corresponding decline in their share of the national income."

Growing concentration of wealth: In *How to Profit From the Next Great Depression* by John L. King (New York: New American Library, 1988), Patrick Moynihan is quoted (in 1981) as saying, "Interest rate payments represent the largest transfer of wealth in history from wages to capital."

Growing concentration of income: BCD, p. 35, says the top 1% of families had average incomes of $212,000 in 1986. Half of Canadian families earned less than $33,000 in 1986. According to StatsCan's *Income Distributions by Size and Type 1991*, families in the top 20% received 40% of all income and families in the bottom 20% received 6.4% of all income.

Short and long cycles: See Chapter 21, and the notes for same, for more information.

9. The Unravelling of the Global Economy

Keynes quote: Re-quoted from **FCG**, p. 209.

Increased dependence on exports: From the *Report of the Business/Labour Task Force on Adjustment*, created by the Canadian Labour Market and Productivity Centre in January 1989, we have the following quote: "The export share of world production has risen steadily. This trend has been particularly pronounced in Canada with the export share of Gross Domestic Product rising from 18 to 33 percent since 1960 [to 1989]" (p. 2).

Global inflation: The International Monetary Fund's *World Economic Outlook* of May 1992 listed average inflation in all developing countries as 57.8% for 1990.

Currency speculation: From "Confidence Crisis Means Low Dollar, Higher Rates" in the *Globe & Mail*, November 19, 1992, pp. A1-2.

Unwise loans: To the argument made in Chapter 8 that undue accumulations of wealth create the negative result of inflation, we can add the negative result of unwise loans. In the mid-1970s, petrodollars from the Arab states added ᴛᴏ accumulations of financial wealth here until North American banks were swimming in a sea of deposits. To invest those huge deposits they made equally huge loans to Third World countries, for extremely questionable purposes.

Third World debt: This debt stood at $1.2 trillion in 1989 — from p. 171, *State of the World 1991* by Lester Brown (New York: Norton, 1991).

Environmental problems associated with Third World debt: See ☛ *Odious Debts: Loose Lending, Corruption, and the Third World's Environmental Legacy* by Patricia Adams (London: Earthscan, 1991), for good information on the social and environmental damages resulting from the initial loan projects, and from the repayment process.

Writing off the debt: North American banks may have written off most of their Third World debt, but they're still doing their best to collect on the loans — and wrecking the Third World in the process.

Community standards: I borrowed the use of the term in this context from Maude Barlow — I don't know where she got it from.

Guy Dauncey quote: In *After the Crash: The Emergence of the Rainbow Economy* (London: Merlin Press, 1989), p. 28.

Dependent Third World economies: See also **FCG** p. 221.

Transnational hardball: See **BOC** pp. 202-207

EEC management: Distinctions between the EEC and the North American Free Trade Zone are itemized in **BOC** pp. 282-284.

Canada-U.S free trade rules: See Maude Barlow's ☛ *Parcel of Rogues* (Toronto: Key Porter, 1991).

Protectionism: In **HTH**, p. 56, Thurow blames the 1930s depression on protectionism, rather than recognizing protectionism as a necessary response to a pre-existing economic collapse.

Need for rules and coherent policies: Lester Thurow discusses these issues on pp. 55-66 of **HTH**. On p. 111, Thurow asserts that if the Europeans can pull off economic integration, they will become the *de facto* rule makers for the world economy.

Global competition: In **FCG**, pp. 209-235, Daly and Cobb do a wonderful job of demolishing the traditional arguments in favour of free trade. See also John Maynard Keynes's "National Self-Sufficiency" in *The Collected Works of John Maynard Keynes*, volume 21, edited by Donald Moggeridge (London: Macmillan, 1933). On pp. 82-83 of **HTH**, Thurow also offers strong cautions on the pitfalls of free trade — and he is a staunch free trader.

10. Limits on Who Works

Anonymous quote: From Help Wanted ads of long ago.

Married women's participation in the labour force: See "Women in the Labour Force, 1911-1986: A Historical Perspective," by Marsha Courchene and Angela Redish, in *False Promises: The Failure of Conservative Economics* edited by Robert C. Allen and Gideon Rosenbluth (Vancouver: New Star Books, 1992)

25% of married women employed: TOA, p. 25, notes that "even in the 1950s and 1960s, about one quarter of wives with children held paying jobs."

Poverty rates for women, seniors and children: On p. 3 of *Poverty in Canada* (Ottawa: Library of Parliament, 1992), Helen MacKenzie states: "Elderly, unattached women still run a high risk of being poor. Indeed, women in general, but particularly single mothers, are more likely to be poor than men." From p. 5: "About two fifths of Canadians aged 65 or over live in or near poverty." From StatsCan's *The Daily* of December 11, 1992. 16% of Canadians live in poverty, but the poverty rate is 18.3% for children, 20% for seniors, and 61% for families headed by single moms.

20% single moms: From StatsCan's *The Daily* of December 17, 1992. Also — the average income of single parents is $22,000 — below the poverty line in much of the country.

Women's wages statistic: From **PEA**, p. 11: "Women still earn, on average, approximately 63% of that earned by men."

Escape From Childhood: By John Holt (Cambridge, Mass.: Pinchpenny Press, 1984).

Centuries of Childhood: A Social History of Family Life by Philippe Aries (New York: McGraw, 1965).

Women's re-entry: From **CYB**, p. 144: women went from making up 34% of the workforce in 1970 to 44% in 1988.

11. Sharing the Work

Samuel Gompers quote: Reported in B.K. Hunnicutt's ☞ *Work Without End* (Philadelphia: Temple University Press, 1988).

History of workweek reductions: In *Futures for Work* edited by Geert Hofstede (London: Martinus Nijhoff, 1979), we have European stats that the average workweek in 1800 was 78 hours. From p. 135: "In the period before the first World War the working week was shrinking at the rate of two hours per decade; afterwards the rate increased to three hours per decade. By the end of the century the working week in the most developed countries will be reduced to 30 hours or less."

History of reductions in the length of the workweek: In *Work and Leisure in Canada* by S.M.A. Hameed and D. Cullen (Edmonton: University of Alberta Press, 1971), we have the following information: U.S. legislation for a 10-hour workday was enacted in 1868, and by 1860 the standard workweek was 60 hours (p. 10). In 1872 trade unions started their campaigns for a 9-hour workday, and by 1887 the Trades and Labour Congress had adopted an 8-hour workday as "basic policy" (p. 14).

30-hour workweek bill: From **TOA**, p. 30. For more details, see *Work Without End* by B.K. Hunnicutt.

European vacation times: See **TOA**, p. 82.

Maternity leaves: Germany now gives 3-year leaves to new mothers. See **HTH** p. 64.

Cost of benefits: From **TOA**, p. 67, U.S. fringe benefit costs were 36.5% of wages in 1987. In *Part-Time Employment: Labour Market Flexibility and Equity Issues* (Kingston, Ont.: Industrial Relations Centre, 1988), Mary Lou Coates reports a very similar figure for Canada: 36.3%.

Comparative costs between overtime and relief staff: If hiring extra workers entails extra benefit packages equivalent to 36% of wages, plus training costs of hiring and severance costs when such workers are laid off, the costs approach those which result when existing workers are paid a 50% overtime premium. Working existing staff overtime is less work for supervisors than hiring and training relief staff, and mitigates employee demands for higher wages.

Relief staffing in Sweden: From "Can We Afford to Work?" Casten von Otter's address to the 1984 annual conference of the Canadian Mental Health Association in Montreal, November 2, 1984.

Work options: The best resource is ☛ *Put Work In Its Place* by modest author Bruce O'Hara (Victoria: Work Well Publications, 1988).

250,000 jobs statistic: In "Combatting Unemployment Through Work Time Reductions" (*Canadian Public Policy*, Vol. 12, No. 2, 1986, pp. 275-285), Frank Reid estimates that work options could create a 2% increase in the number of employed Canadians (for an employed labour force of 12,208,000, this works out as 244,160). Reid estimates that about half the hours opened up by significant work time reductions will turn into new employment. See also *Sharing the Work* by Noah Melz, Frank Reid, and G. Swartz (Toronto: University of Toronto Press, 1981).

Limits on the use of flexible work schedules: Barney Olmsted and Suzanne Smith of New Ways to Work in San Francisco, in personal communication with me, have reported that interest in, and availability of, flexible work schedules has gone up and down in sync with unemployment levels during the 20 years they have been promoting such schedules.

12. Consuming Addictions

Edward Abbey quote: From *Peter's Quotations* by Laurence J. Peter (New York: William Morrow, 1977).

Economic expansion in the 1950s and 1960s: Using figures from **CGA**, p. 177, the growth of the Canadian gross domestic product averaged 5.2% in the 1960s and 4.7% in the 1970s. By the 1980s, growth had fallen to 2.4% a year. Thus far in the 1990s we have negative average growth.

Ideologies of growth: In 1955, according to John L. King, author of *How to Profit From the Next Great Depression* (New York: New American Library, 1988, p. 27), "W.W. Rostow developed new economic theories that suggested everlasting growth and the concomitant banishment of depressions."

Numbers of advertising messages: In *Advertising in Canada* (Toronto: Wiley, 1984) p. 3, Rene Darmon gives an estimate of 1500 commercial messages per day.

Wordsworth quote: From Miscellaneous Sonnets Part 1, No. 33.

Happiness and things: From **TOA**, p. 116, the proportion of the population that reports being "very happy" in surveys has never regained the peak it reached in 1957. Things do not make us happy.

World defence spending: From the *Universal Almanac 1990* edited by John Wright (New York: Andrews & McMeel, 1989), p. 534: total world military expenditures are quoted as exceeding $1 trillion per year since 1987.

Hazel Henderson and the GNP: See pp. 21-23 of her book *Creating Alternative Futures* (New York: Perigee, 1980). She includes a lovely quip from Ralph Nader on the subject: "Every time there is an automobile accident the GNP goes up."

Canadian defence spending: From **CGA**, p. 195, Canadian military expenses in 1992 were $12.8 billion, 11% of federal tax revenue, or 8% of federal spending.

22% public sector statistic: StatsCan's *The Daily* of August 17, 1992, lists public sector employment of 2,710,800, with a payroll of $94.2 billion. With an employed labour force of 12,253,000 (see **KEY**) this represents 22% of all jobs in Canada.

Tax costs: In the Fraser Institute's *Fraser Forum*, July 1992, we have the information that Canadians must work till July 7 to pay their portion of all government expenses, including the public deficit. The average total taxes paid by Canadians is listed at 44% of total family income.

Per capita costs and jobs in public vs. private health care: U.S. health care in 1990 cost 12.1% of GDP, or US$2566 per American, while the Canadian system cost only 9.2% of GDP, or US$1730 (**BOC**, p. 148). From **BOC**, p. 153: "The scale of waste among private carriers is illustrated by Blue Cross/Blue Shield of Massachusetts, which covers 2.7 million subscribers and employs 6682 workers — more than work for all of Canada's provincial health plans, which together cover more than 25 million people."

Comparison of Canadian and U.S. government expenditures: From **HTH**, p. 269, we have U.S. taxes consuming 30% of GDP, and Canadian taxes 34% of GDP. If we subtract 80% of health care costs from Canadian taxes (which would roughly equalize the share of health care costs paid by both governments), the Canadian rate drops to 26% of GDP, or 10% less than what the Americans spend — despite Canada's better social programs!

Per capita federal debt: From **BOC**, p. 125: the federal debt by early 1993 was projected at $450 billion. Divided among 10 million Canadian households this works out as $45,000 per household.

Provincial and municipal debt: The *Financial Post* of May 2, 1992, on p. 6, in "Canadians Double Debt Load," reported that in 1991 the per capita share of provincial debt was $5500 and of municipal debt, $1400. For a population of 27.3 million, these two debts total $188 billion. 1992 provincial deficits of $21 billion pushed this figure up to the $209 billion mark, which divided by 10 million households is $20,900 per household.

Corporate and personal debts: StatsCan's *The Daily* of November 23, 1992, listed corporate debts of $344 billion, and personal debts of $431 billion. Consumer debt was 21% of personal disposable income, and mortgage debt 62%, for a total of 83%. From these figures we can interpolate consumer debt of $109 billion and mortgage debt of $322 billion. Dividing each by 10 million households gives a household share of corporate debt of $34,400, consumer debt of $10,900 and mortgage debt of $32,200.

Household share of debt charges: Most public and private debt is held at an interest rate of 10% or better, so the individual household's share of the debt is 143,000 x .1 = $14,300. On an average family income of $53,535 this works out as 26.7%.

Perils of growth: See ☛ *The Growth Illusion: How Economic Growth Has Enriched the Few, Impoverished the Many, and Endangered the Planet* by Richard Douthwaite (Dublin: Lilliput Press, 1992).

13. Producing Solutions

Keynes quote: Requoted from p. 98 of *Steady-State Economics* by Herman Daly (Washington: Island Press, 1991)

John Maynard Keynes: *The General Theory of Employment, Interest and Money* (London: Macmillan, 1933).

Falling interest rates: Free-falling interest rates in the early 1990s are not evidence of emerging economic health, but are rather like the defibrillator shocks given a patient who has gone into cardiac arrest!

Interest rates and inflation: See ☛ *Interest and Inflation-Free Money*, by Margit Kennedy (Steyerberg, Germany: Permaculture Institute Publications, 1988).

The Luddite response: See Robert Reid's *Land of Lost Content: The Luddite Revolt of 1812* (London: Heineman, 1986).

14. Solutions for Some

Samuelson quote: From **BOC**, p. 178.

Corporate concentration background: See **BOC**, pp. 180-189. For a more general discussion see ☛ *The Bigness Complex* by Walter Adams and James Brock (New York: Pantheon, 1987). From *The Wrong End of the Rainbow*, by Eric Kierans and Walter Stewart (Toronto: Collins, 1988) comes this amazing statistic: "Nine families alone control 46% of the value of all the 300 most important companies listed on the Toronto Stock Exchange."

Soap industry background: see p. 80 of Kirkpatrick Sale's *Human Scale* (New York: Coward, McCan & Geoghegan, 1980).

Rationalization: "Rationalization" involves streamlining the production process in a number of ways. Old or inefficient factories are removed from the merged unit until the remaining factories operate near full capacity. Where several name brands of a similar product are being sold, they are often all produced in the same factory, merely altering the production formula for particular brands, and using different labels.

Corporate concentration and profitability: Technological improvements often increase production although no new factories are built, so overcapacity can build up even when a corporate oligarchy restricts the building of new plants. Similarly, when markets contract, as they have in the early 1990s, overcapacity can emerge like a reef on a falling tide, and corporate profits disappear quickly.

75% statistic: In 1988, 0.1% of Canadian corporations controlled 74.9% of all corporate assets in Canada, from **BOC**, p. 181.

Corporate political donations: From **BOC** p. 258: "Corporations contributed some $8.5 million to the federal Conservatives in 1988, representing some 65% of the party's disclosed funding." The estimate is also made that big business and governments spent an additional $40 million promoting free trade.

Three times the selling commission cost statistic: From "Winnipeg Realtors Quietly Give Themselves a Big Raise" in the *Financial Post*, July 23, 1966, we have sales commissions of 4%. Today the MLS sales commissions are 7% — or 1.75 times what they were. From the *Royal Trust Survey of Canadian House Prices* for April 1983 and Fall 1992, a detached bungalow in Richmond in 1974 cost $47,000 ($151,000 in 1992 dollars), but by 1992 the price had risen to $240,000 — or 1.59 times the 1974 cost. Combining a rate increase of 1.75 times a real increase in house prices of 1.59 equals 2.78 times the comparable commission cost for the mid-sixties.

Education and competence: Questions as to how more education affects competence are explored in humorous detail in Chapter 5 ("The Not-So-Expert

Expert") of *The New Contrarian Investment Strategy* by David Dreman (New York: Random House, 1982).

Educational qualifications for psychologists: Because psychologists are near-at-hand subjects for other psychologists, we have a wealth of information about them. The general conclusion is that further education creates a tiny improvement in competence, and a big increase in confidence. *The New Contrarian Investment Strategy* gives numerous examples. Robert R. Carkhuff's research on counselling skills and counselling outcomes presents similar findings.

15. Non-Solutions I: Canada's Trade Policies

Brian Mulroney quote: From "The Wilson Depression" in *Canadian Forum* of December 1992, p. 5.

Protective tariffs cut from 30% to 3.3%: taken from the 1992 Canadian government pamphlet "The Global Trade Challenge."

The exports/imports balance: From p. 112 of the Ministry of Finance's *Quarterly Economic Review* of June 1991, we have the following figures (in billions of dollars) which show imports creeping up in step with exports:

Year	1982	1983	1984	1985	1986	1987	1988	1989	1990
Exports	84	90	111	119	120	126	138	141	146
Imports	66	73	91	102	110	115	128	134	135

The government likes to crow about our multi-billion dollar trade surplus with the U.S. What the government doesn't mention is that Canadian branches of U.S. firms ship a roughly equivalent amount in earnings to the United States. Canada needs a trade surplus in order to earn back the money that U.S. ownership takes out of our economy — hardly a matter for self-congratulation.

Parcel of Rogues: By Maude Barlow, (Toronto: Key Porter, 1991).

Clayton Yeutter quote: Quoted in *The Dictionary of Canadian Quotations* by John Robert Columbo (Toronto: Stoddart, 1991).

Job losses: From Duncan Cameron's "The Wilson Depression" in *Canadian Forum*, December 1995, p. 5.

96% of foreign investment: This statistic is from p. 75 of *Parcel of Rogues*. To make matters worse, Barlow also reports that "between 1974 and 1986, almost 80 percent of the increase in foreign direct investment was financed in Canada." In other words, foreign companies are buying out Canadian companies with Canadians' money!

Job creation: From BOC, p. 79, we have net job creation of 876,000 for Canadian-owned firms and a net job loss of 11,400 for foreign-owned firms from 1978-85.

Lester Thurow quote: HTH p. 201.

Branch plant staffing: From BOC, p. 80: 339 times the employment from Canadian vs. U.S. firms per $1 billion in profits.

Transfer pricing: See BCD pp. 76-78, and BOC, pp. 73-77.

Mel Hurtig quote: BOC, p. 80.

16. Non-Solutions II: Canada's Job Policies

Small business job creation: From PEA, p. 4, we find that 75% of the net growth in employment in the period 1978-85 came from small businesses. The revolving door nature of entrepreneurship is seen in the fact that 3.8 million jobs were created, but 2.5 million jobs disappeared. Two thirds of the new jobs were offset by job losses elsewhere.

76,000 bankruptcies: StatsCan's *The Daily* of February 6, 1992, p. 1, listed 75,773 bankruptcies for 1991. (76,000 bankruptcies were also reported for 1992.)

Supply-side theory: See Milton Friedman's *Essence of Friedman* (Stanford, California: Hoover Institution Press, 1987)

Increased immigration: From **CGA**, p. 43, net immigration in the period 1981-86 was 23,000. In the period 1986-91, net immigration had skyrocketed to 756,000. From StatsCan's *The Daily* of December 10, 1992, we have the information that Canada's annual population growth rate is 1.5% — among the highest in the industrialized world.

Growth in gross domestic product: Corrected for inflation, per capita GDP fell by almost 6% between 1989 and 1992, as reported in "The Only Thing Growing is the Economist's Hype" by Bud Jorgensen in the *Globe & Mail* of January 8, 1993. In truth, the economy has been stagnant for a full decade. From **CGA** we have the following:

	1981	1991	1992
GDP (in $millions)	$355,994	$679,203	$687,334
GDP (in 1992 $millions)	$541,779	$687,937	$687,334
Per Capita GDP	$22,256	$25,201	$24,934

Per capita GDP grew at a paltry 1.3% per year between 1981 and 1991, whereas GDP grew at 2.7%.

LFDS: Is described in reasonable detail in the Canada Employment and Immigration *Annual Report 1990/91*.

LFDS funding: Part of the reason for shifting UI monies into training is to make job-creation spending look larger and UIC outflows look smaller. While this is arguably a better use of UI funds, its prime purpose is to hide how little the federal government actually spends on job creation.

17. A Short History of Work

Stone Age Economics: By Marshall Sahlins (Hawthorne, N.Y.: Aldine de Gruyter, 1972).

99% statistic: Human beings have been around for somewhere on the order of 1 million years, and for all but the past 10,000 years lived as hunters and gatherers: 990,000/1,000,000 = 99%.

Work hours: From **TOA**, p. 45, a thirteenth-century peasant worked 1440 hours per year — or 28 hours per week.

The Chalice and the Blade: By Riane Eisler (San Francisco: Harper San Francisco, 1988).

Thomas Paine quote: From *The Rights of Man*, p. 190 (Harmondsworth: Penguin, 1976; originally published 1791).

180 holy days statistic: From *Time Wars: The Primary Conflict In Human History* by Jeremy Rifkin (New York: Touchstone, 1989).

Work hours: From **TOA**, p. 55, factory workers worked 75 to 90 hours per week in 1825.

Service sector jobs: "In Canada . . . the service sector now accounts for 75.6% of employment and 72.4% of Gross Domestic Product," George Radwanski writes in *The Ontario Study of the Service Sector* (Toronto: Ontario Ministry of Treasury and Economics, 1986).

18. The Addiction to Busyness

Juliet Shor quote: From **TOA**, p. 112.

The scope of work addiction: Lindsay Scotton makes the following observation in "How We Have Become Suckers for Work" in the Toronto *Star*, May 29, 1988: "One in ten Canadians in the labour force works 50 hours or more per week. Across the country, nearly half a million people who are already working full time are looking for second jobs." Among addictions counsellors, the consensus is that roughly 10% of the population are workaholics and 10% alcoholics.

Workaholism: The chapter title is a corruption of the title of a book by Canadian Barbara Killinger, *Workaholics: The Respectable Addicts* (New York: Simon and Shuster, 1992). Much of the conceptual basis for this section is adapted from ☛ *Working Ourselves to Death: The High Cost of Work Addiction and the Rewards of Recovery* by Diane Fassel (San Francisco: Harper San Francisco, 1990).

The great chain of being: The table is one I developed for workshop use, but the basic concept comes from somewhere else — I have no idea who I borrowed the metaphor from!

The Addictive Organization: Why We Overwork, Cover Up, Pick Up the Pieces, Please the Boss and Perpetuate Sick Organizations: By Anne Wilson Schaef and Diane Fassell (San Francisco: Harper San Francisco, 1990).

Productivity of workaholics chart: The chart given is my own, and is conceptual rather than empirical, but it mirrors the pattern of burnout described in the research literature.

The Neurotic Organization: Diagnosing and Changing Counterproductive Styles of Management: By Manfred DeVries and Danny Miller (San Francisco: Jossey-Bass, 1984).

When Society Becomes An Addict: By Anne Wilson Schaef (San Francisco: Harper San Francisco, 1987).

Work-obsessed lifestyle: Cycles described here are drawn from my experience as a counsellor.

Cues for identifying work addiction in others

- external referencing of worth
- multiple addictions
- denial of personal problems
- inability to relax — obsessive or driven quality
- perfectionistic
- gets freaked out by silence or inactivity
- emotional numbness
- has a private or hidden stash of work
- insomnia
- denial of work addiction
- strong need to be in control
- thinks of self as indispensable at task
- tends to create files, piles, and do lists

🌢 addiction of some kind in family of origin

🌢 isolated — lacks intimate connection with self or others

🌢 lacks a sense of lightness or playfulness

🌢 life feels one-dimensional — emotionally or spiritually shallow

19. Work and Self-Worth

Neil Postman quote: From *Amusing Ourselves to Death* (New York: Viking, 1984).

Self-worth and possessions: From John K. Galbraith's *The Affluent Society* (New York: Mentor, 1958), p. 126, comes the idea that contemporary society "evaluates people by the products they possess . . . The urge to consume is further fostered by the value system."

The Sane Society: By Erich Fromm (New York: Henry Holt, 1990).

Shame: See *Facing Shame: Families in Recovery* by Merle Fossum and Marilyn Mason (New York: Norton, 1986).

Everyday hypnosis: See *Frogs Into Princes* by Richard Bandler and John Grinder (Moab, Utah: Real People Press, 1979) for a good discussion of trance states in everyday life.

Shaw story: I was unable to track down a source for this story — but I've heard it repeatedly.

Externalized costs: Economists refer to environmental and social costs as externalities. See also **FCG** pp. 51-58.

Ideal man, woman, and human: "Sex-role stereotypes and clinical judgments of mental health" by I. Broverman, D. Broverman, F. Clarkson, P. Rosenkrantz, and S. Vogel was published in the *Journal of Consulting and Clinical Psychology*, January 1970, pp. 1-7, and is usually referred to as the "Broverman study" in the literature.

Deathbed quote: Someone else's idea — but I don't know whose!

Amusing Ourselves to Death: By Neil Postman (New York: Viking, 1984).

Shopping as recreation: From **TOA**, p. 106: Americans spend 3 to 4 times as many hours per year shopping as Europeans do. Americans spend 6 hours per week shopping, according to Alan Thein Durning in "Are We Shopping Our Planet to Death?" (*E* magazine, January, 1993, p. 31).

Invisible hand: Adam Smith's term. See **FCG**, pp. 139 and 215.

"A system so perfect . . . ": Is T.S. Eliot's wry sense of humour (re-quoted from **FCG**, p. 140).

Charles Darwin: *The Origin of Species* (Buffalo, New York: Prometheus Books, 1991).

Herbert Spencer: *The Evolution of Society: Selections From Herbert Spencer's Principles of Sociology* edited by Robert Carneiro (Chicago: Midway Reprint Series, 1984).

Cooperation: See **HTH**, p. 33, for Thurow's description of the communitarian economies of Europe and Japan, economies which are a careful mixture of competition and cooperation.

20. The Politics of Scarcity

Alvin Toffler quote: *Future Shock* (New York: Random House, 1970).

Hoarding: Thurow touches on this issue on p. 92 of **HTH**.

One quarter of manufacturing jobs lost: See Maude Barlow and Bruce Campbell's *Take Back the Nation* (Toronto: Key Porter, 1991).

Union activism: For more information on when unions made work hours a major issue, see **TOA**, pp. 74-81.

Frank Reid's research: See "Combatting Unemployment Through Work Time Reductions" (*Canadian Public Policy*, Vol. 12, No. 2, 1986, pp. 275-285).

Corporate political contributions: Maude Barlow outlines the extent to which corporate financial contributions affected the 1988 election on p. 9 of *Parcel of Rogues* (Toronto: Key Porter, 1991). Corporate Canada spent more than $19 million to promote free trade — Shell Canada alone shelled out $250,000.

Surplus Powerlessness: The Psychodynamics of Everyday Life and the Psychology of Individual and Social Transformation: By Michael Lerner (Atlantic Highlands, N.J.: Humanities Press International, 1991).

21. Default Future: Where Are We Headed?

James Dale Davidson quote: *The Great Reckoning* (New York: Summit Books, 1991), p. 12.

Economic cycles: ☛ *The Great Reckoning: How the World Will Change in the Depression of the 1990s* by James Dale Davidson and William Rees-Mogg (New York: Summit Books, 1991) is excellent when it is descriptive and falls short when it tries to be analytic. (Its explanation for the occurrence of depressions at 50-year intervals is basically: "Shit happens.") See also Robert Beckman's *Downwave: Surviving the Second Great Depression* (London: Pan Books, 1983).

Commodity prices: From **HTH**, p. 41: in real terms, commodity prices have dropped 40% since 1970.

How to Profit From the Next Great Depression: By John L. King (New York: New American Library, 1988).

'Slow 1929': From *The Next Left* (New York: Henry Holt, 1986).

Government intervention: On p. 18 of **HTH** Thurow blithely admits that without strong government intervention, the stock market crash of 1987, S&L bankruptcies, and the crash in the North American real estate market each had the capacity to produce a panic and/or economic crash reminiscent of 1929.

Strategy chart: I have arbitrarily assigned importance ratings (small, medium, or large, being represented by 1, 2, or 3 faces) for these various strategies based on my own estimates. Other commentators might quibble about the relative impact of each individual strategy, but few would argue with the overall result.

Workforce history chart: This chart is conceptual in nature, but accurate to within about about a 10% margin of error.

22. How Do We Fix It?

Lester Thurow quote: From p. 66, *Zero-Sum Society: Solving the Economic Problems of the 1980s* (New York: Basic, 1980).

Labour and business in Europe and Japan: See **HTH** for an overview.

Lowest business profits: From p. 88 of *A New and Better Canada* by Mel Hurtig (Toronto: Stoddart, 1992)

23. The 4-Day Workweek

David Riesman quote: From p. 67 of *Selected Essays from Individualism Reconsidered* (New York: Free Press, 1954).

Overtime usage: From *Hours of Work and Overtime in Ontario: The Dimensions of the Issue* by Frank Reid (Toronto: Government of Ontario, 1987) we have statistics that Ontario employees work an average of one hour per week of overtime; overtime represents 2% of work hours; and the usual distribution is that about 12% of the workforce works an extra 8 hours per week.

Salary staffing: From **TOA**, p. 68: 40% of workers are salaried.

Annual hours programs: See *Put Work In Its Place* by Bruce O'Hara (Victoria: Work Well Publications, 1988).

Desires for reduced workweek: A survey conducted for Hilton Hotels reported that nearly half of those polled said they'd be willing to trade a day's pay for an extra day of free time (reported in "The Death of Leisure" in the *Globe & Mail*, May 25, 1991). One can only presume that survey results would be higher still if the loss in take-home pay were only 5%. From **TOA**, p. 164, in a 1989 poll almost two thirds of workers were willing to give up pay for time off — an average of 13% less pay. One can only presume that the vast majority of workers would be willing to give up 5% of their pay for 16% time off.

Why a 15% pay increase?: The 15% increase in the hourly wage which I have proposed is the best compromise I could find in terms of the arrangement being affordable for both employee and employer. A higher increase would makes it very easy for the individual but very difficult for the employer. It also would run a risk of pushing our fragile economy over the edge into a depression, and/or causing a return of inflation. A lower increase would make the change more affordable for employers, but more difficult for the working population. In addition, a lower rate would not increase aggregate demand sufficiently to ease overcapacity problems.

Employee wages: I have not made any allowance for lower taxes in these figures — in recognition that workers with incomes over $25,000 will gain somewhat less than 3% back from UIC.

Employer costs: I have knocked down the savings on UIC from 4.2% to 3%, in recognition of the ceiling on UI contributions. 30% benefit costs for 8% more workers will add 2.4% to the employers' wage bill (benefit costs are lower without UIC).

Aggregate demand: If we guesstimate that the 8% new hires would double their incomes, and that 86% of the workforce would have 5% less to spend, the change in demand works out as 8% — (.86 x 5%) = 3.7%.

Productivity: From *A Shorter Workweek in the 1980s* by William McGaughey (White Bear Lake: Thistlerose Publications, 1981), p. 141, we have data that during the 1973 coal miner's strike in Great Britain the government imposed a 3-day workweek for 3 months, but industrial output dropped only by 6% due to higher productivity and lower absenteeism. A Danish study found that 34% of the production loss associated with shorter working hours is made up in higher productivity. From **TOA**, pp. 155-157, we see that shorter hours at Kellogg's, Medtronics, and Ideal Industries all boosted productivity.

Frank Reid's research: See "Combatting Unemployment Through Work Time Reductions" (*Canadian Public Policy*, Vol. 12, No. 2, 1986, pp. 275-285) and also *Sharing the Work* by Noah Melz, Frank Reid, and G. Swartz (Toronto: University of Toronto Press, 1981).

Moonlighting: There were 604,000 Canadians who were multiple job-holders in November 1992 according to StatsCan's *The Labour Force* for that month. "Moonlighters" by Maryanne Webb, *Perspectives*, Winter 1989, does give a number of statistics which put moonlighting in perspective. Almost half of Canadian moonlighters are self-employed for one of their jobs; many of the rest are people holding multiple part-time jobs. More than half of moonlighters earned less than $20,000 in 1987, suggesting that moonlighting was more often a function of need than greed.

Training needs: Canada's unemployed can be roughly divided into three groups: one third with both ability and training, one third with ability but limited training, and one third with limited abilities and no training. According to Gary Cohen's "Today's Unemployed" in StatsCan's *Perspectives* of Spring 1991, a majority of Canada's unemployed have at least some high school education, 29% have at least some college education, and 7% have university degrees.

24. Going All the Way

Juliet Shor quote: TOA, p. 2.

Unemployment estimates: Officially technology is only increasing productivity by 1.2% per year — but this is in an economy with high levels of overcapacity and lots of marginal employment. If we reduce consumption for environmental reasons, and if women, teens, and seniors continue to enter the labour force rapidly, the true level of unemployment might grow by as much as 3% per year.

Take-home pay: Working 87.5% as much time at 105% of former pay would yield gross income 92% of previous levels. A 20% reduction in income taxes would lift take-home pay to about 95% of previous.

Double shifting: John Ward Pearson's ☛ *The Eight-Day Week* (New York: Harper & Row, 1973) gives lots of good detail.

European vacation times: See **TOA,** p. 82.

25. Take Back The Nation!

Take Back the Nation!: Is the title of Maude Barlow and Bruce Campbell's new book (Toronto: Key Porter, 1991).

Mel Hurtig quote: BOC, p. 338.

International Trading Organization: See **HTH,** p. 237.

Withdrawal from Canada-U.S. Free Trade Agreement: Article 2106 of the agreement says: "This agreement shall remain in force unless terminated by either party upon 6-month notice to the other party."

26. Undoing the Damage

The need for electoral reform: See ☛ *A Capital Scandal* (cited below) and also **BOC,** pp. 252-278.

Statistics on women in parliament: 40 of 295 members of parliament, or 13.5%, are women, from *A Capital Scandal: Politics, Patronage and Payoffs — Why Parliament Must Be Reformed* by Robert Fife and John Warren (Toronto: Key Porter, 1991), p. 213.

Affirmative action: One simple way to institute affirmative action in the Canadian parliament would be to require that in each of the next three federal elections one third of the seats would be open only to female candidates. A different third of the seats would be closed to men each time, with the remaining seats open to either gender. This would guarantee that an least one third (and probably closer to 50%) of the seats went to women. The sole restriction on each voters' freedom is that in one election they would not have the option of voting for a male candidate. By the time three elections had passed there would be enough incumbent female MPs to establish new norms around electing women.

Non-Partisan free trade campaign: See the note under "Corporate myopia" in Chapter 20.

Employee stock ownership: See ☛ *Taking Stock: Employee Stock Ownership at Work* by Michael Quarry *et al.* (Cambridge, Mass: Ballinger, 1986).

Daly quote: In **FCG,** pp. 49-50, Herman Daly gives a concise and eloquent explanation of why corporate concentration occurs, and why it must be broken up.

Small-scale vs. megaprojects: In *Cities and the Wealth of Nations* (New York: Random House, 1984), Jane Jacobs argues against megaprojects, or "transplants" as she calls them, on pp. 93-104, and suggests a smaller-scale model on pp. 228-229.

Local exchange trading systems: See *After The Crash: The Emergence of the Rainbow Economy* by Guy Dauncey (London: Greenprint, 1989), pp. 52-69, for more information about LETS. Michael Linton, originator of the LETSystem concept, can be reached by phone at (604) 338-0213, or by mail at Landsman Community Services Ltd., 1600 Embleton Cres., Courtenay, B.C.

Declining regions: From **HTH**, p. 78: two thirds of America's 3000 counties are losing population.

Co-housing: This is a model of community-oriented living which retains an element of privacy for residents. The main features of co-housing include: participation by residents in the design and planning process; a physical design which fosters a strong sense of community; extensive common facilities to supplement private living areas; and complete resident management of the resulting residential environment.

Real estate taxes: In **FCG**, pp. 257-259, the suggestion is made that land taxes that approached the rental value of the land would curtail land speculation. (Buildings and improvements on land would be subject to low taxation rates.)

Carter report: See Neil Brooks's *The Quest for Tax Reform: the Royal Commission on Taxation Twenty Years Later* (Scarborough: Carswell, 1988).

Kenneth Dye quote: From *Report of the Auditor General to the House of Commons* (Ottawa: Supply and Services, 1986), p. 10.

Cost of tax breaks: Data in **BCD**, p. 16, indicates that most tax breaks for corporations cost far more than they deliver. On **BCD**, p. 10, we have the estimate that tax breaks cost the government about as much as the current annual federal deficit, and that these tax breaks go overwhelmingly to the wealthy. From **BCD**, p. 85, corporations received $11 billion in tax breaks in 1984.

Wealth taxes: From **BCD**, p. 232. Of the industrial nations, Canada, New Zealand, and Australia are the only countries that now have no wealth tax.

Mel Hurtig quote: From a presentation to the Senate Standing Committee on Banking, Trade and Commerce.

Maintaining low unemployment: Anyone who still believes that the unemployment rate is outside a nation's control should read Göran Therborn's delightful *Why Some Peoples Are More Unemployed Than Others* (London: Verso, 1986).

Guaranteed employment: On the surface, guaranteed employment sounds not unlike workfare, described on pp. 203-206 of Lester Thurow's *Zero-Sum Society* (New York: Basic, 1980). However, I see two essential differences. First, workfare still contains overtones of public charity and the shamefulness of welfare. Secondly, workfare typically provides incomes far below those of individuals who have "real" jobs. A guaranteed employment program would be required to pay employees of the program at least the legal minimum wage.

27. Protecting the Environment

Wendell Berry quote: From "Word and Flesh" in the Spring 1990 issue of the *Whole Earth Review*.

Green taxes: Green Taxes, sometimes called eco-taxes or Pigovian taxes, are broadly supported within environmental literature. Laurence Solomon has suggested the idea of a sliding tax based on warranty duration in *The Conserver Solution* (New York: Doubleday, 1978), p. 181. See also **FCG**, pp. 51-60.

Adbusting: Another idea from *The Conserver Solution*, pp. 114-128.

Vancouver Telecommuting information: Was gathered by the author at the International Society for Work Options annual conference in Vancouver in May of 1993. Vancouver commuting information is available from the Greater Vancouver Regional District. Steve Finlay's unpublished monograph "Benefits, Costs, and

Policy Strategies for Telecommuting in Greater Vancouver" is available through the Simon Fraser University Library. Information on BC Tel's satellite office can be found in BC Tel's internal report "Satellite Office Trial Final Report" by Don Rouse.

Recycling information: The percentages for components of household garbage are taken from p. 106 of *The Canadian Green Consumer Guide* by Pollution Probe (Toronto: McClelland and Stewart, 1989).

28. A New Worth Ethic

Studs Terkel quote: *Working* (New York: Avon Books, 1983).

Models for change: I also like Doris Longacre's phrase that we can be signs of contradiction to the toxic values of mainstream culture (her book is cited below).

Workaholics Anonymous: c/o Bart Craig, 23732 - 54A Avenue, Langley, B.C. V3R 7N6. Phone (604) 534-1315.

Right livelihood: See *Do What You Love and the Money Will Follow: Discovering Your Right Livelihood* by Marsha Sinetar (New York: Dell, 1989)

Simple living: See ☛ *Living More With Less* by Doris Longacre (Scottsdale, Pa.: Herald Press, 1971) and ☛ *Your Money or Your Life: Transforming Your Relationship With Money and Achieving Financial Independence* by Joe Dominguez and Vicki Robin (New York: Viking Penguin, 1992).

Image vs. substance: In ☛ *The Beauty Myth: How Images of Beauty are Used Against Women* (New York: Morrow Books, 1992), Naomi Wolf looks at how advertising creates impossible images for women.

The Gift: Imagination and the Erotic Life of Property: By Lewis Hyde (New York: Random, 1983).

Women hold up half the sky: Is a quote from Mao Zedong.

Value of women's work: From *Somebody Has to Do It: Whose Work Is Housework?* by Penny Kome (McClelland & Stewart, Toronto, 1982): "Recognizing housework as an important and meaningful adult activity will restore women's status in society and make it easier for them to move into other occupations as well."

Women's wages two thirds of men's: From **PEA**, p. 11: "Women still earn, on average, approximately 63% of that earned by men."

European-North American wage differentials: From Lester Thurow's *The Zero-Sum Society* (New York: Basic Books, 1980), p. 7: "If you look at the earnings gap between the top and the bottom 10 percent of the population, the West Germans work hard with 36% less inequality than we, and the Japanese work even harder with 50% less inequality." On p. 138 of **HTH** we find that American CEOs are paid 119 times what the average worker makes, vs. 18 times in Japan.

29. The Rehabilitation of Pleasure

Buffy St. Marie quote: Is also the name of one of her songs.

Anhedonia: See Alexander Lowen's *Bioenergetics* (New York: Penguin, 1965).

Wendell Berry: Berry explores community rootedness in an article titled "Word and Flesh" in the Spring 1990 *Whole Earth Review*.

Rewarding teamwork: The U.S. employee turnover rate is 4% per month, versus 3.5% per year in Japan, according to **HTH**. Bonuses in Japan are based on how well the whole corporation does (**HTH**, p. 140).

☛ *Deep Ecology: Living As If Nature Mattered* by Bill Devall and George Sessions (Salt Lake City: Gibbs M. Smith, 1985). The Gaia concept comes from James Lovelock's *The Ages of Gaia: A Biography of our Living Earth* (New York: Norton, 1988).

States of Grace: Spiritual Grounding in the Post-Modern Age: By Charlene Spretnak (San Francisco: Harper San Francisco, 1991).

Original Blessing: Is the title of a book by Matthew Fox. See ☛ *Creation Spirituality: Liberating Gifts for the People of the Earth* by Matthew Fox (San Francisco: Harper San Francisco, 1991).

Protestantism and capitalism: For a healthier attitude see *Global Economy: A Confessional Issue for the Churches?* by Ulrich Duchrow (Geneva: WCC Publications, 1987), pp. 158-162.

Time Enough for Love: Is the name of a science fiction story by Robert Heinlein (New York: Ace Books, 1981).

Rethinking leisure: A fun resource for rethinking leisure is *The Joy of Not Working* by Ernie Zelinski (Edmonton: VIP Books, 1991).

30. The Politics of Abundance

Michael Lerner quote: *Surplus Powerlessness* by Michael Lerner (Atlantic Highlands, N.J.: Humanities Press International, 1991).

Paradigm shift: See *The Structure of Scientific Revolutions* by Thomas Kuhn (Chicago: University of Chicago, 1970).

Reframing: See *Frogs Into Princes* by Richard Bandler and John Grinder (Moab, Utah: Real People Press, 1979).

Nudging: Involves use of the "Broken Record" technique from *When I Say No I Feel Guilty* by Manuel Smith (New York: Bantam, 1985).

Work Well Network: Mailing address is Box 3483, Courtenay, B.C. V9N 6Z8. Phone (604) 334-0998.

Study circle guides: *Working Harder Isn't Working* can easily be used as a study guide, with groups reading two, three, or four chapters each week to provide a basis for discussions. Work Well is currently at work on a study guide to accompany *Working Harder Isn't Working*. Work Well also has workshop kits on "The Four-Day Workweek Solution," "The Addiction to Busyness," and "The Addictive Organization," available at $20 each.

Church involvement: Bishop Remi de Roo of Victoria and the Catholic bishops have shown a willingness to take a strong stand on economic issues within Canada. Other churches have been moving in that direction.

Want To Work Union: I am told by my Australian partner that Australia has such a union for the unemployed. In Canada there is an Unemployed Workers' Union which receives at least token union financial support — a start, perhaps.

Re-inventing the Corporation: Is the title of a book by John Naisbitt and Patricia Aburdene (New York: Warner Books, 1986).

31. What to Do Until the Revolution Comes

Al Giordano quote: From "Red Emma" on the Citizens Band audiotape "Smash the State — and Have a Nice Day."

Norman Cousins: *Head First: The Biology of Hope* (New York: E. P. Dutton, 1989).

☛ *Your Money or Your Life: Transforming Your Relationship With Money and Achieving Financial Independence* by Joe Dominguez and Vicki Robin (New York: Viking Penguin, 1992).

Action Canada Network: c/o Council of Canadians, Suite 1006, 251 Laurier Avenue West, Ottawa, Ont. K1P 5J6. Phone (613) 233-2773

Eric Hoffer quote: From p. 37 of *The Temper of Our Time* (New York: Harper & Row, 1967). The original quote had a previously explained term, "the automated machine," in place of [technology].

Index

About the Author

In 1983, the frequent juxtaposition of unemployed and overworked individuals among his counselling case load convinced Bruce O'Hara that there had to be a better and more balanced way to apportion work hours. He founded **Work Well,** Canada's first work option resource centre, to promote voluntary arrangements to reduce or restructure work times: job sharing, phased retirement, permanent part-time, banked overtime, flextime, and telecommuting. O'Hara's self-help guide to work options, *Put Work In Its Place,* has become a widely recommended resource. A new edition will be published by New Star Books in 1994.

As a work scheduling specialist, O'Hara explored work issues with employers, union leaders, economists, bureaucrats, social planners — and thousands of ordinary Canadians. Like many others, he was struck by a strange paradox: futurists were united in predicting the coming of an age of leisure and abundance, yet most Canadians were, instead, finding themselves working more and more — for less and less. It was then that a subversive idea emerged: Prosperity/ leisure is not an either/or choice; in the 1990s, we will create the means to have them both — or we will end up with neither.

In 1990, O'Hara took time out from Work Well to research and write *Working Harder Isn't Working.* He has since resumed his role as Executive Director of **Work Well,** and now coordinates the **Work Well Network,** a grassroots coalition of individuals and organizations dedicated to making the four-day workweek a reality. O'Hara is an experienced and stimulating media guest, conference presenter, workshop leader, and public speaker.

As part of his (non-exhaustive) research into work scheduling, O'Hara has worked four-day (or three-day) workweeks for most of the past decade — and he reports that it's every bit as wonderful as you might think! When not working, Bruce and his partner, Lynne, like to explore the waterways around Vancouver Island in their 21-foot sailboat, the *Bunyip.*

Bruce O'Hara can be reached through the Work Well Network at Box 3483, Courtenay, B.C. V9N 6Z8. Phone (604) 334-0998.

5648